PAREIDOLIA:
FACES IN EVERYDAY OBJECTS
By Markus Baker

Published by R-and-Q.com.
Copyright © 2018 Mark 'Markus' Baker and R-and-Q.com

All rights reserved.

ISBN: 978-0-9933275-4-4

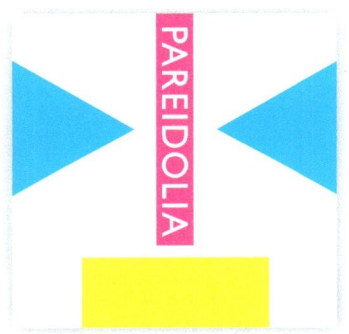

PAREIDOLIA

Introduction

Pareidolia is finding faces in everyday objects. This passion has grown into an obsession over the last few years and as a result, I've collected many photos some of which are shared in this book.

The location mentioned next to each face represents where I was in the world when the face in the everyday objected looked back at me.

As an illustrator, I have developed some of the faces from around the world into a set of characters which you can see throughout this book. You can learn more about these characters at www.the-mettas.com

I hope you enjoy the faces as much as I did finding them.
Markus

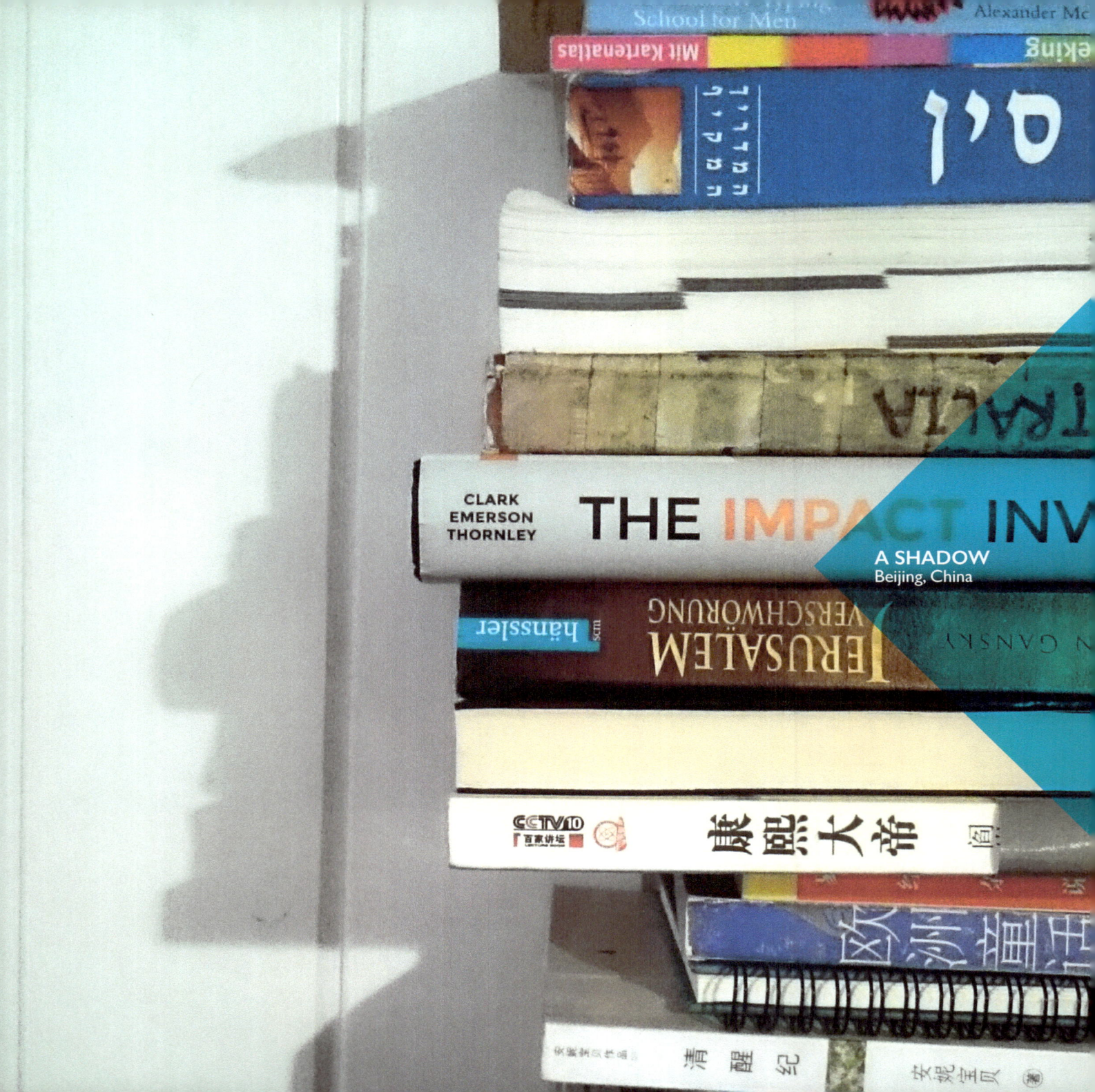

A SHADOW
Beijing, China

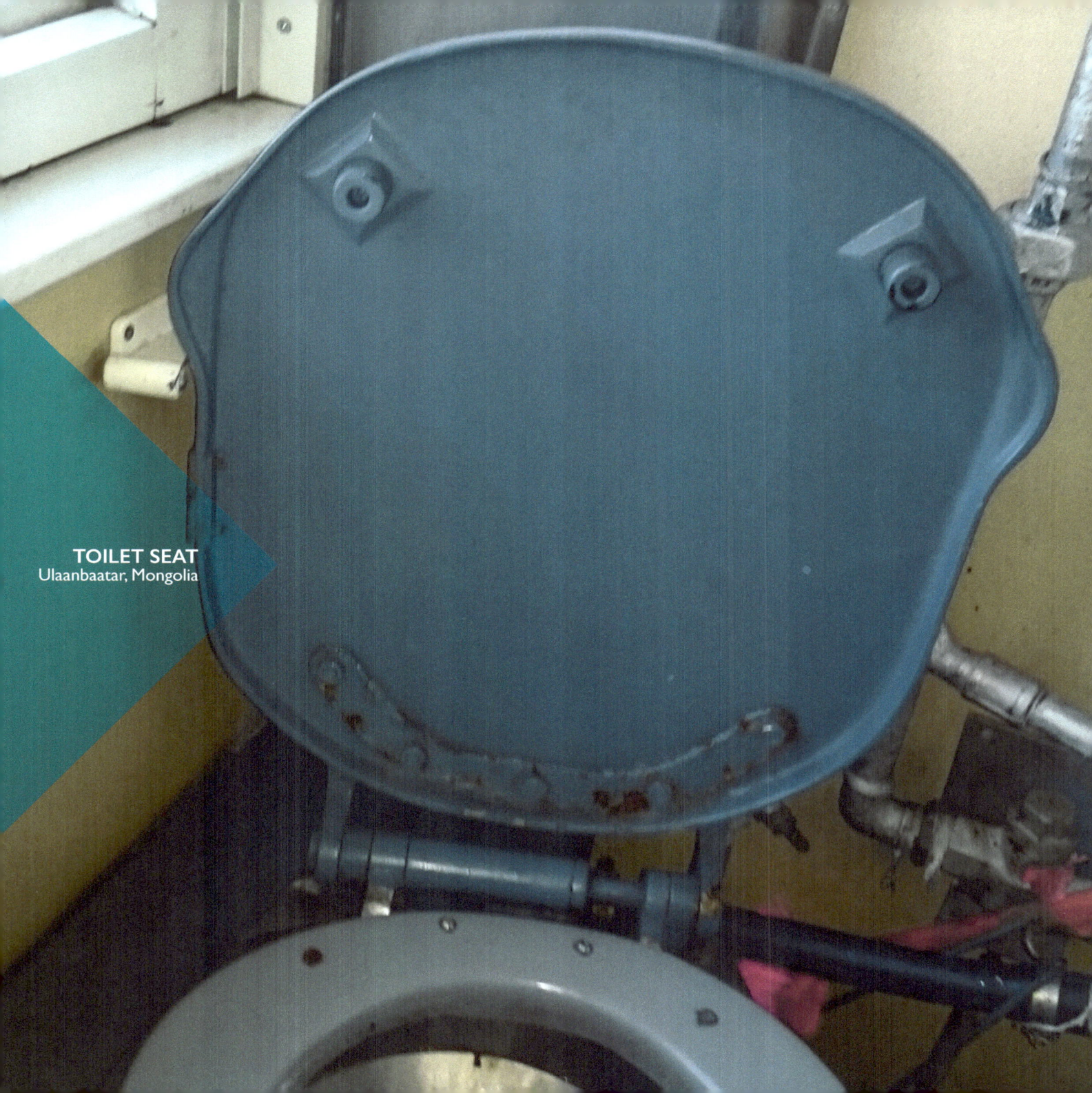

TOILET SEAT
Ulaanbaatar, Mongolia

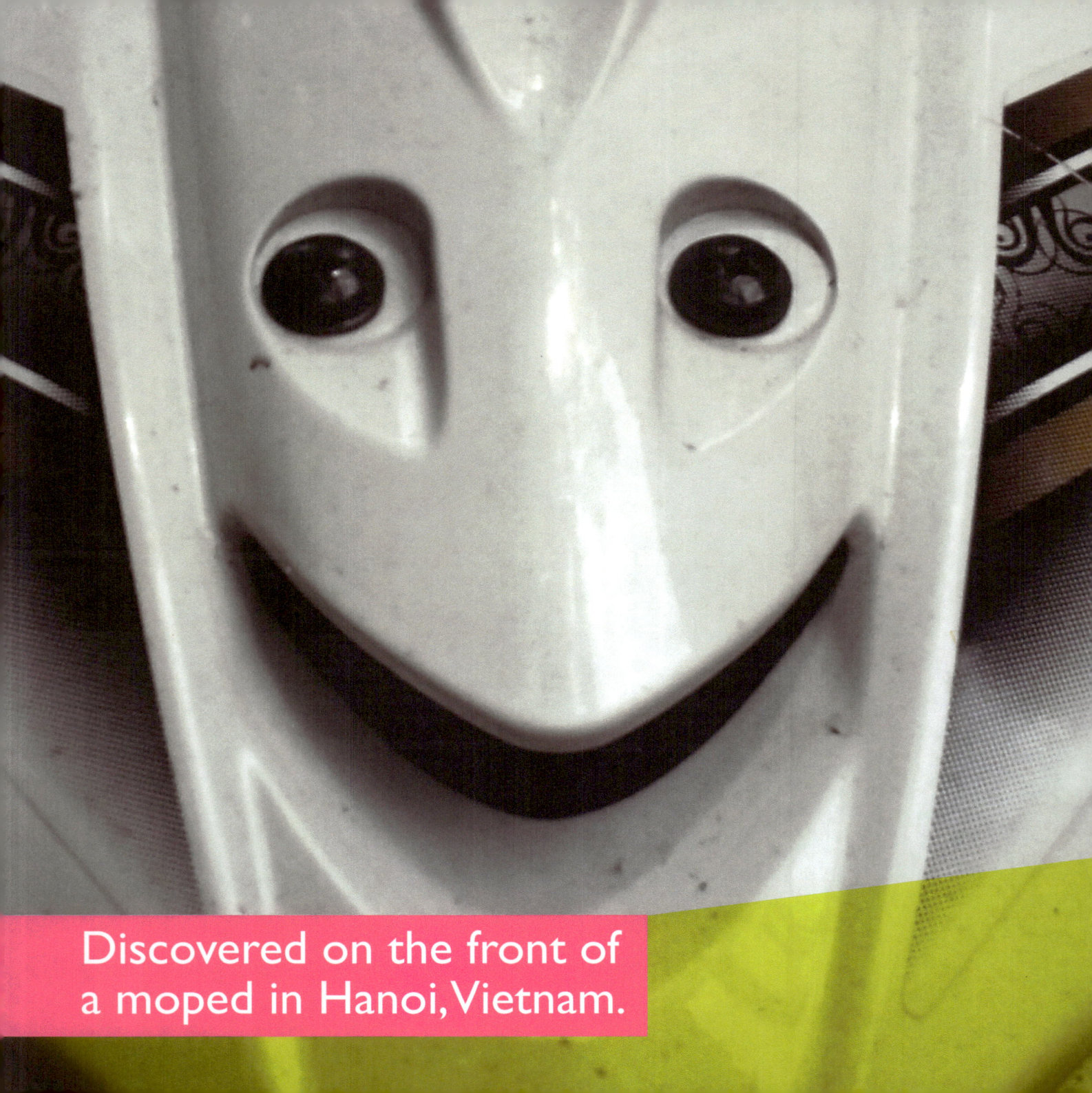

Discovered on the front of a moped in Hanoi, Vietnam.

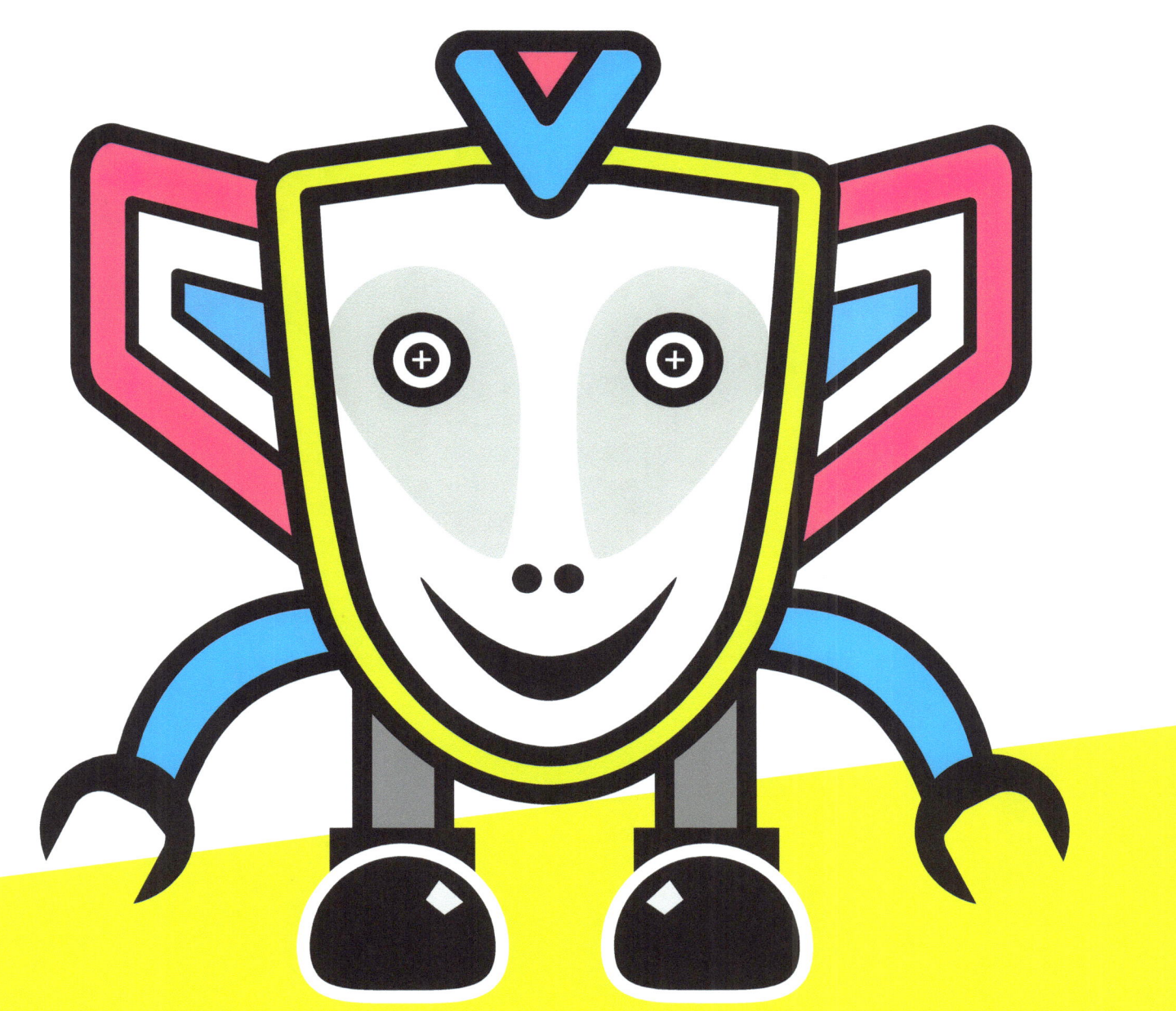

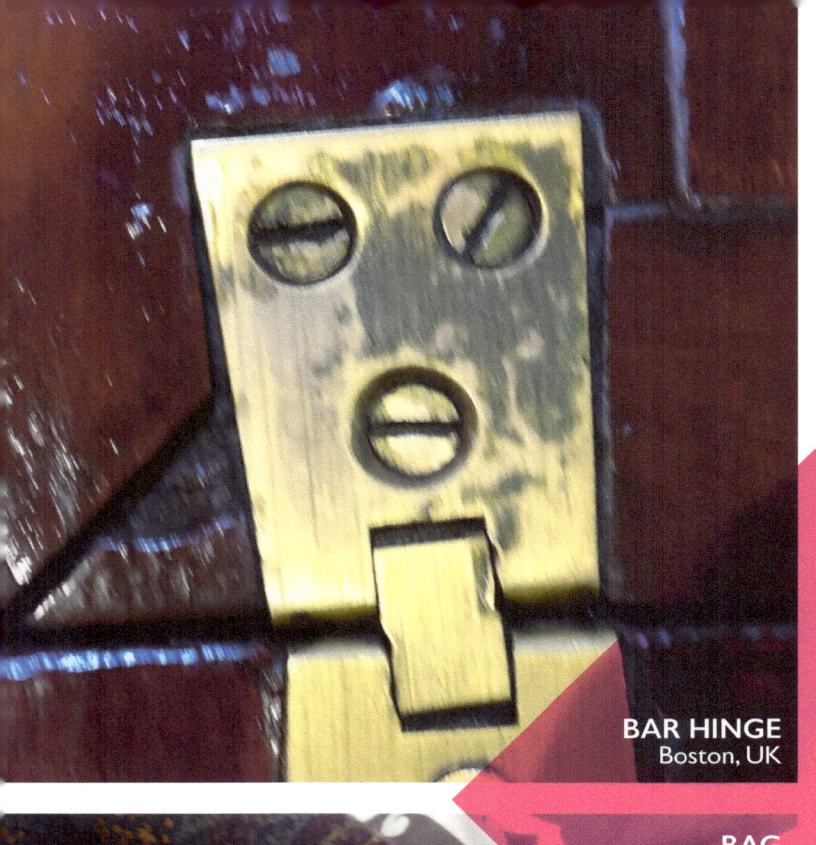

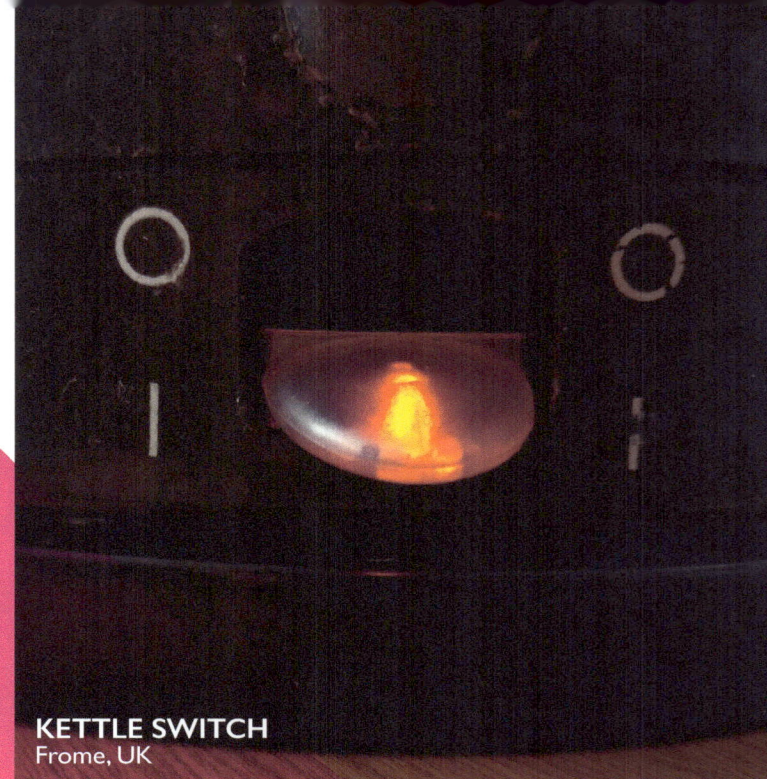

BAR HINGE
Boston, UK

KETTLE SWITCH
Frome, UK

BAG
Varanasi, India

PAPER STAND
New York, USA

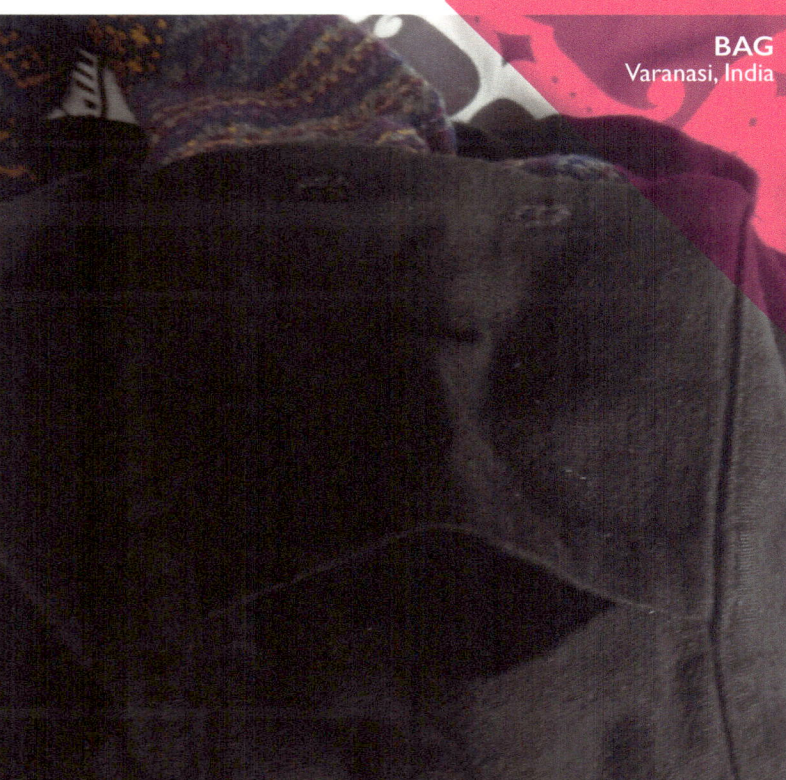

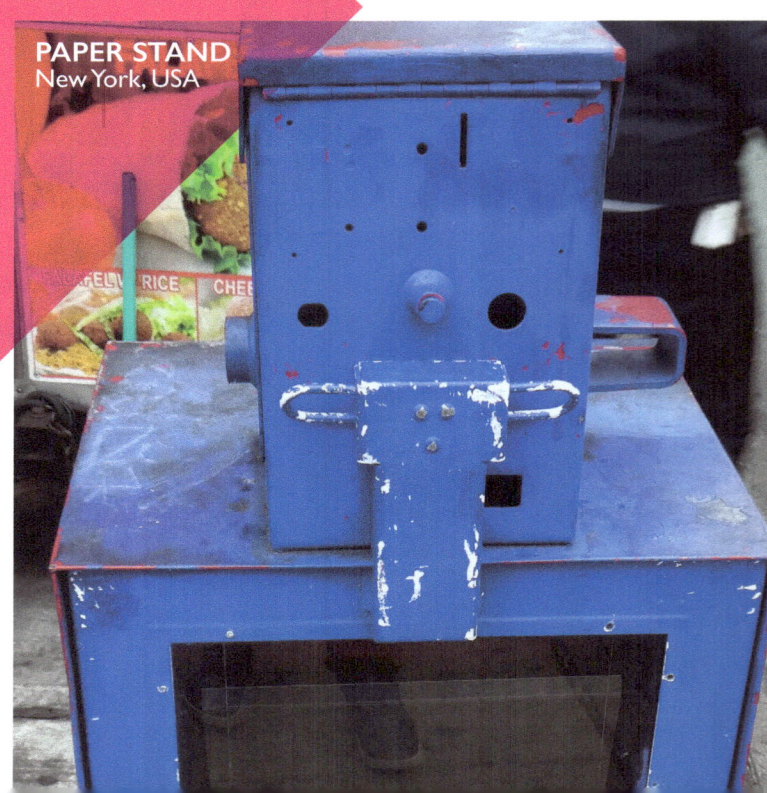

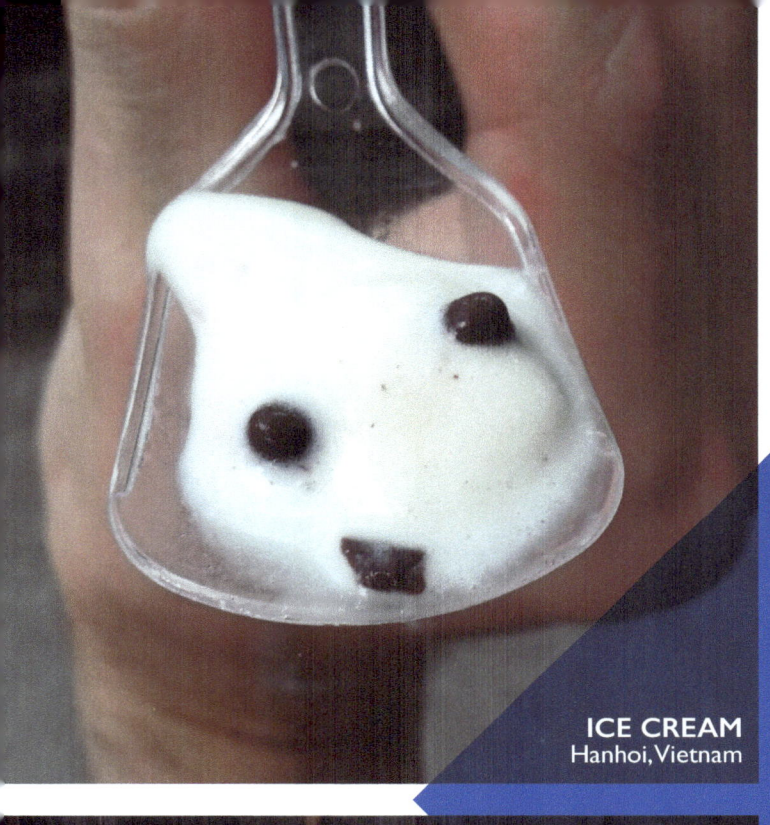

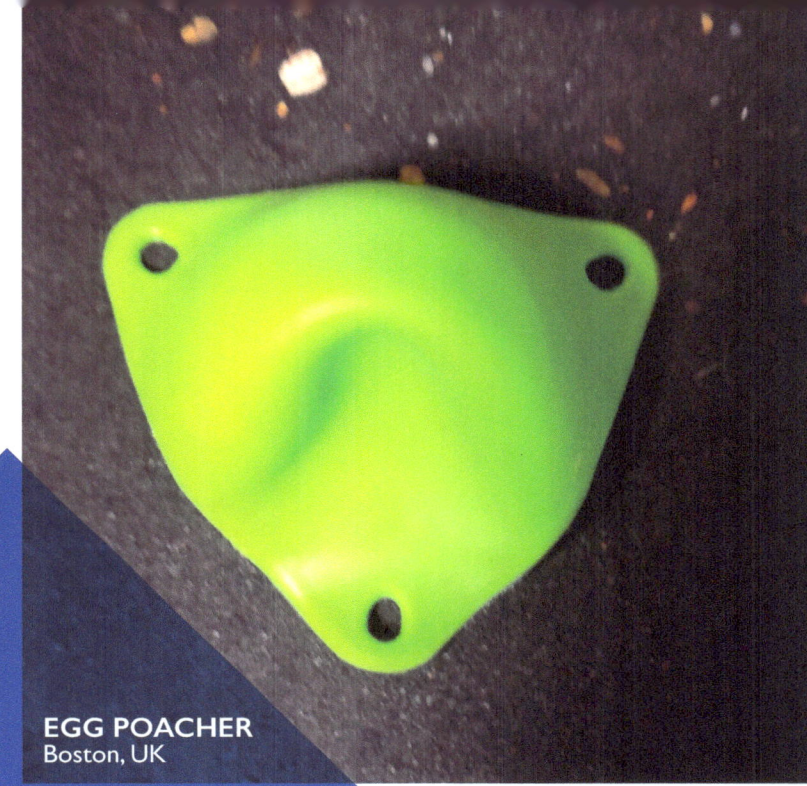

ICE CREAM
Hanhoi, Vietnam

EGG POACHER
Boston, UK

DRAWERS
Boston, UK

TAP
Beijing, China

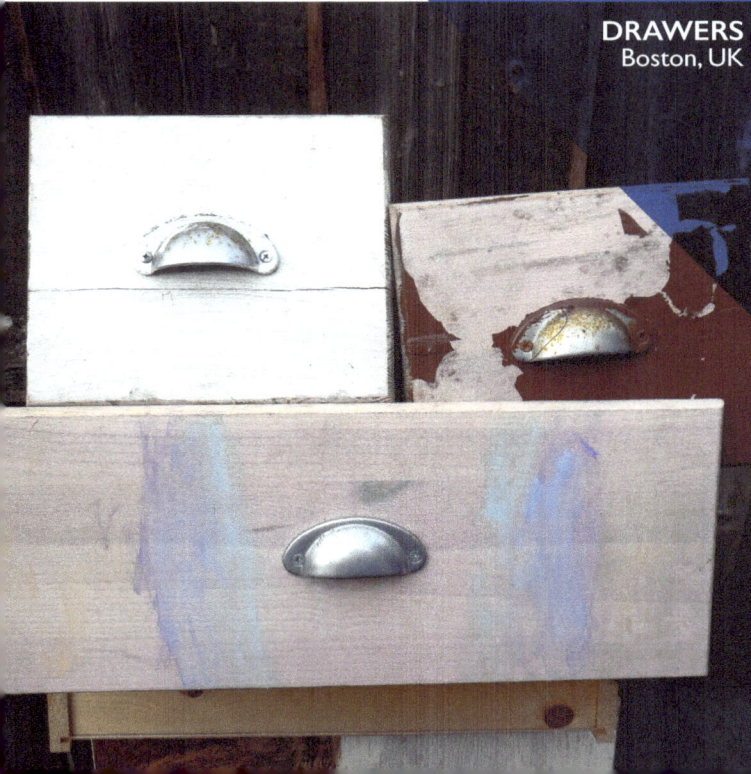

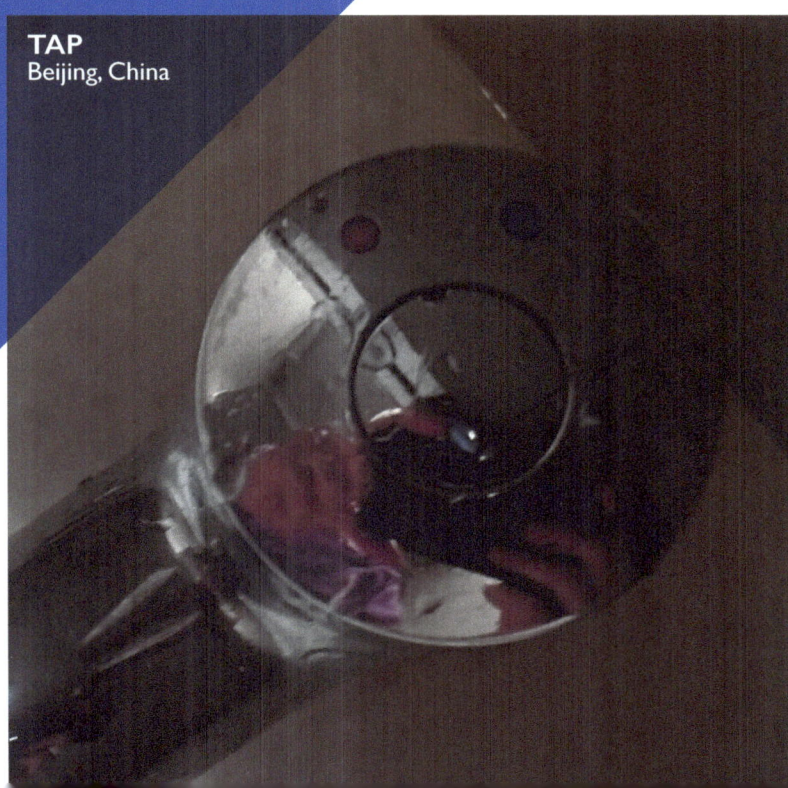

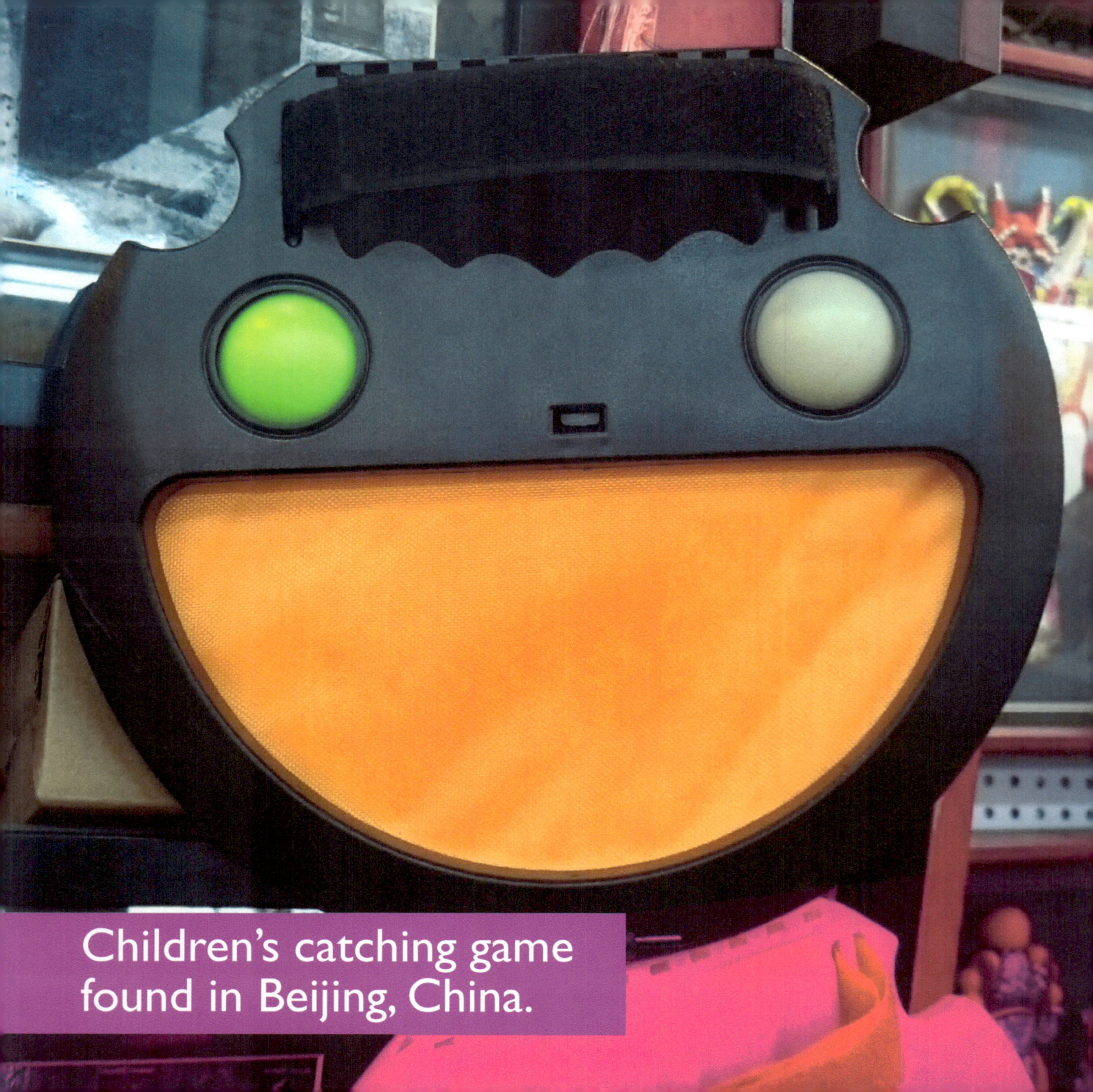

Children's catching game found in Beijing, China.

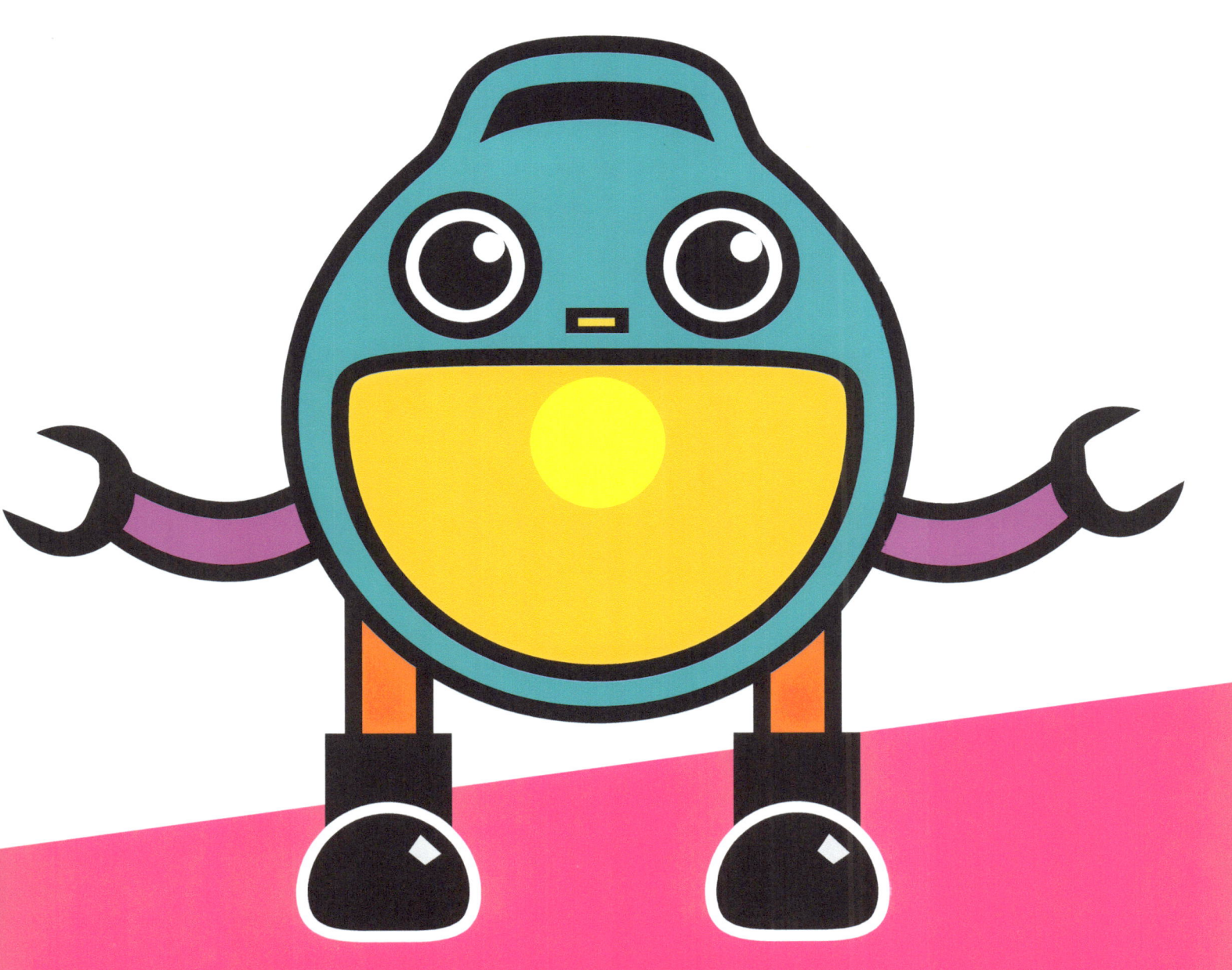

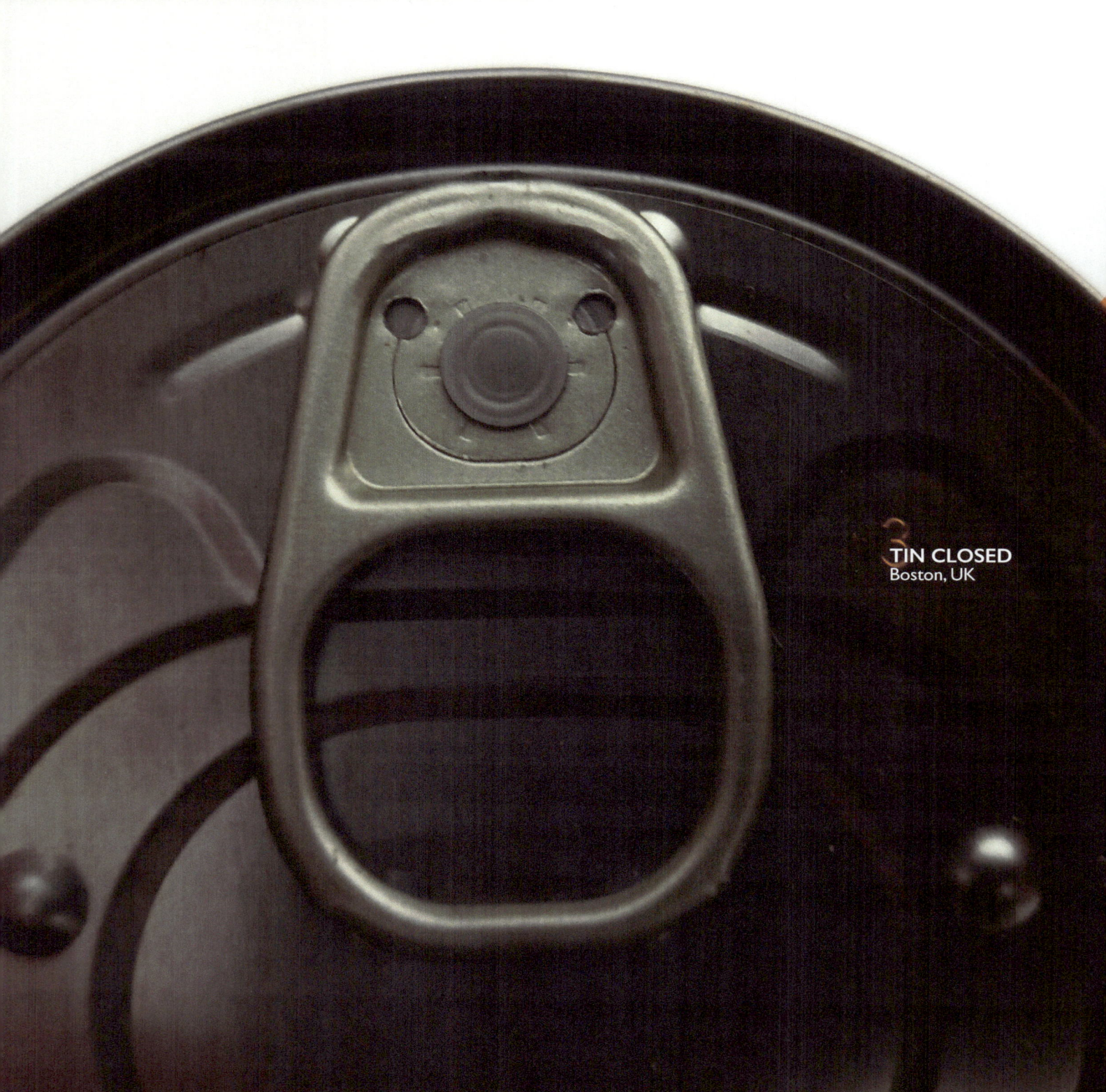

TIN CLOSED
Boston, UK

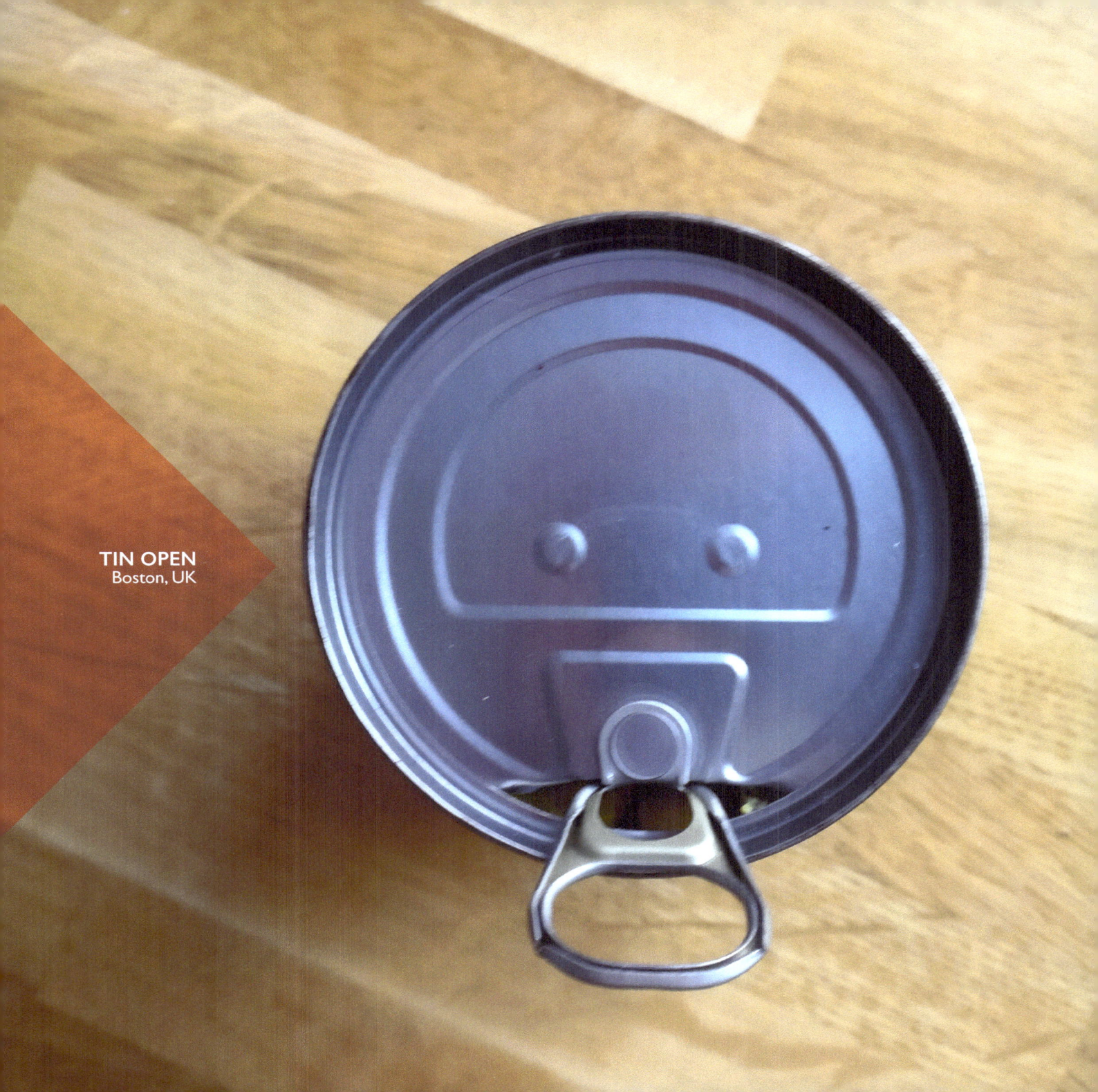

TIN OPEN
Boston, UK

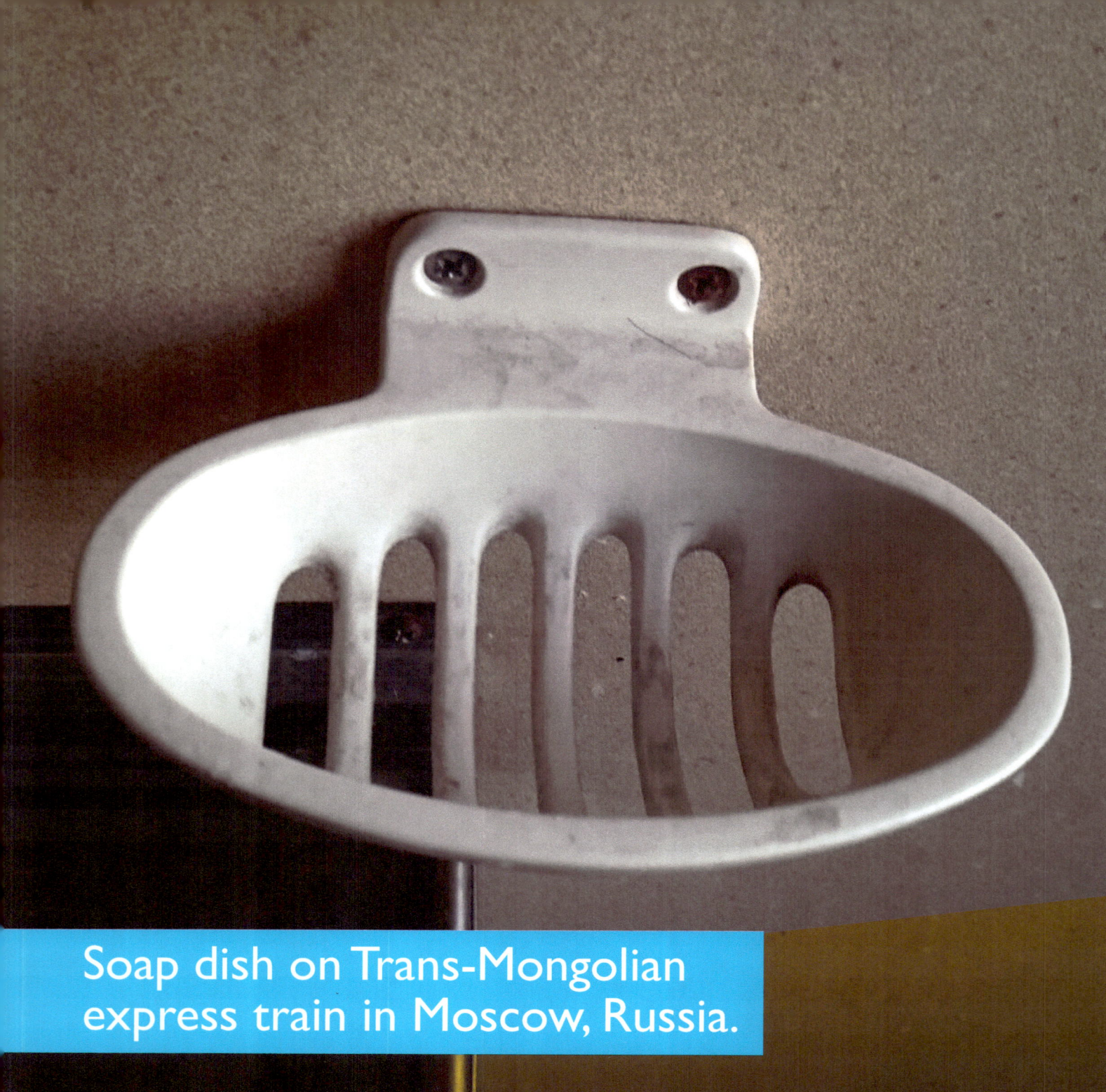

Soap dish on Trans-Mongolian express train in Moscow, Russia.

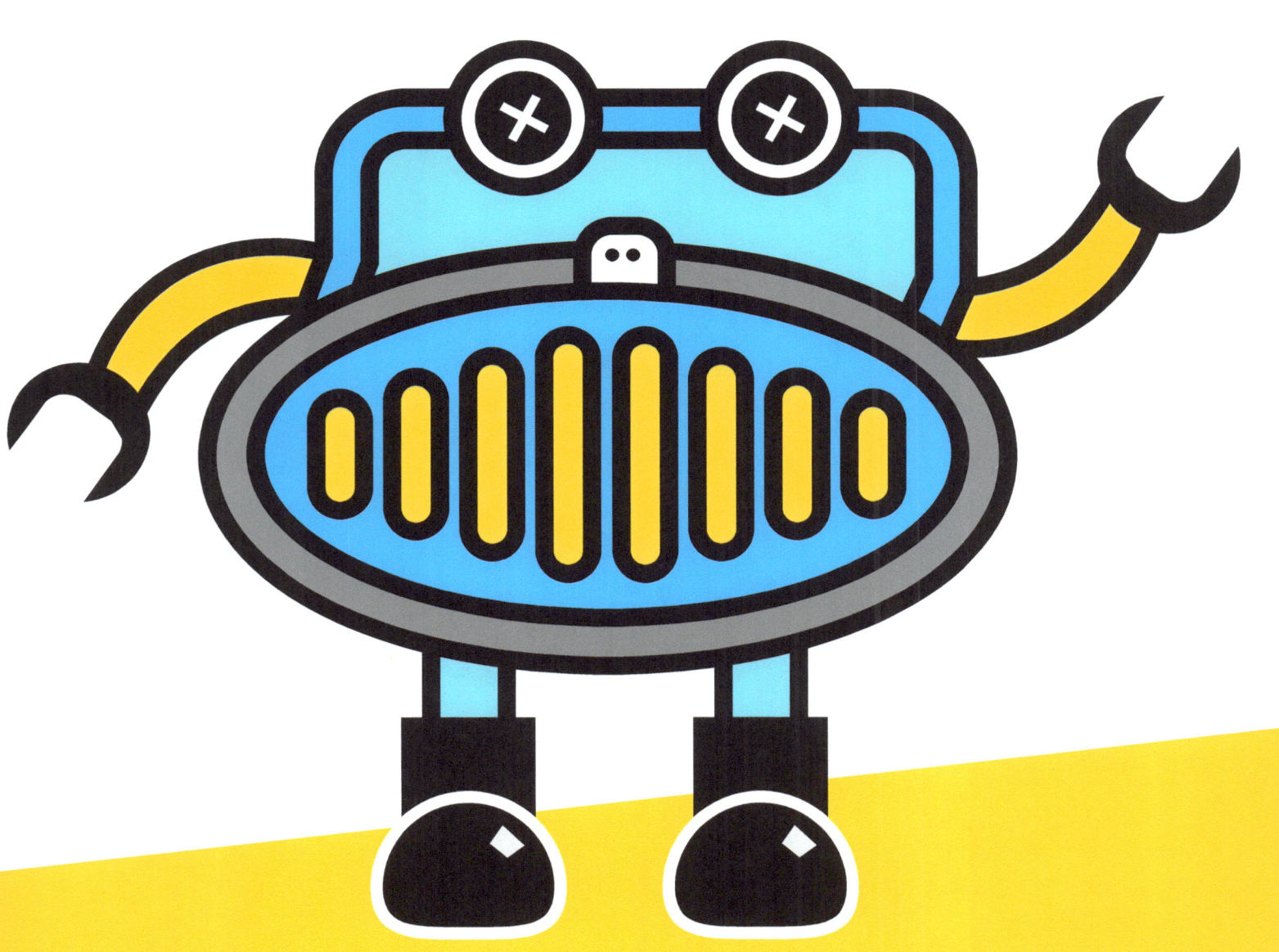

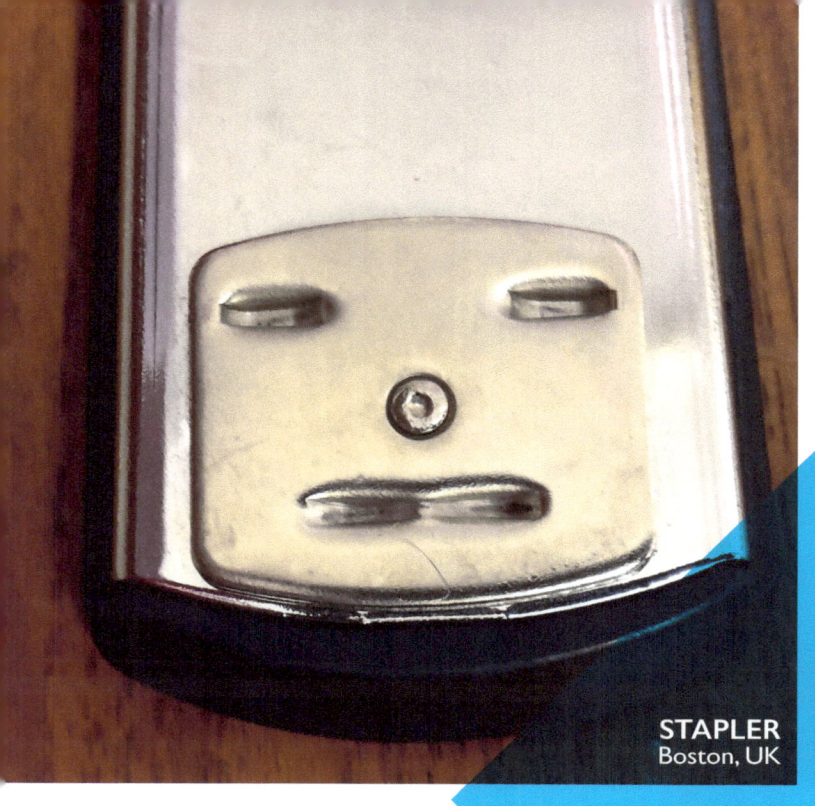

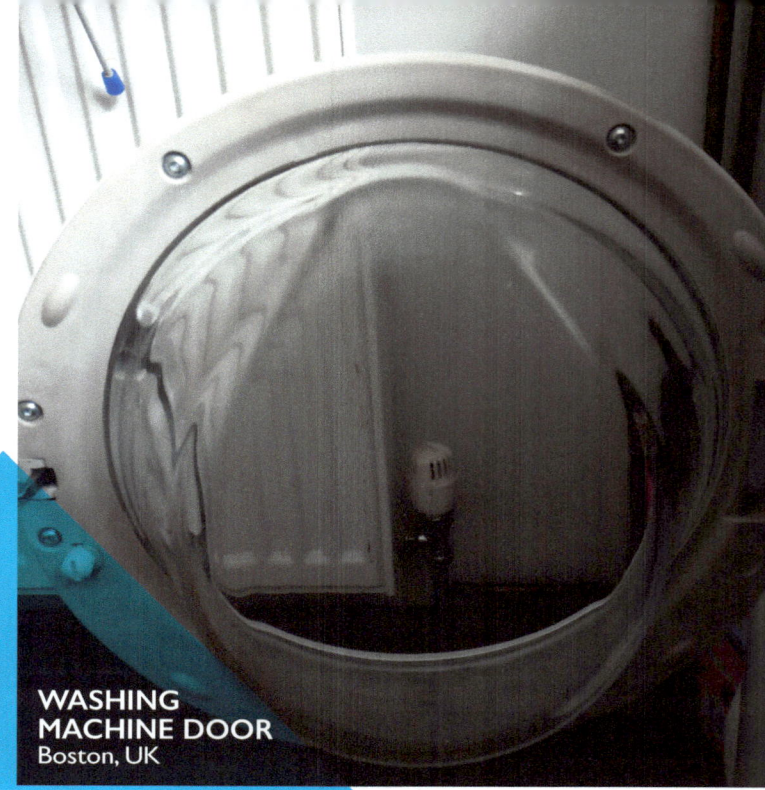

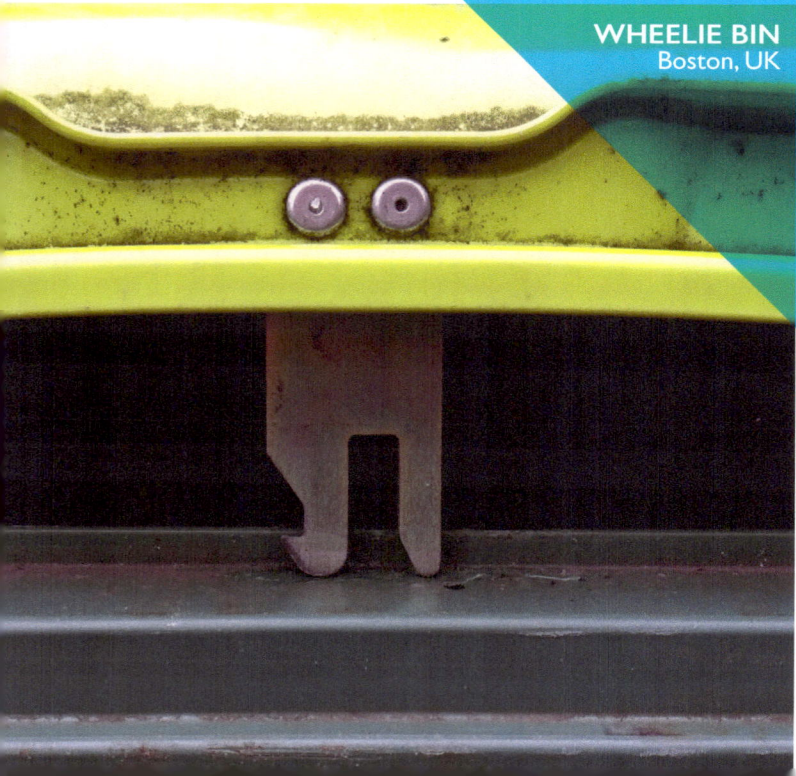

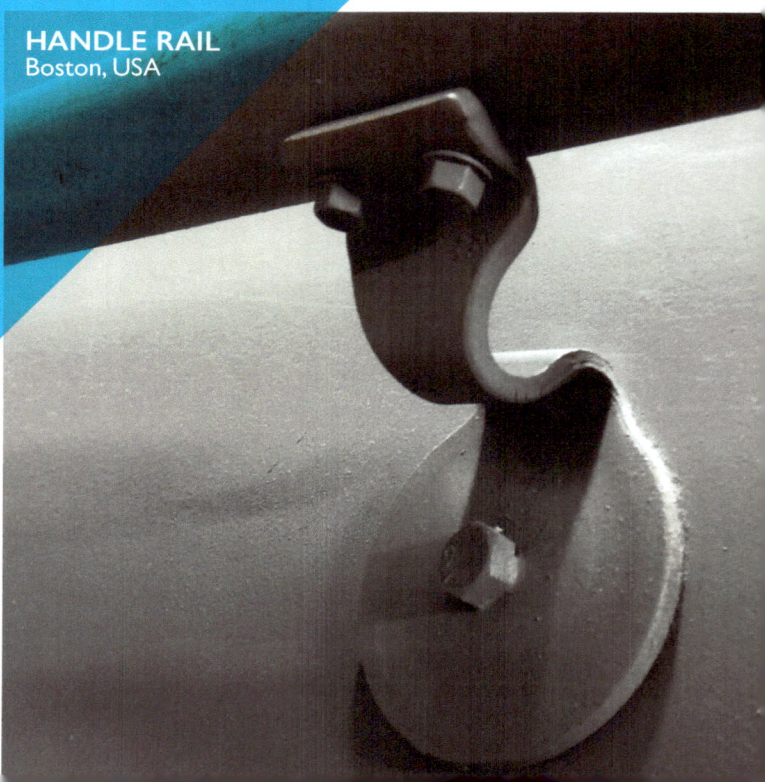

STAPLER
Boston, UK

WASHING MACHINE DOOR
Boston, UK

WHEELIE BIN
Boston, UK

HANDLE RAIL
Boston, USA

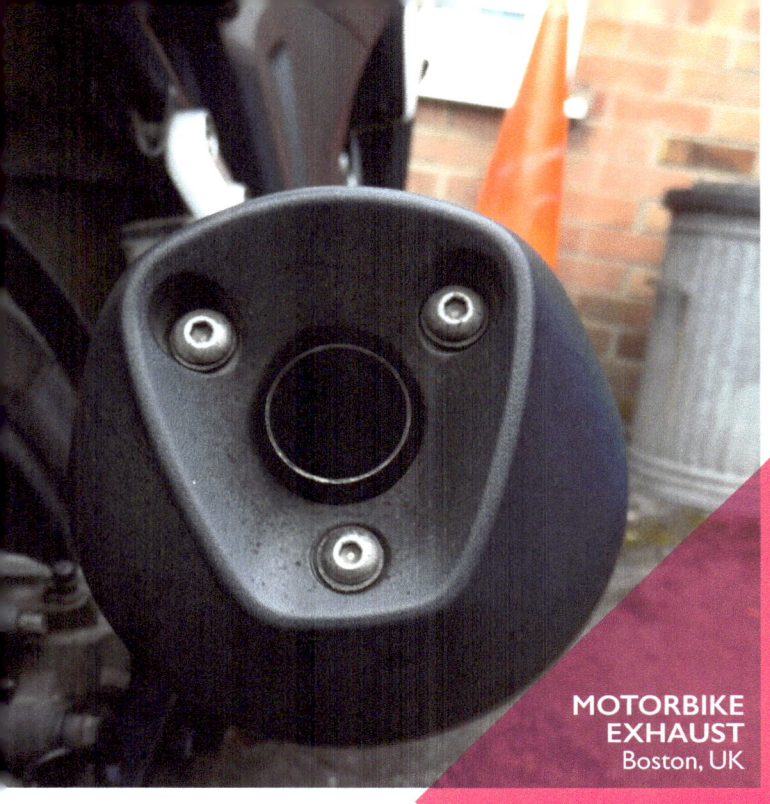

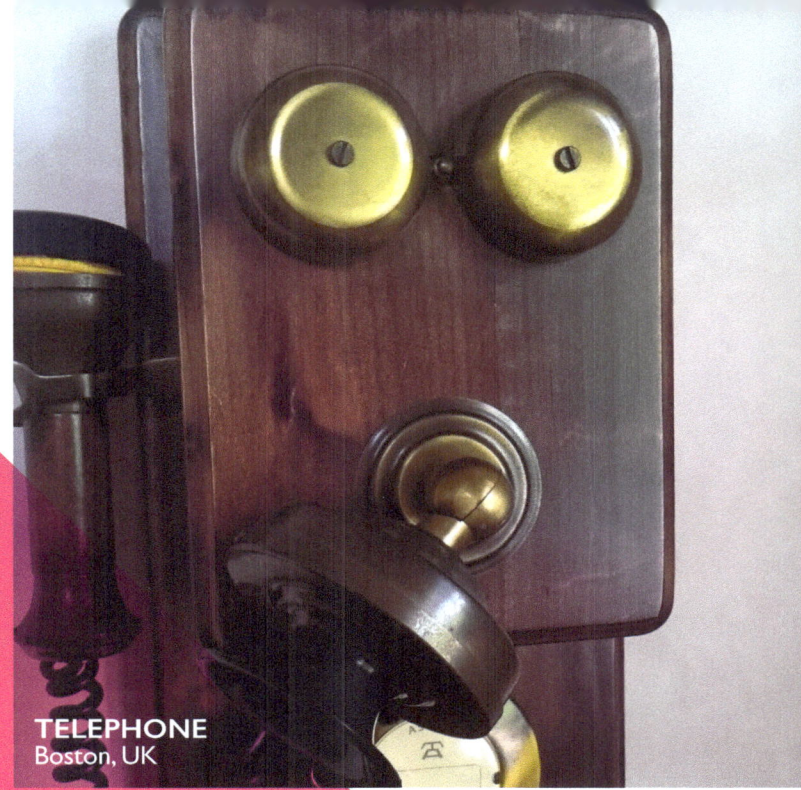

MOTORBIKE EXHAUST
Boston, UK

TELEPHONE
Boston, UK

PACKAGING
Boston, USA

ECO CONTROL
Boston, USA

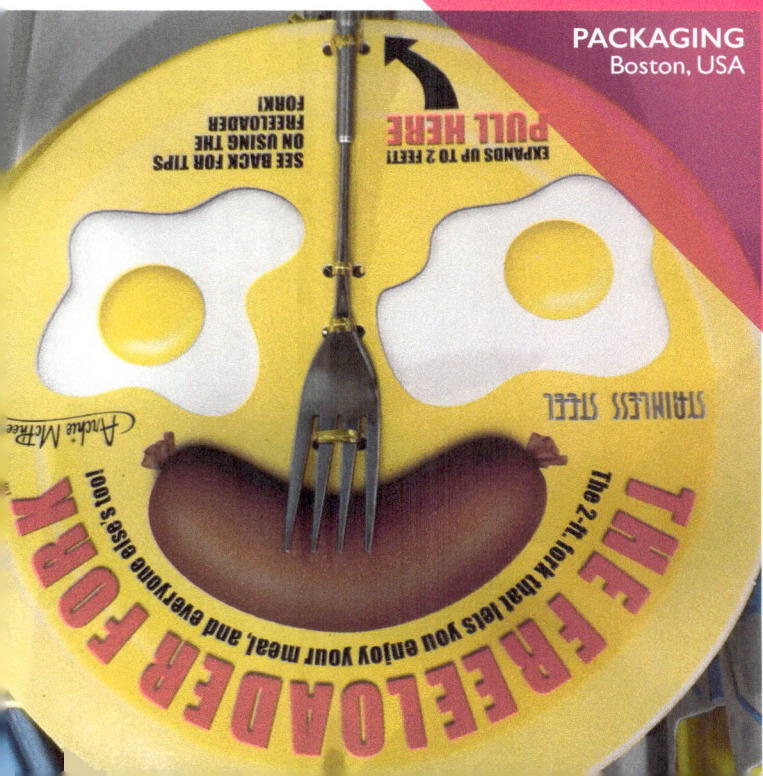

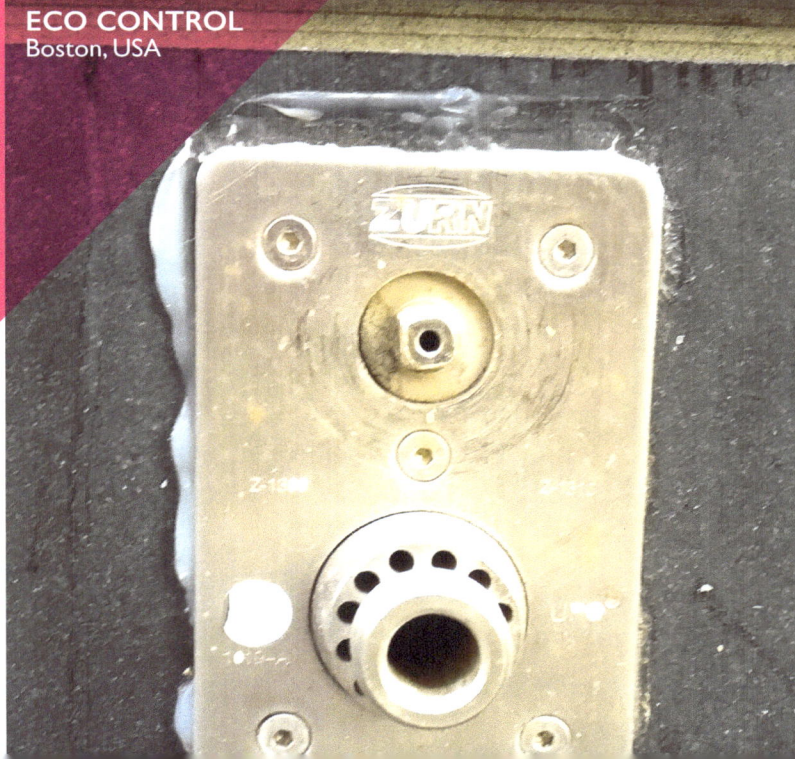

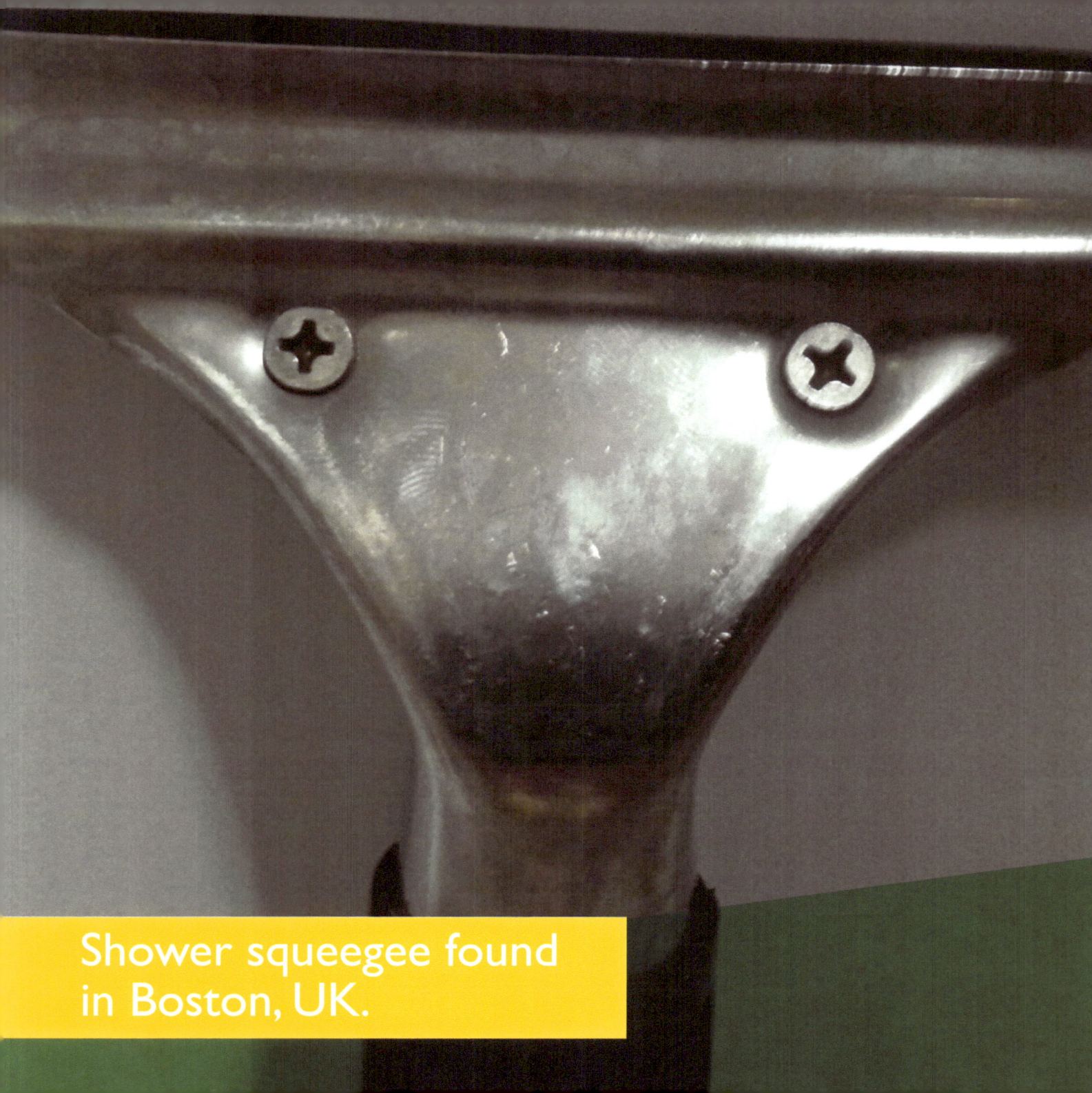

Shower squeegee found in Boston, UK.

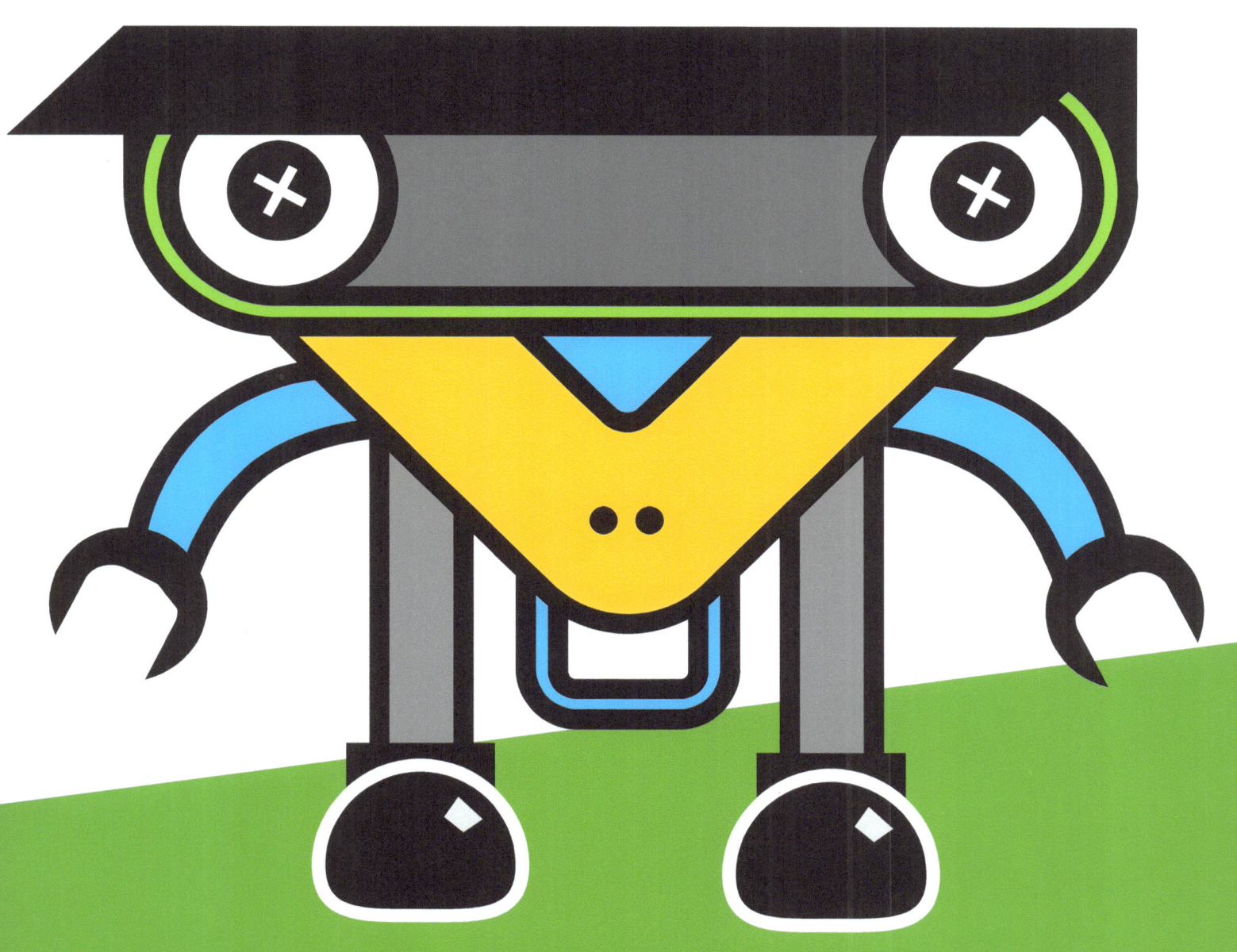

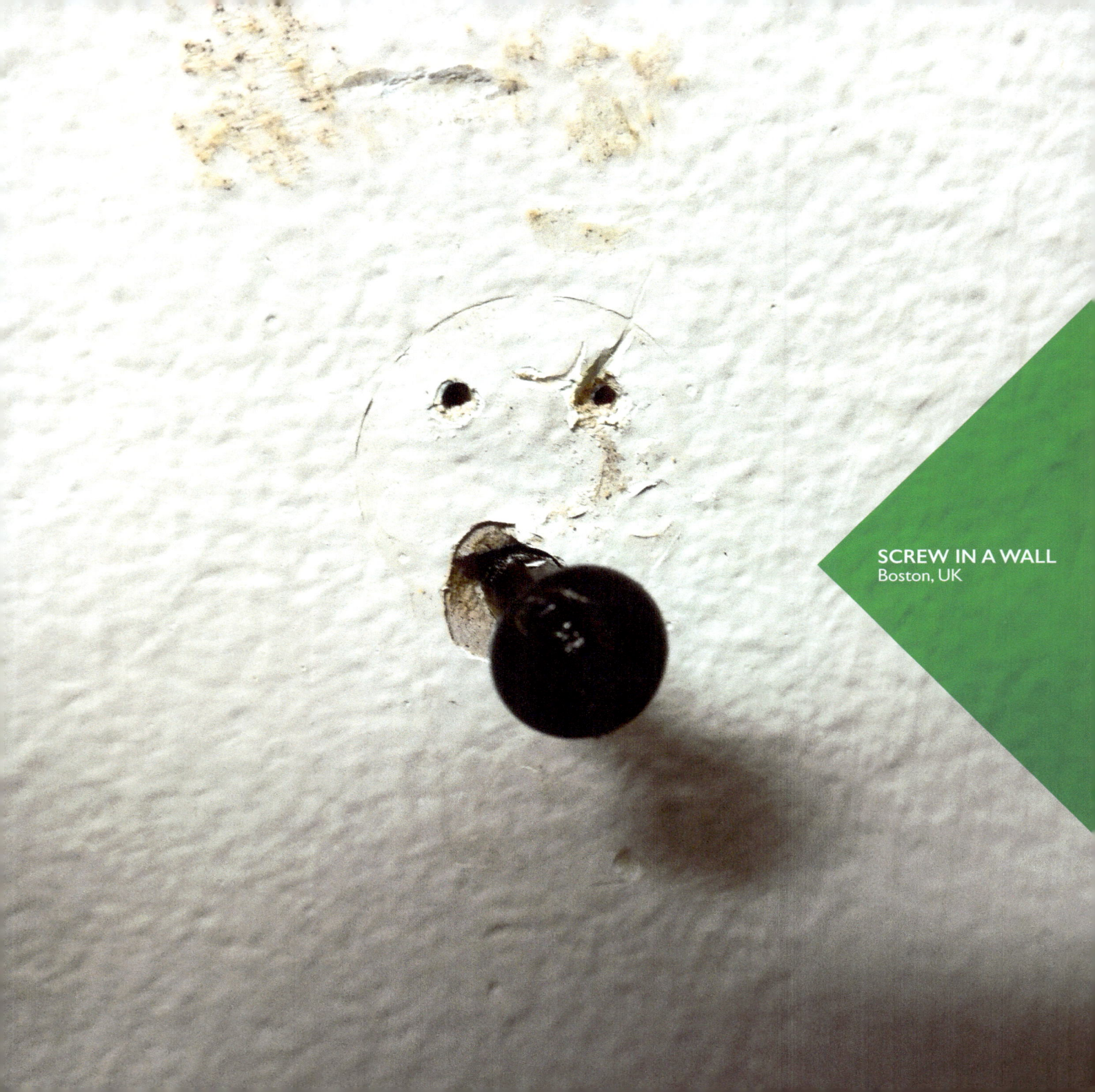

SCREW IN A WALL
Boston, UK

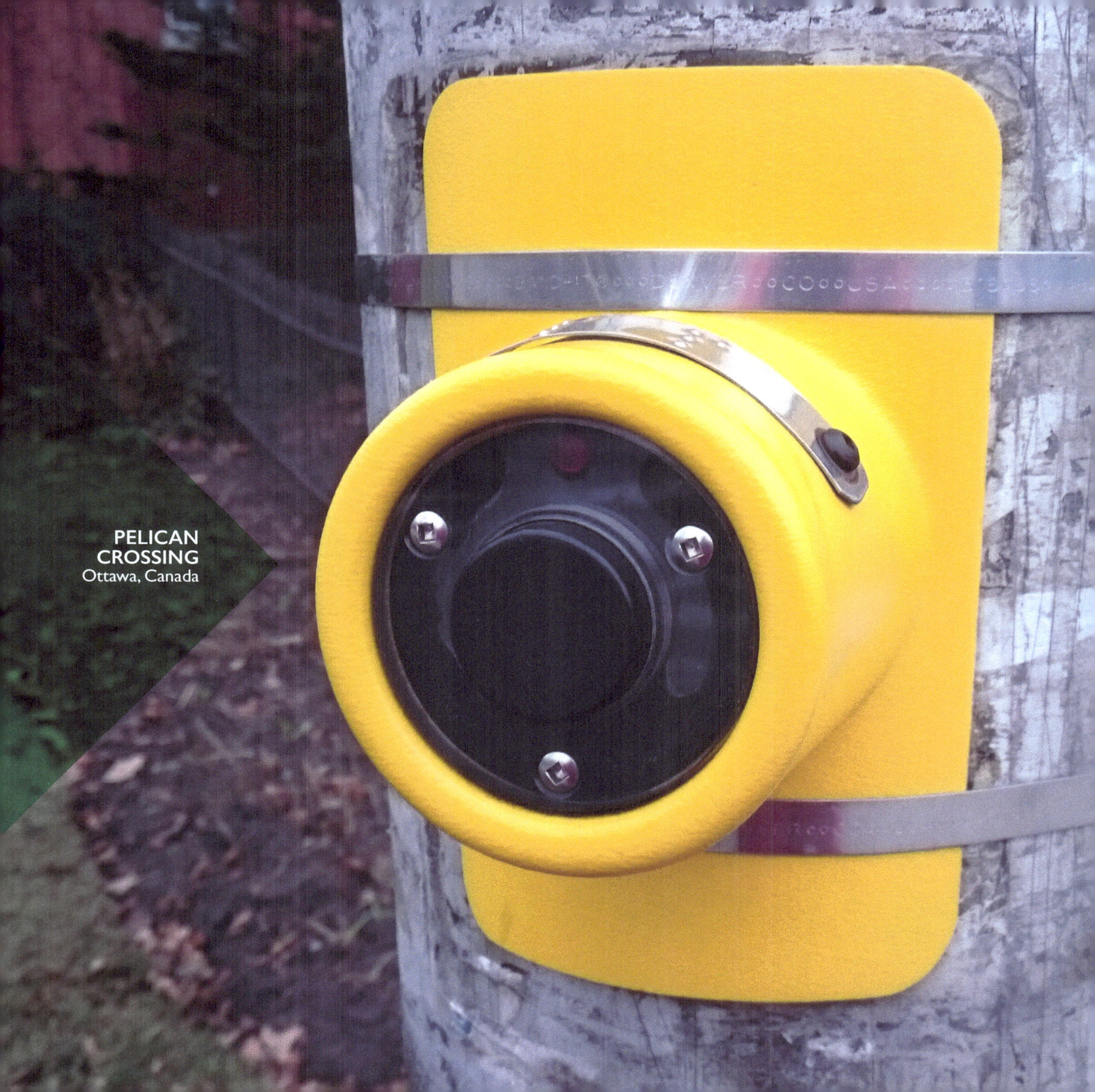

PELICAN
CROSSING
Ottawa, Canada

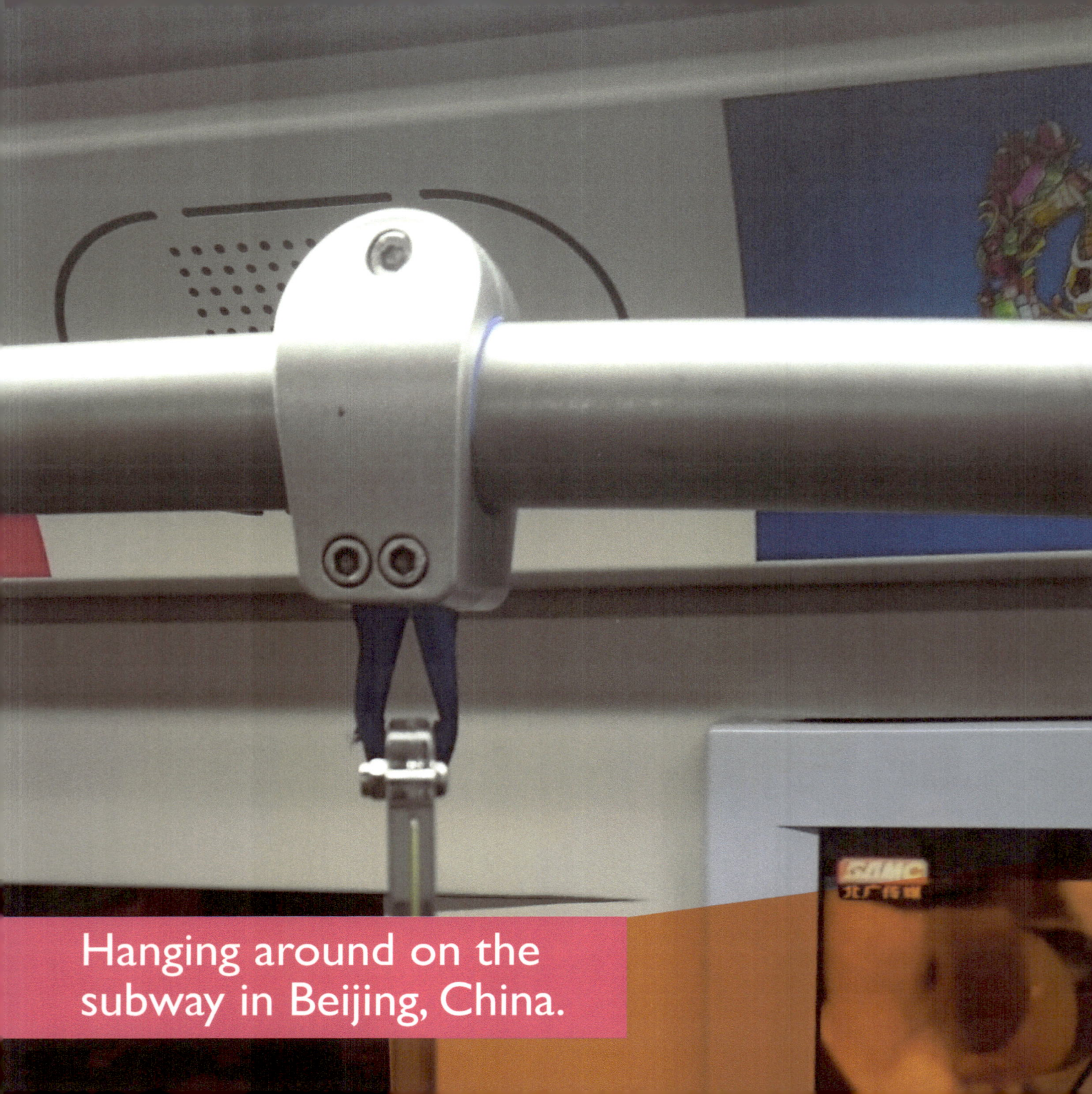

Hanging around on the subway in Beijing, China.

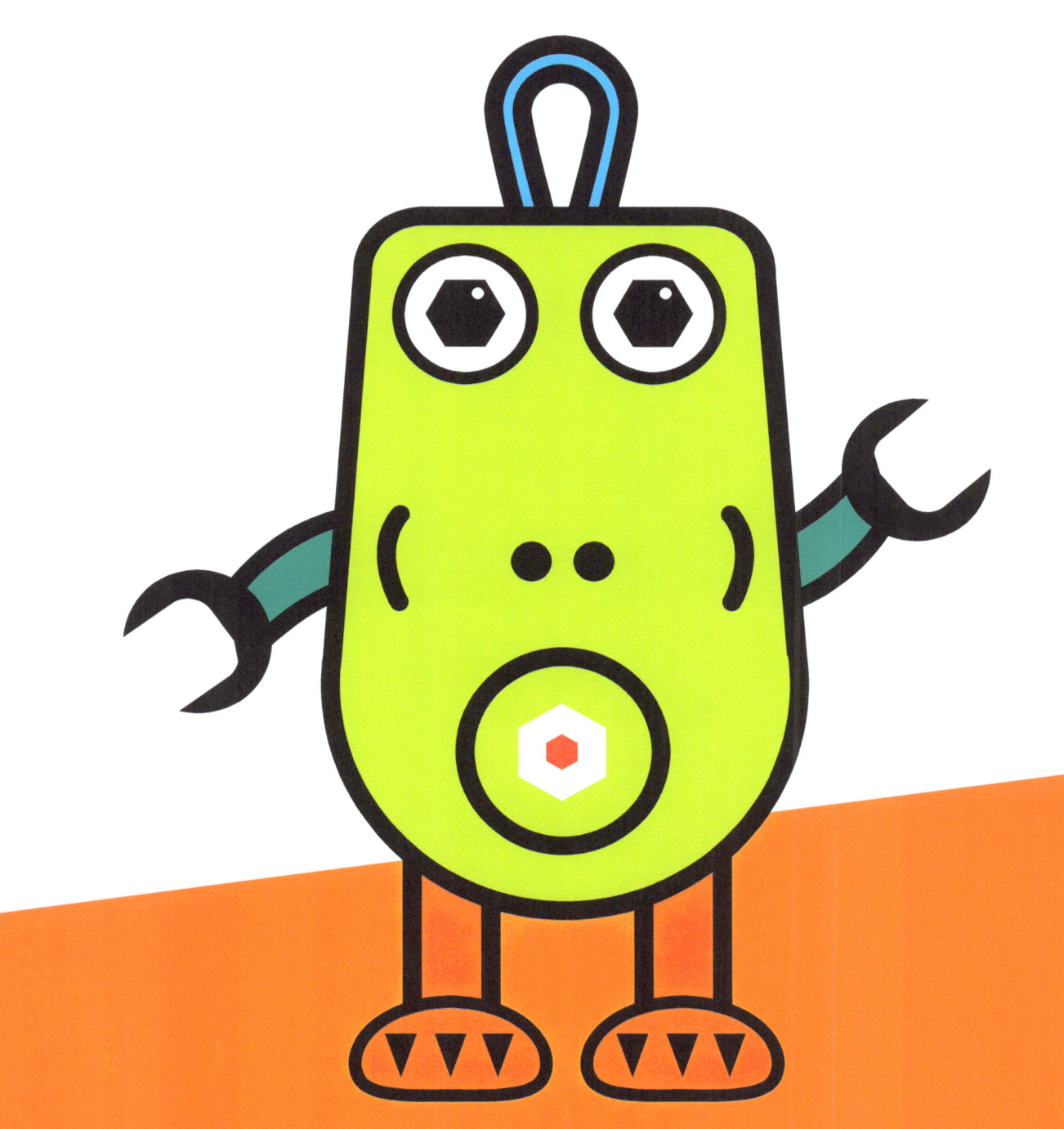

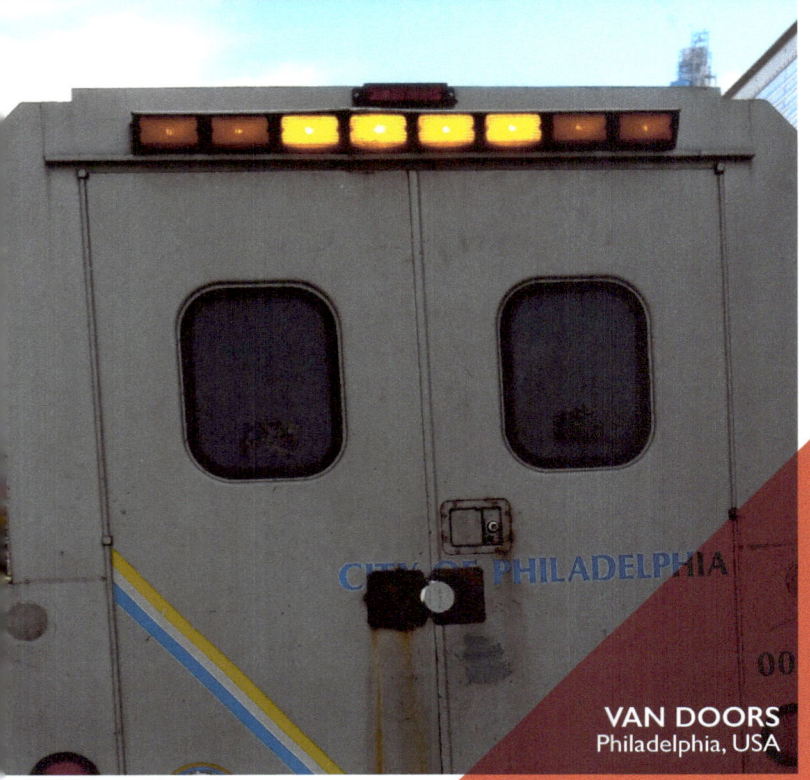

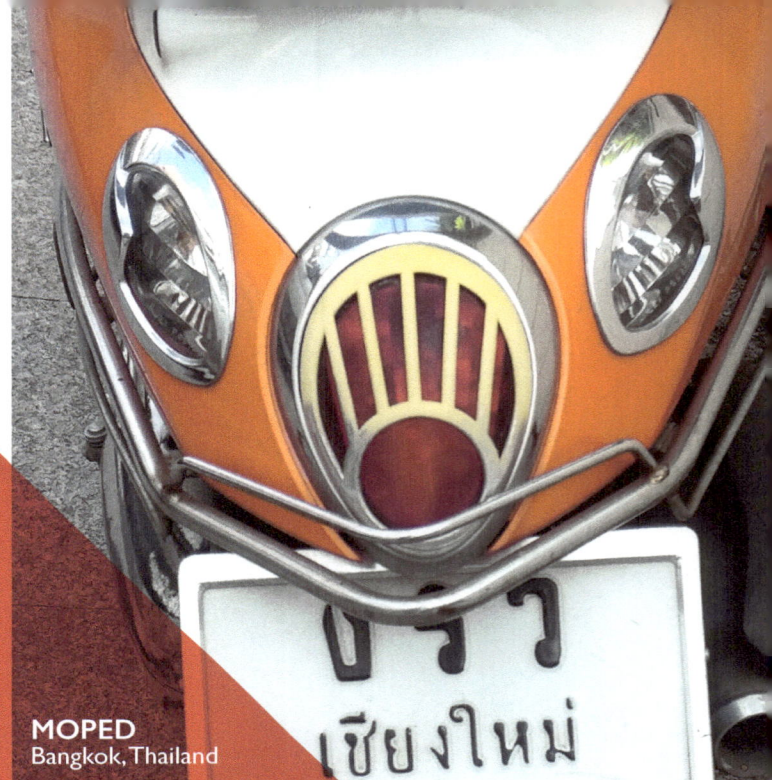

VAN DOORS
Philadelphia, USA

MOPED
Bangkok, Thailand

PLUG SOCKET
New York, USA

DOOR HANDLE
Boston, UK

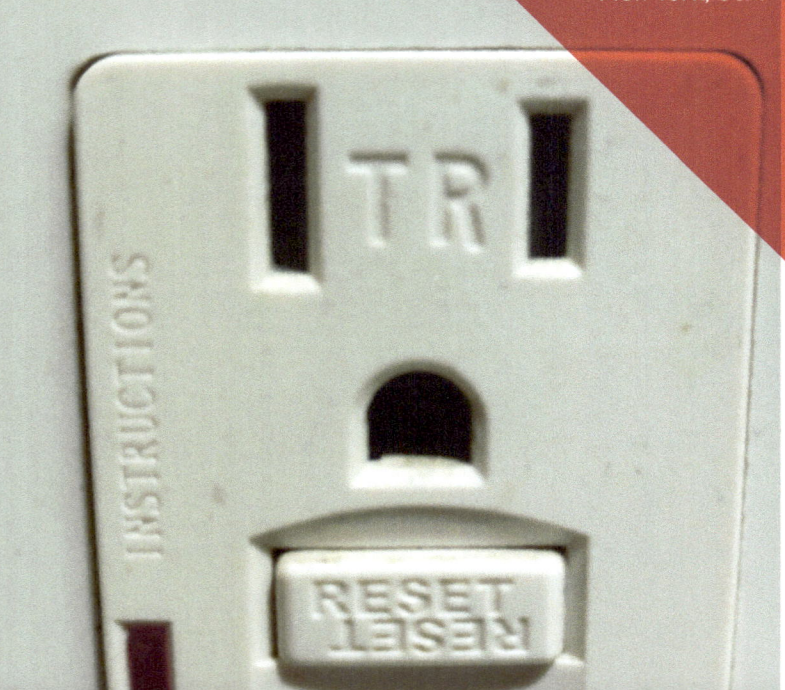

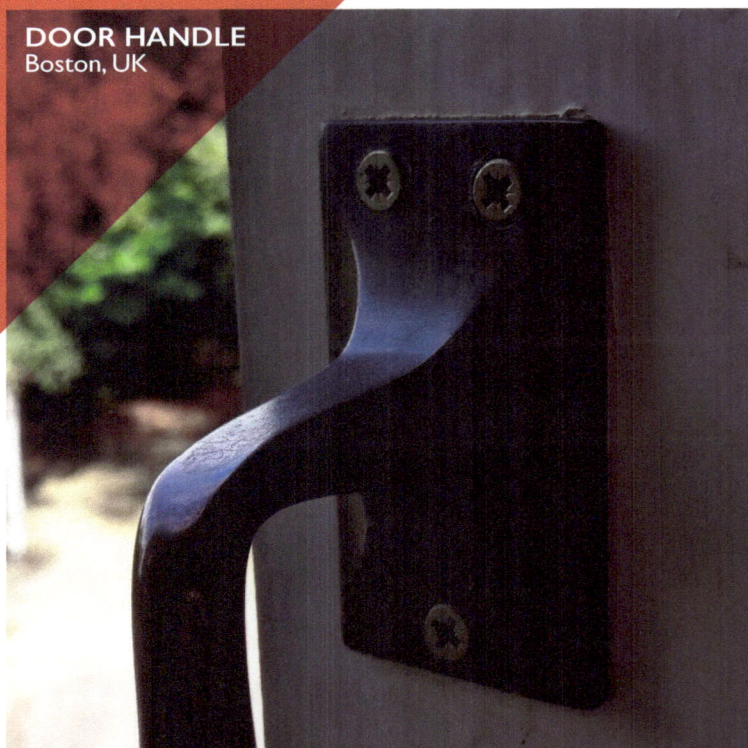

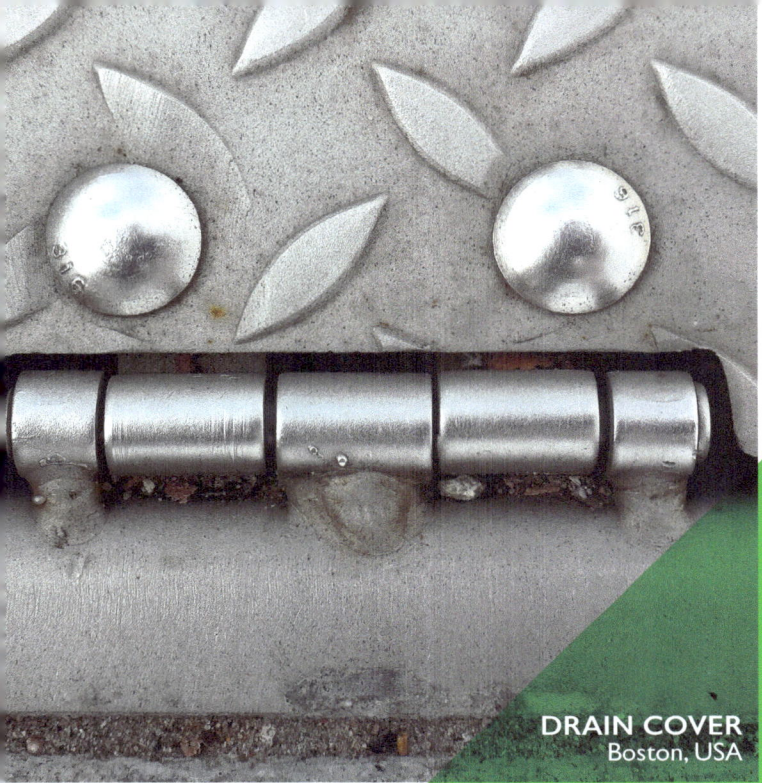

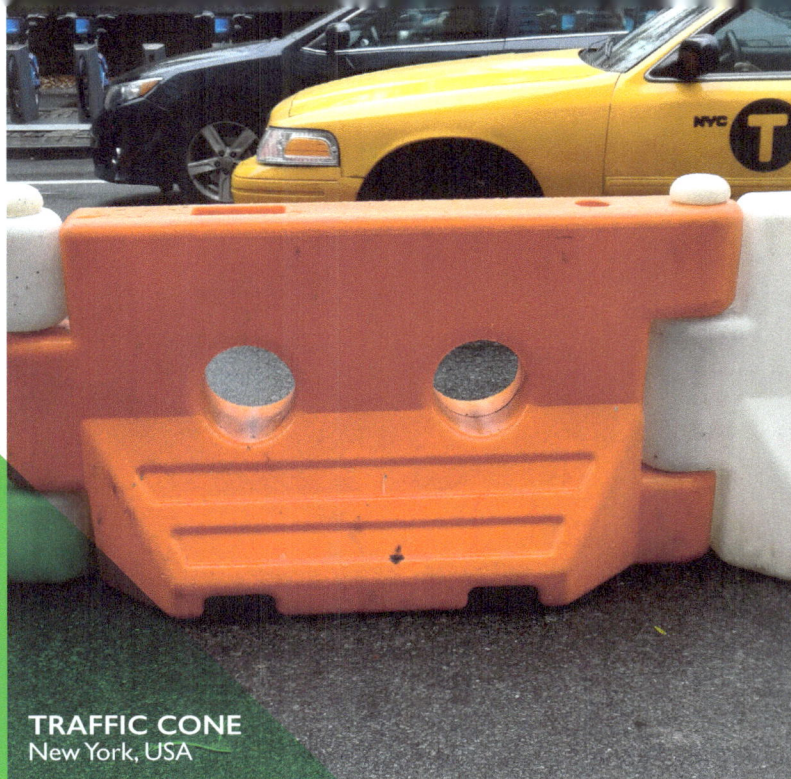

DRAIN COVER
Boston, USA

TRAFFIC CONE
New York, USA

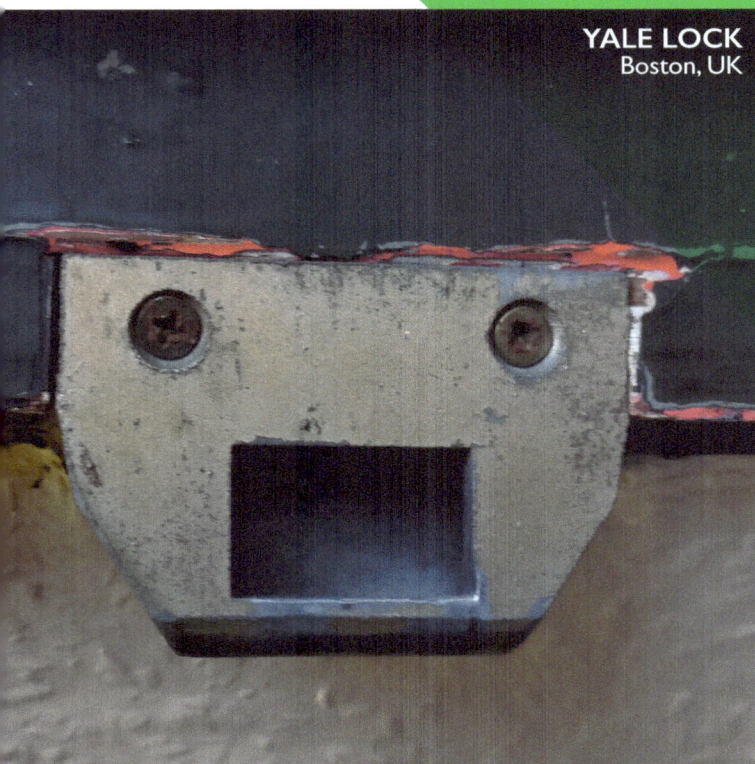

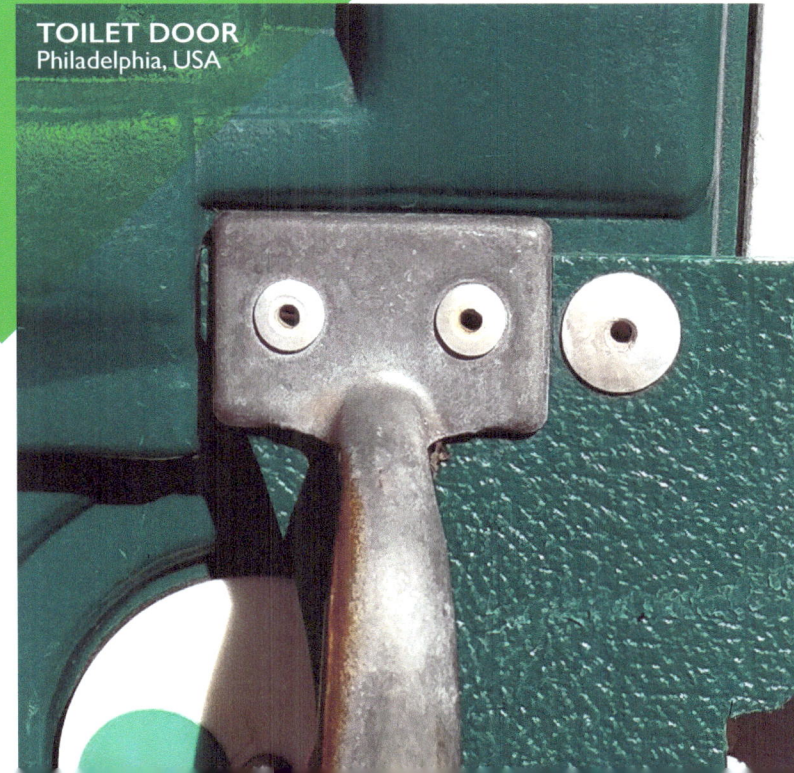

YALE LOCK
Boston, UK

TOILET DOOR
Philadelphia, USA

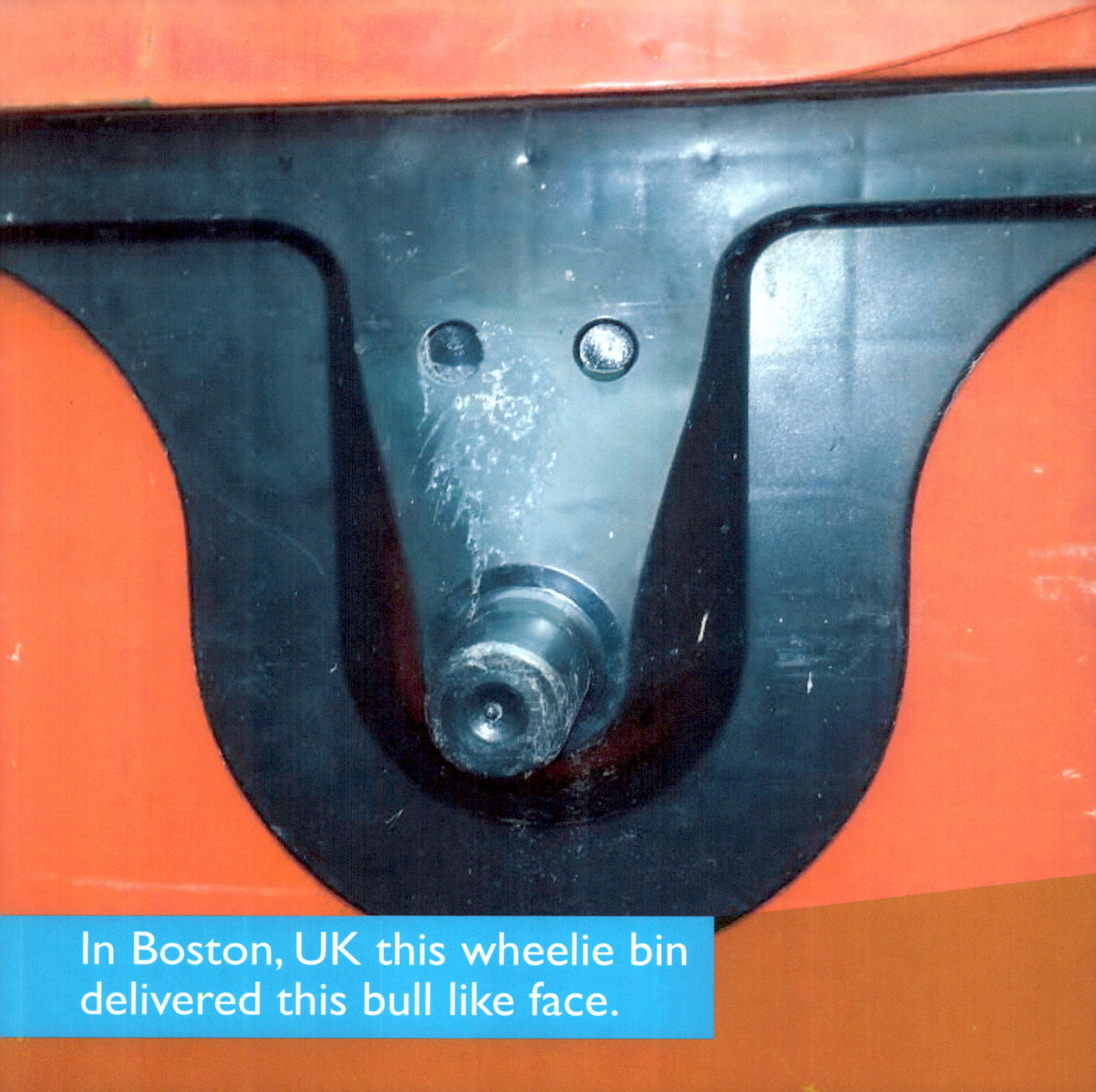

In Boston, UK this wheelie bin delivered this bull like face.

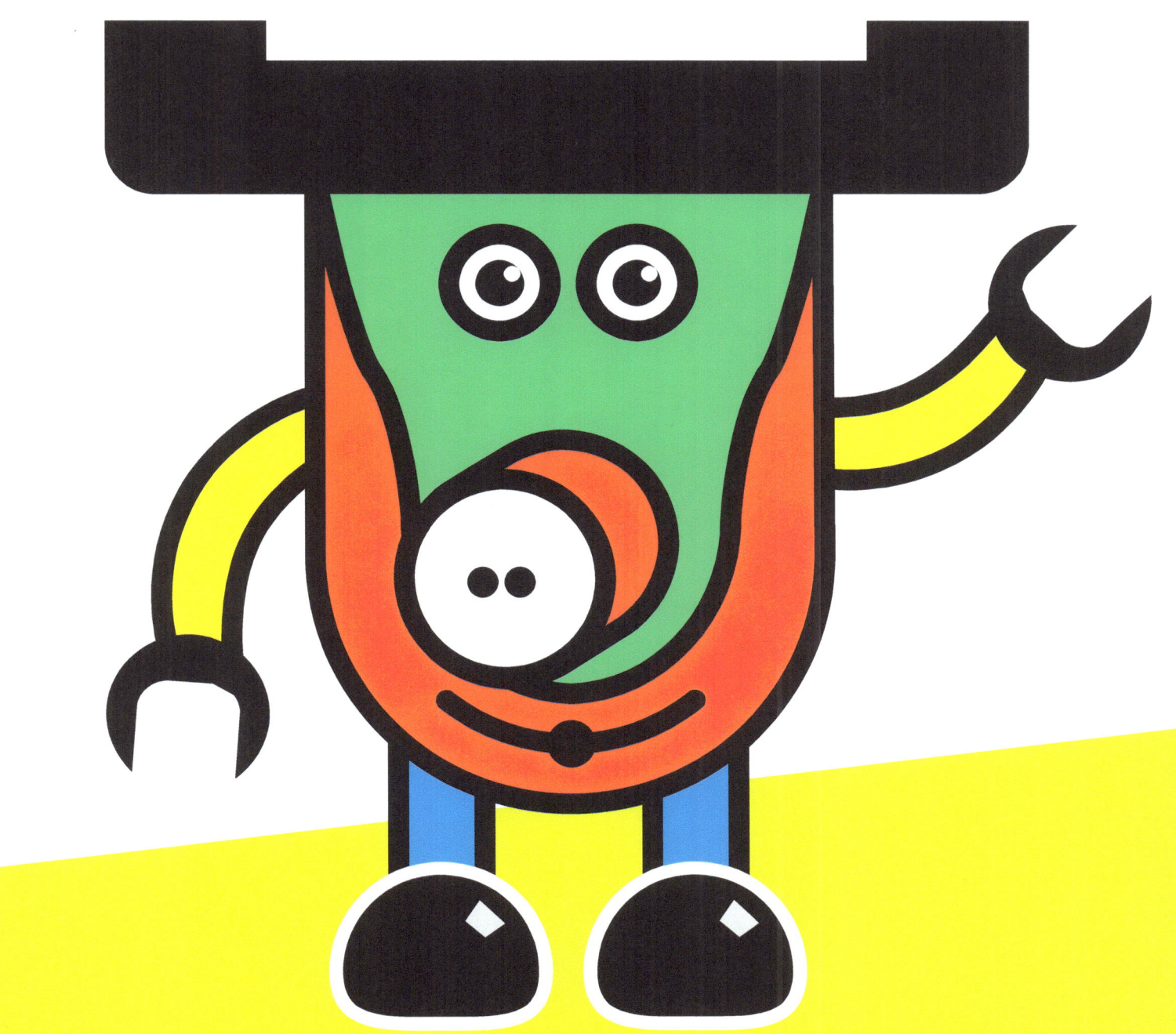

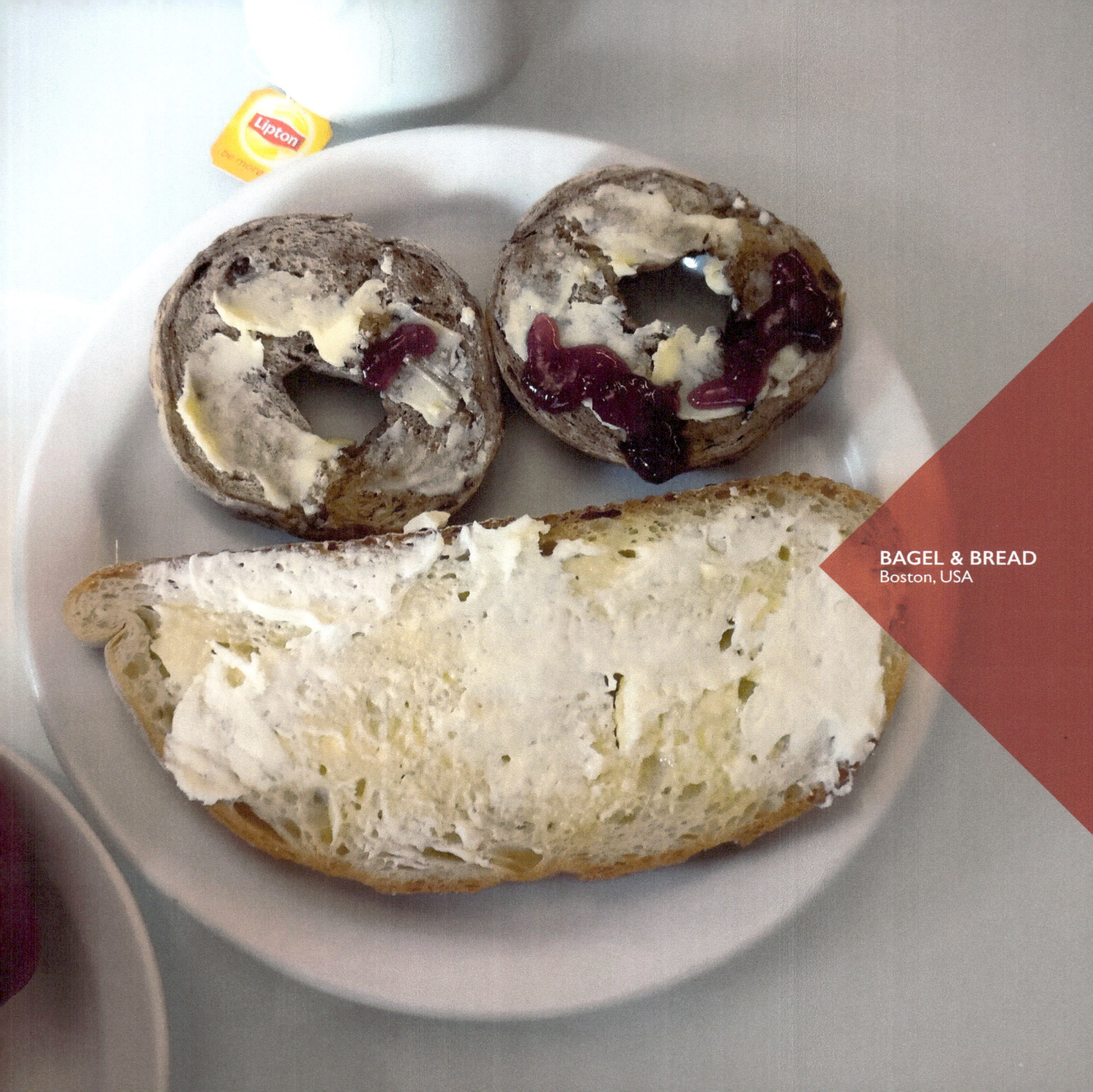

BAGEL & BREAD
Boston, USA

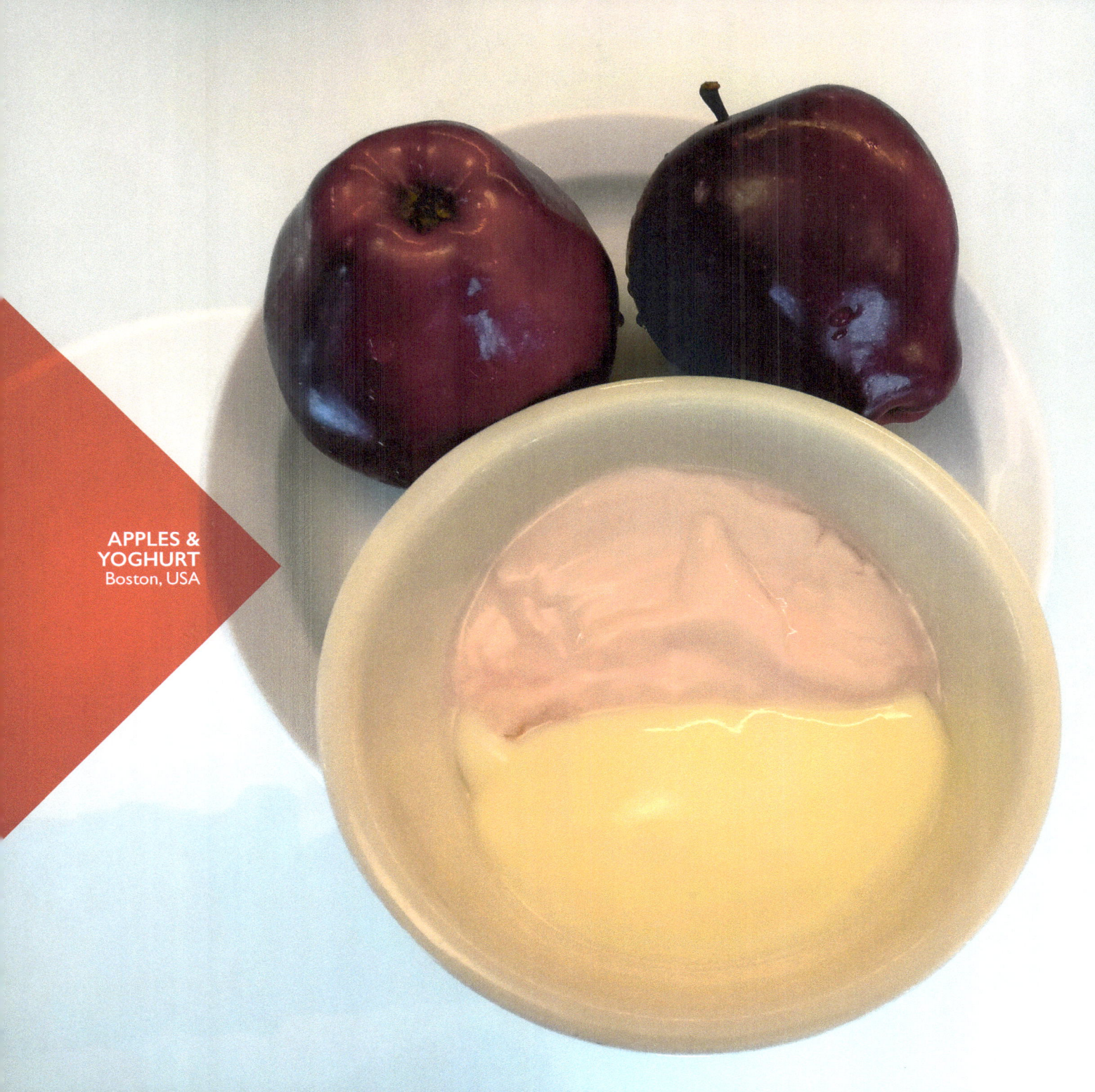

APPLES &
YOGHURT
Boston, USA

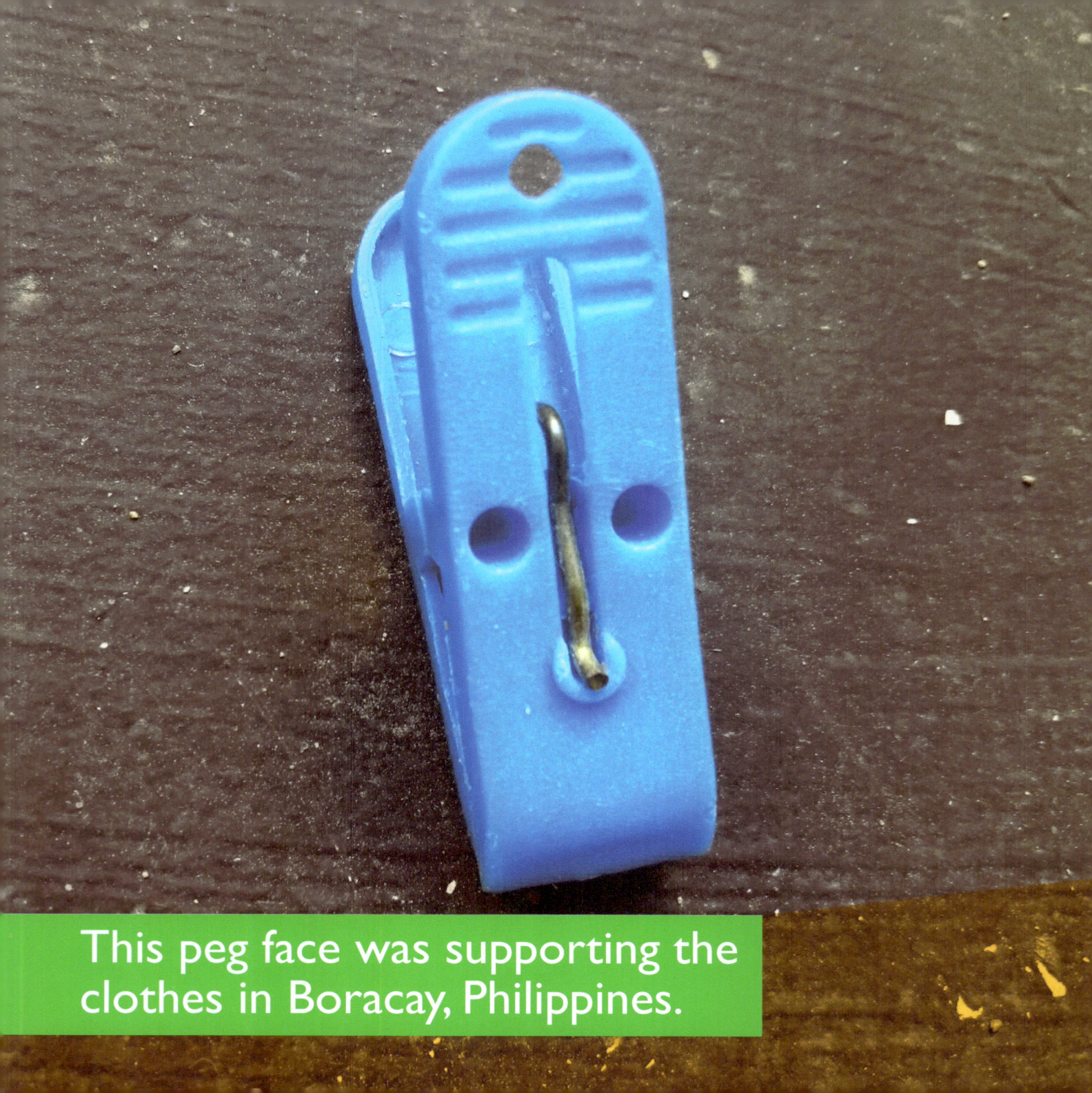

This peg face was supporting the clothes in Boracay, Philippines.

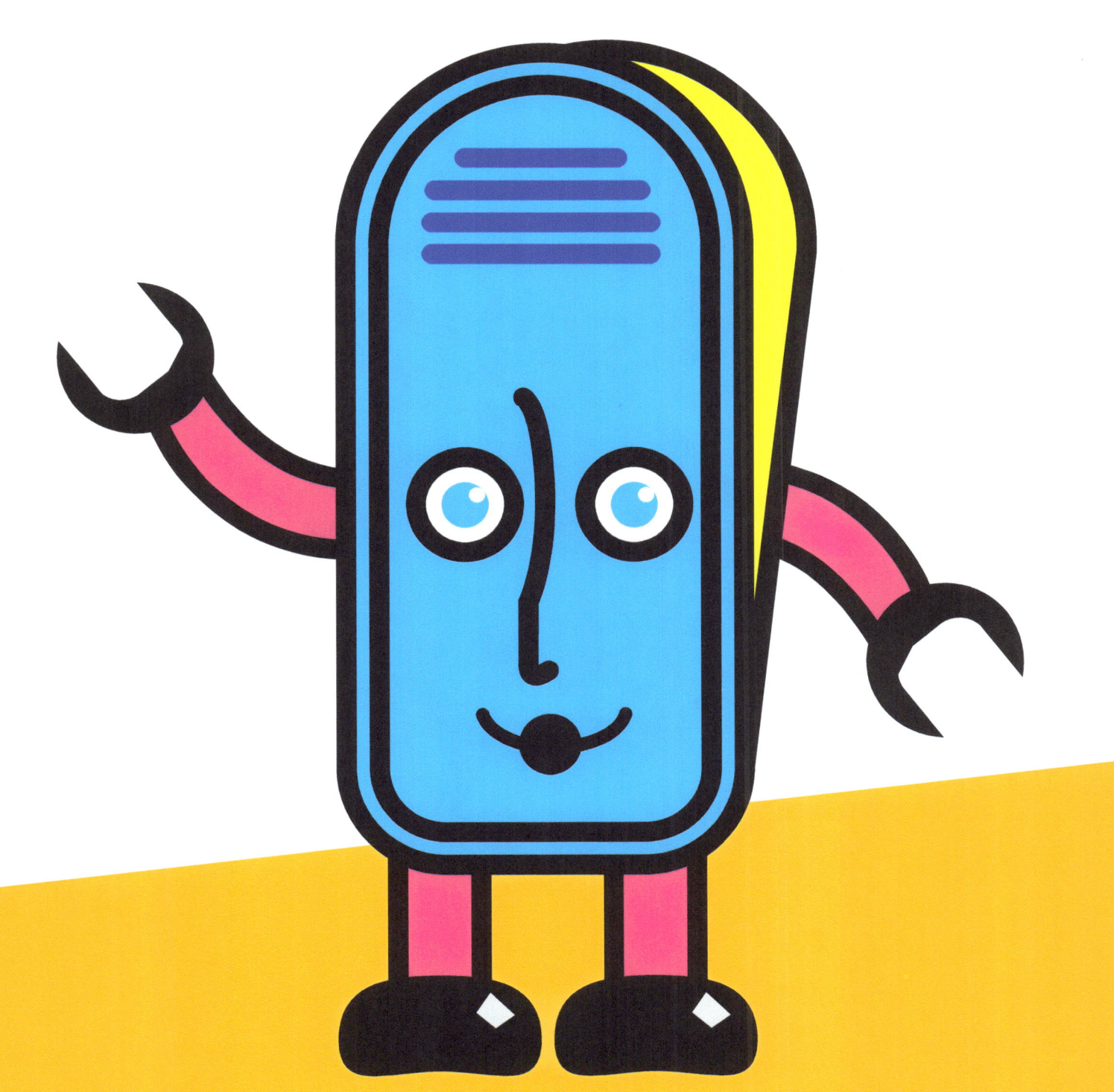

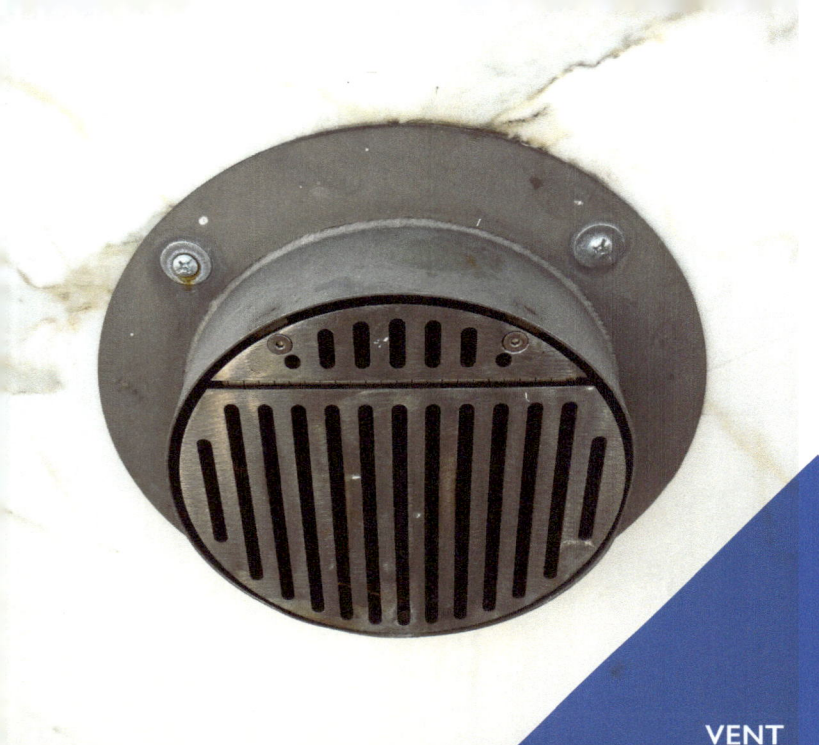

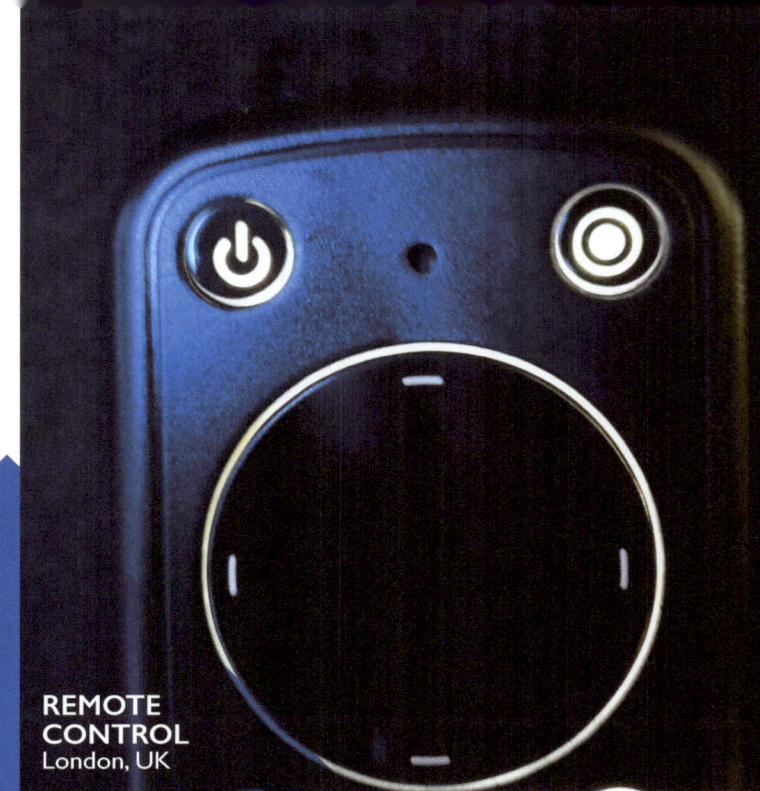

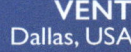

VENT
Dallas, USA

REMOTE CONTROL
London, UK

DOOR STOP
Reno, USA

CAP
Chicago, USA

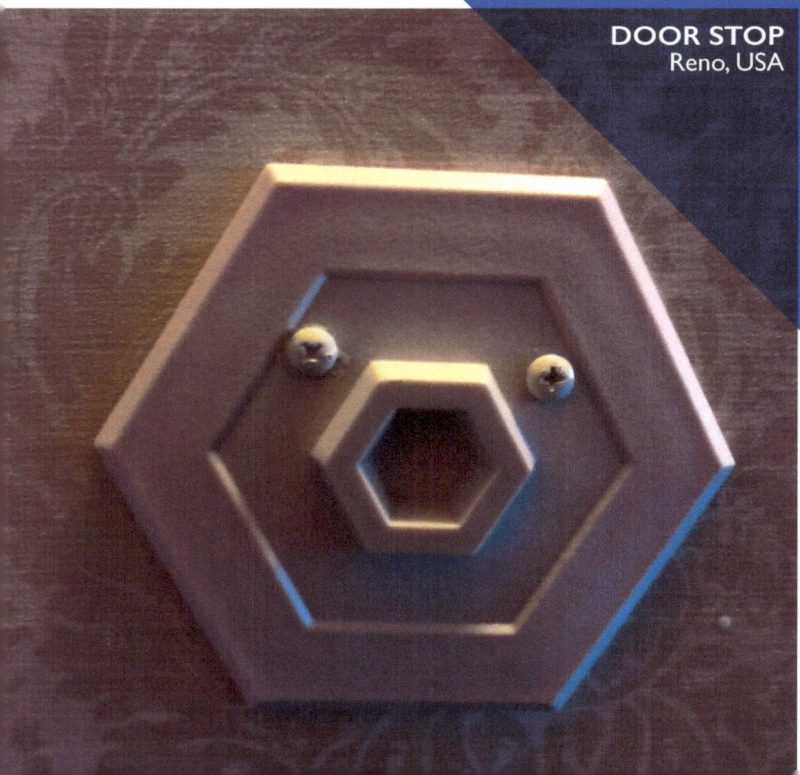

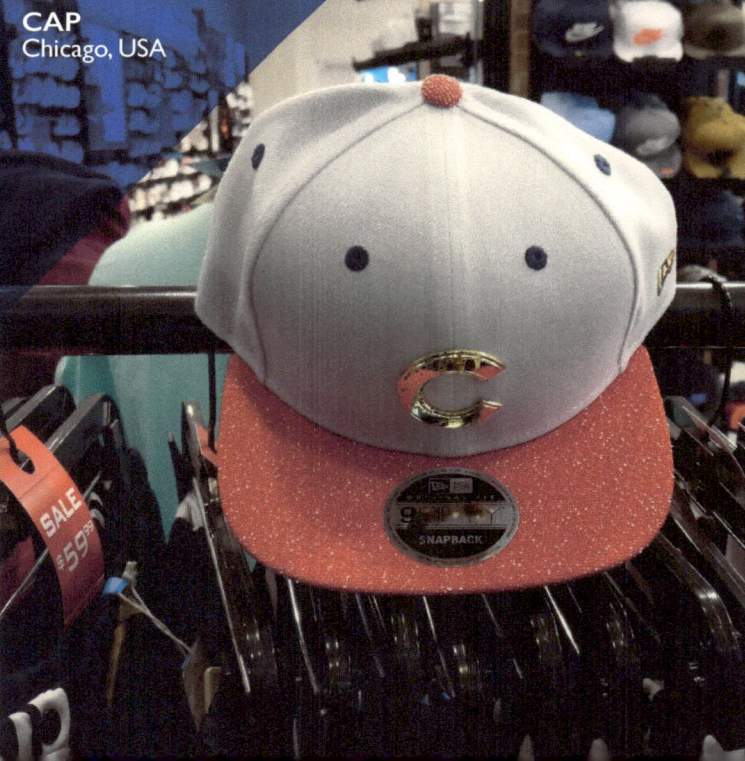

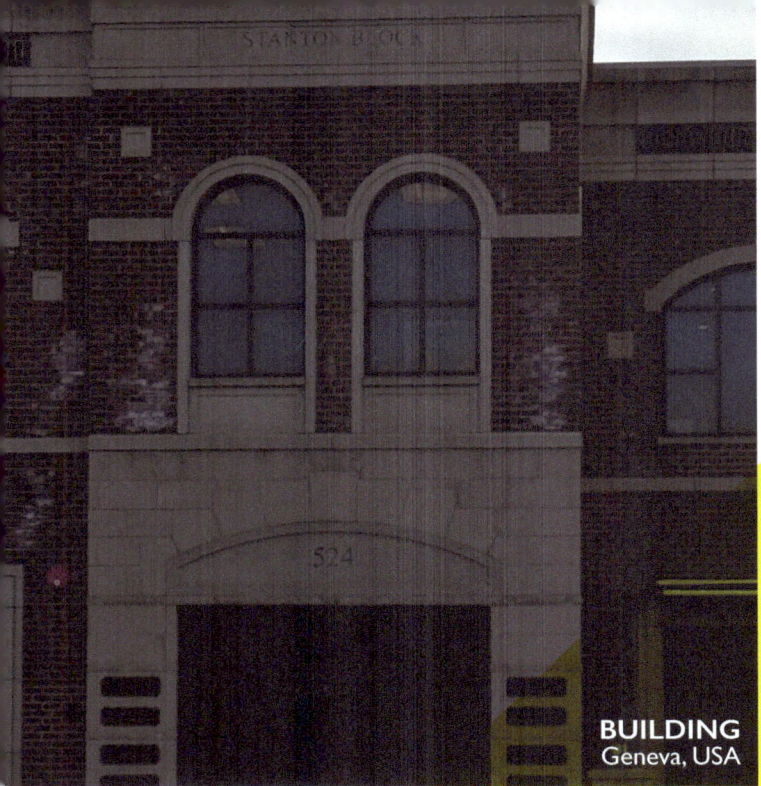
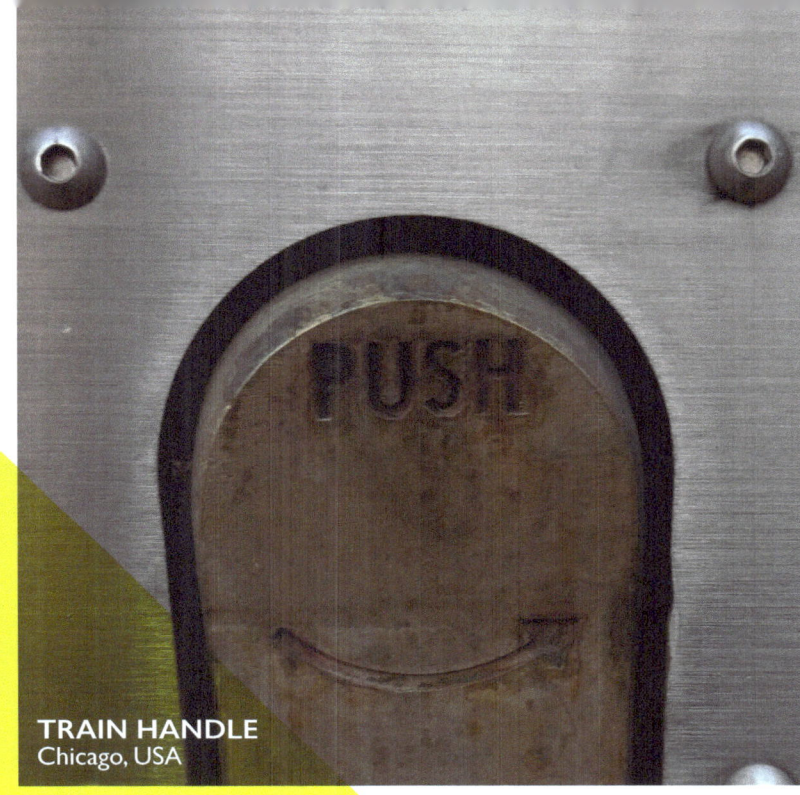

BUILDING
Geneva, USA

TRAIN HANDLE
Chicago, USA

BROKEN LOCK
San Jose, USA

FOOT PUMP
San Francisco, USA

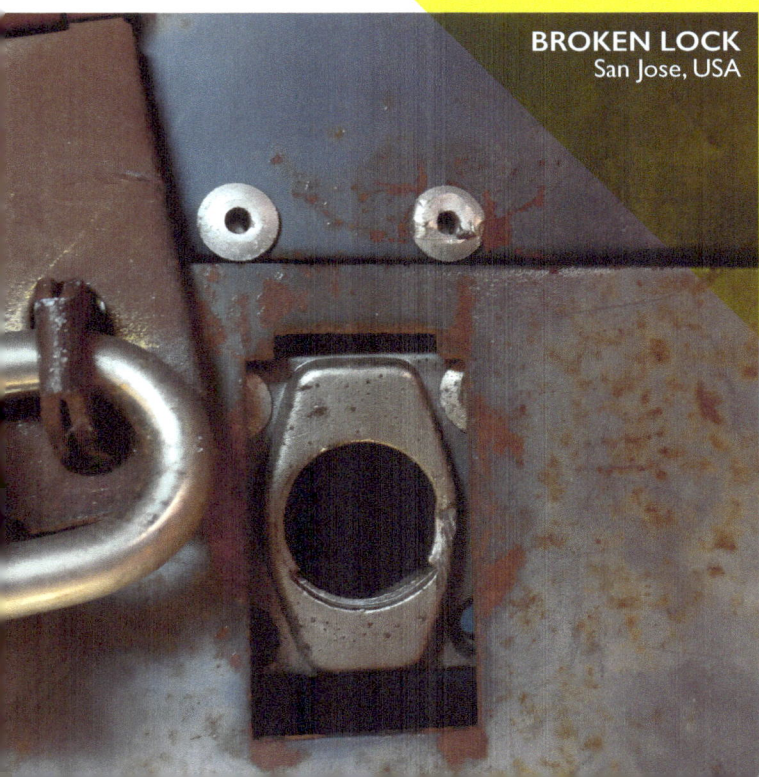
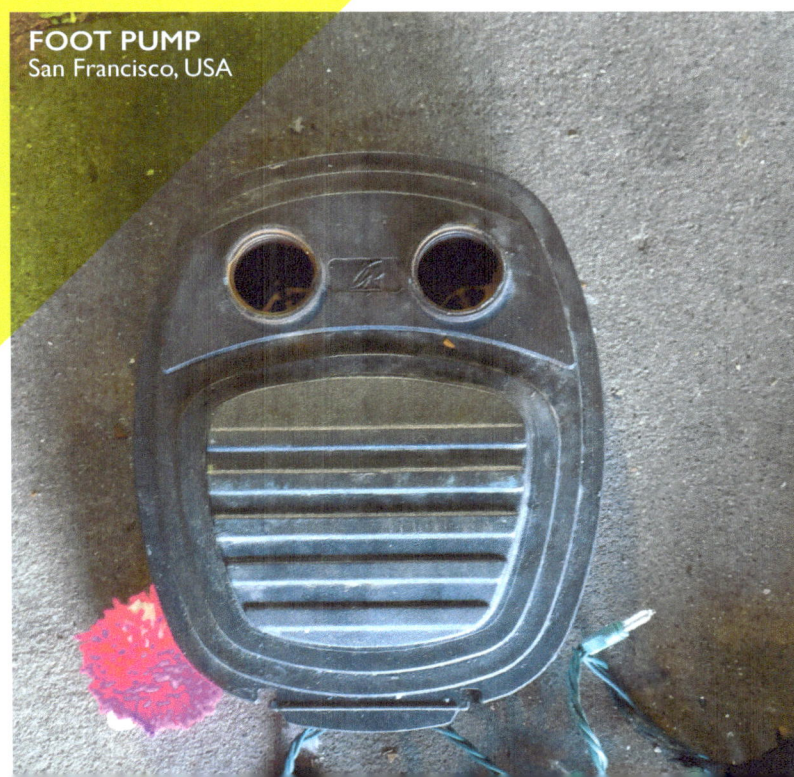

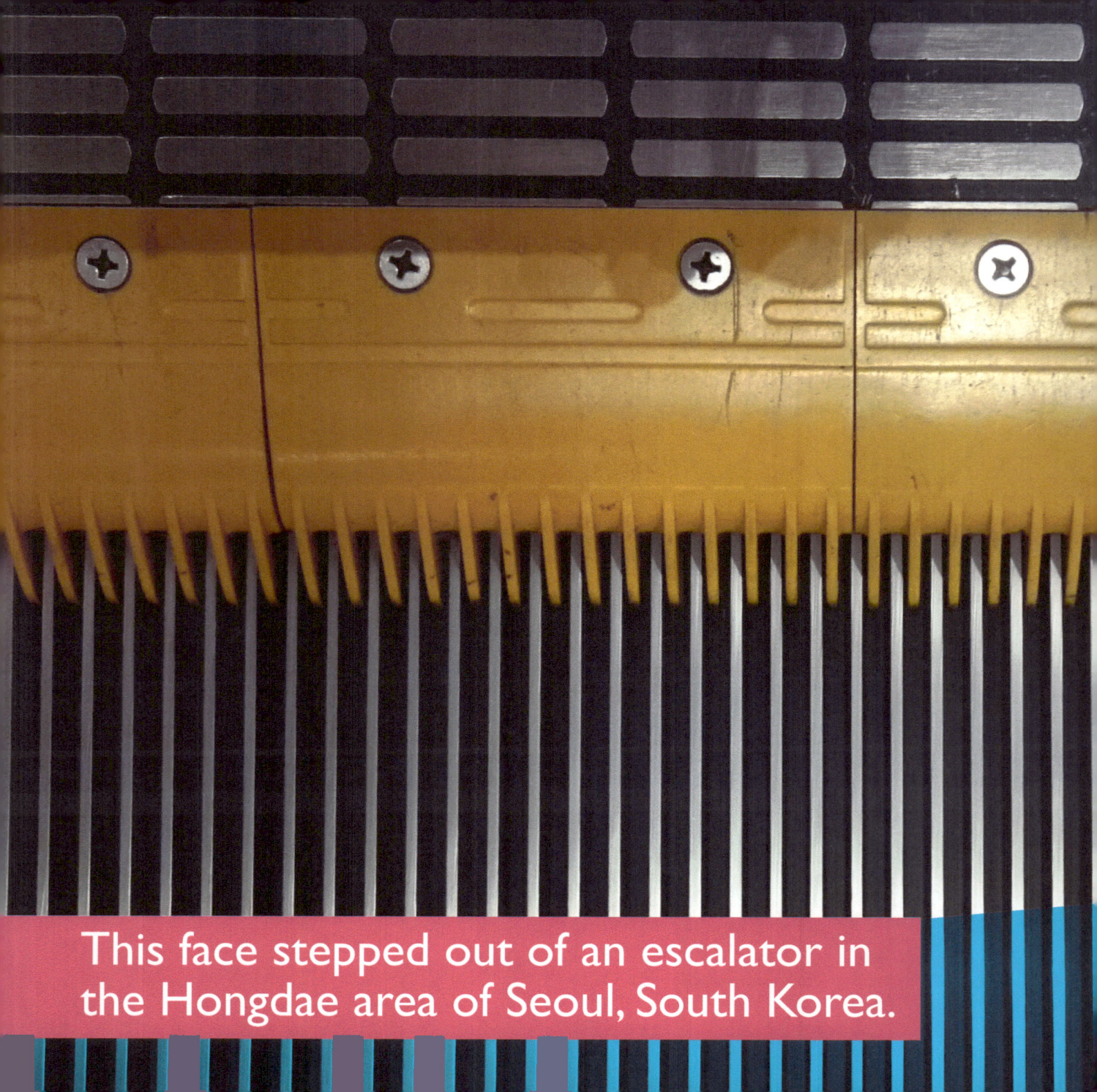

This face stepped out of an escalator in the Hongdae area of Seoul, South Korea.

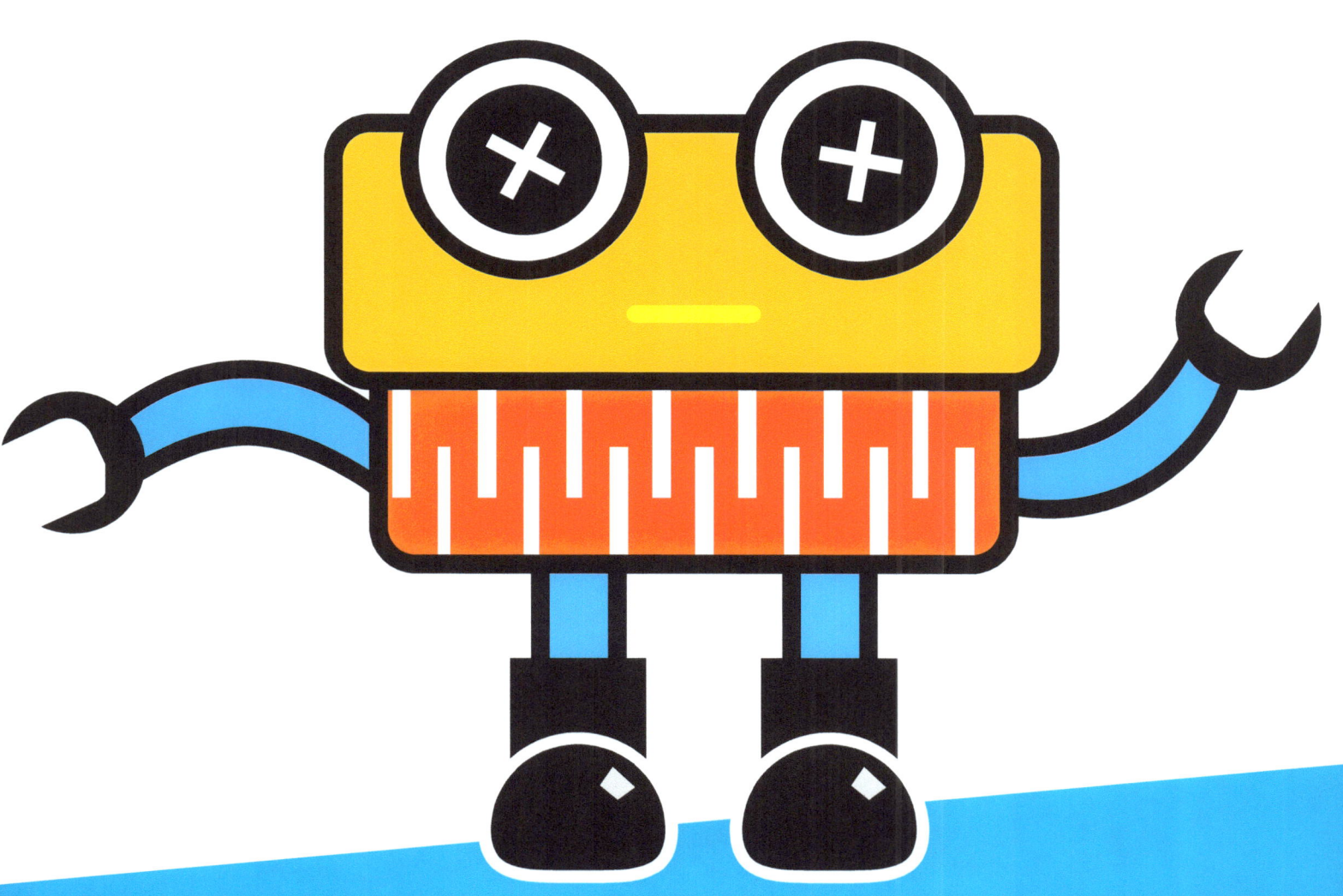

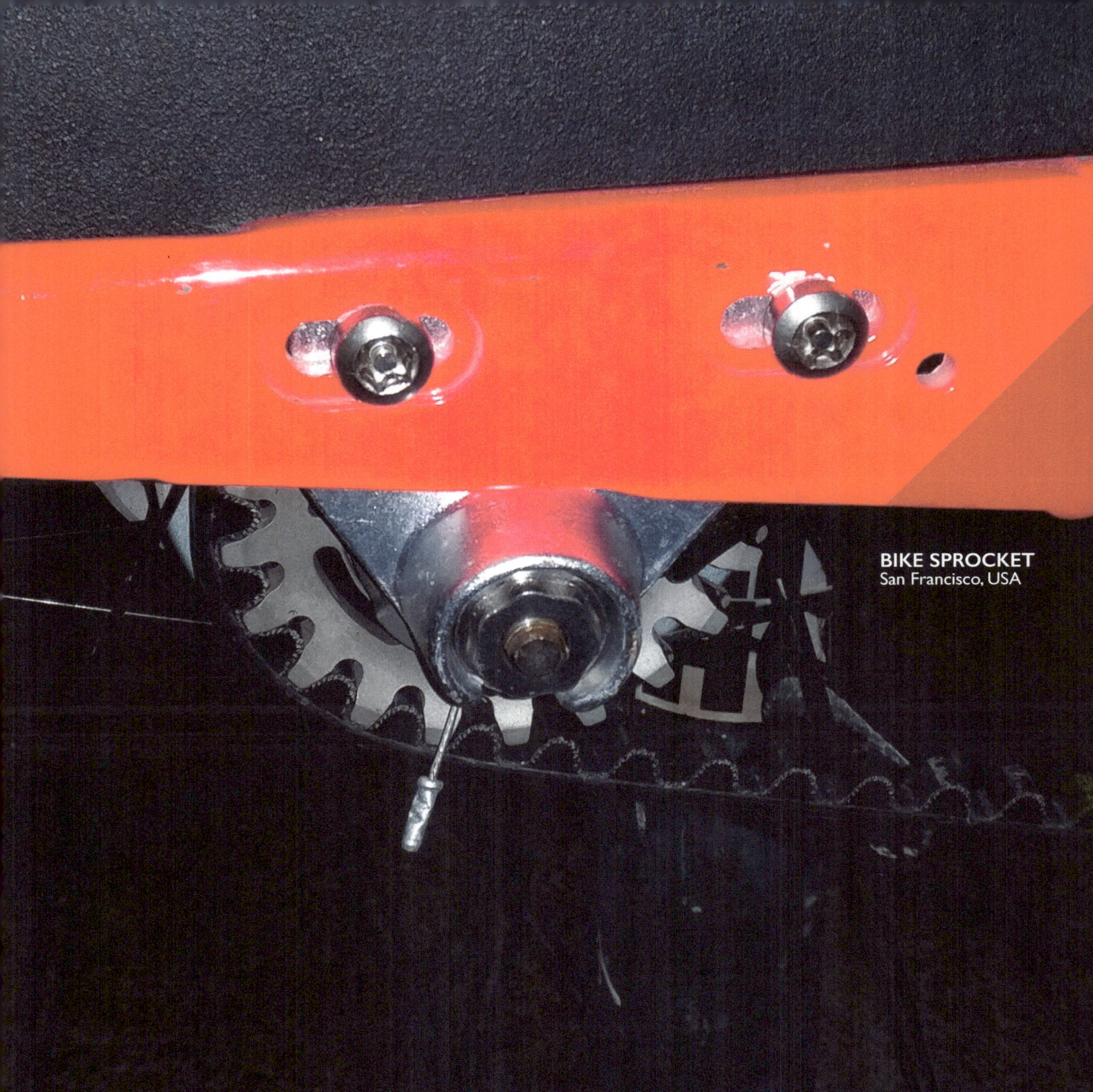

BIKE SPROCKET
San Francisco, USA

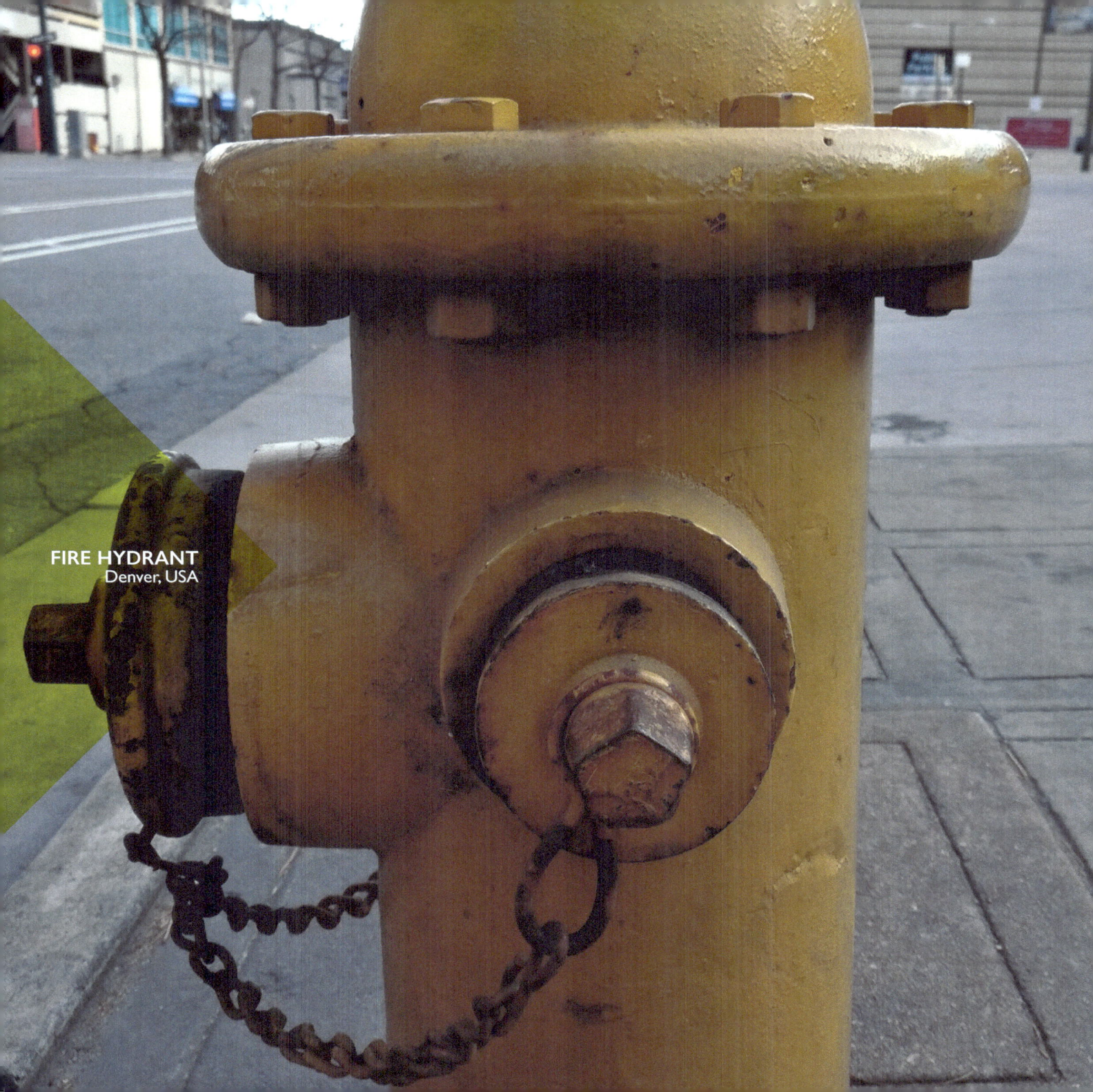

FIRE HYDRANT
Denver, USA

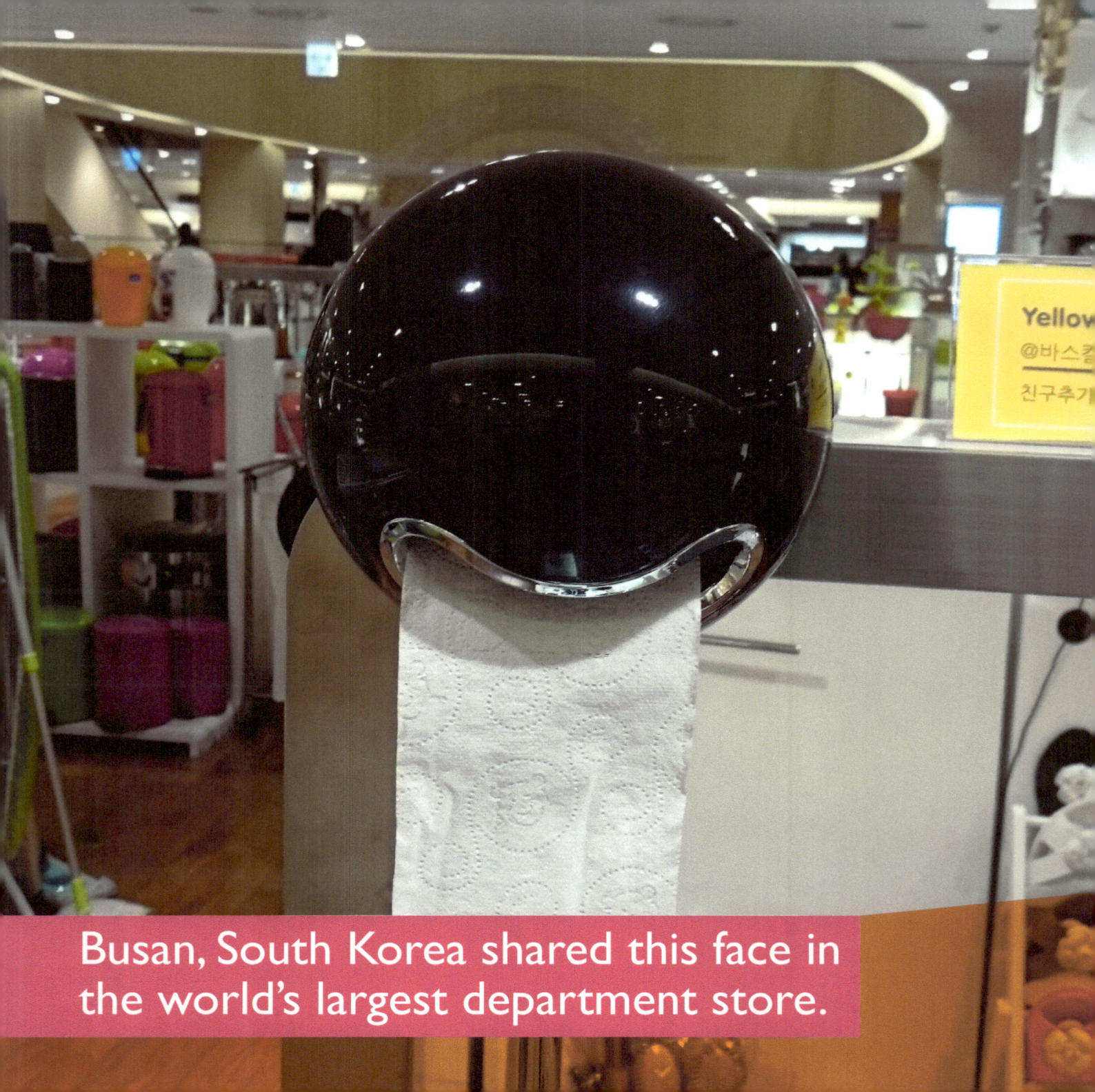

Busan, South Korea shared this face in the world's largest department store.

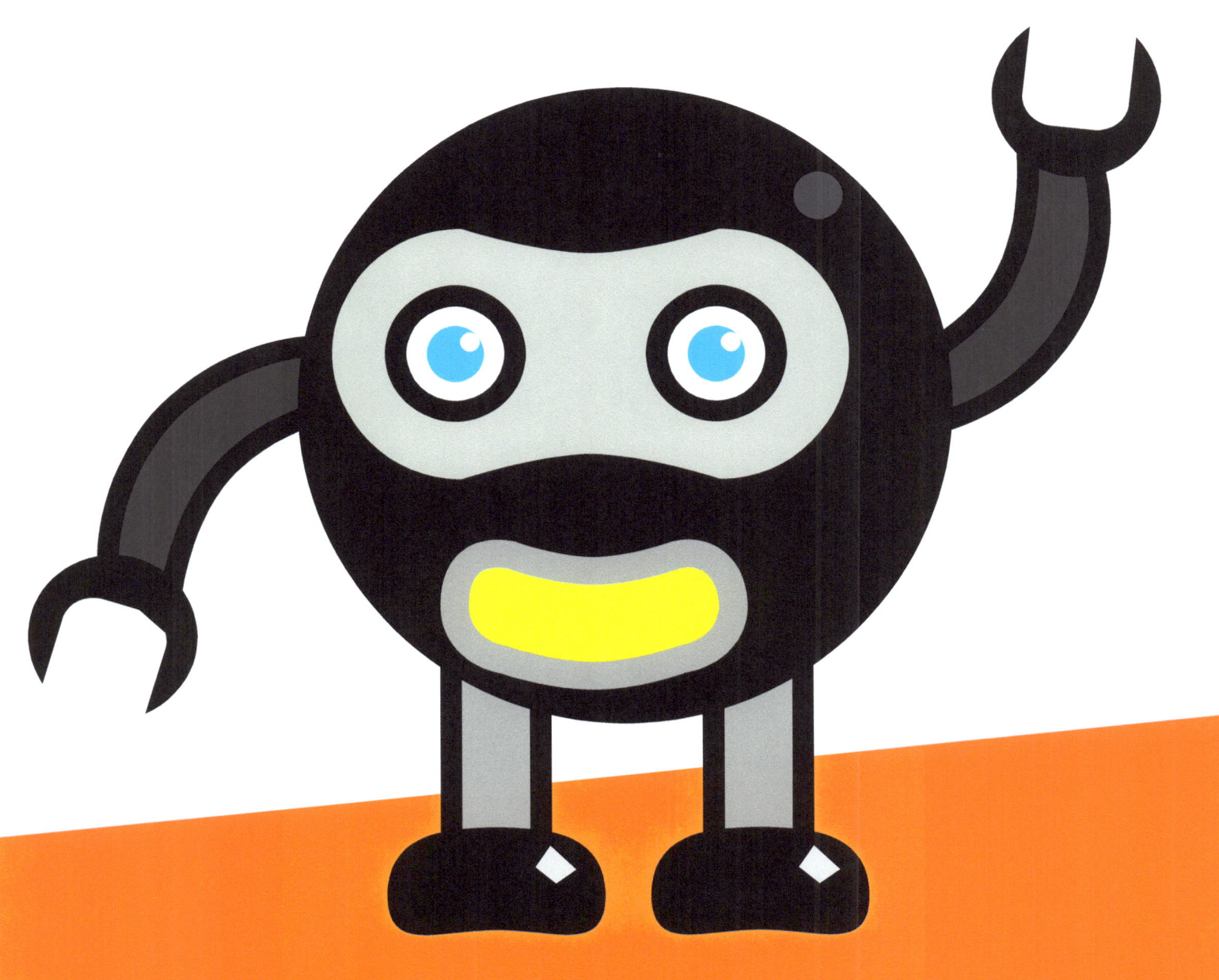

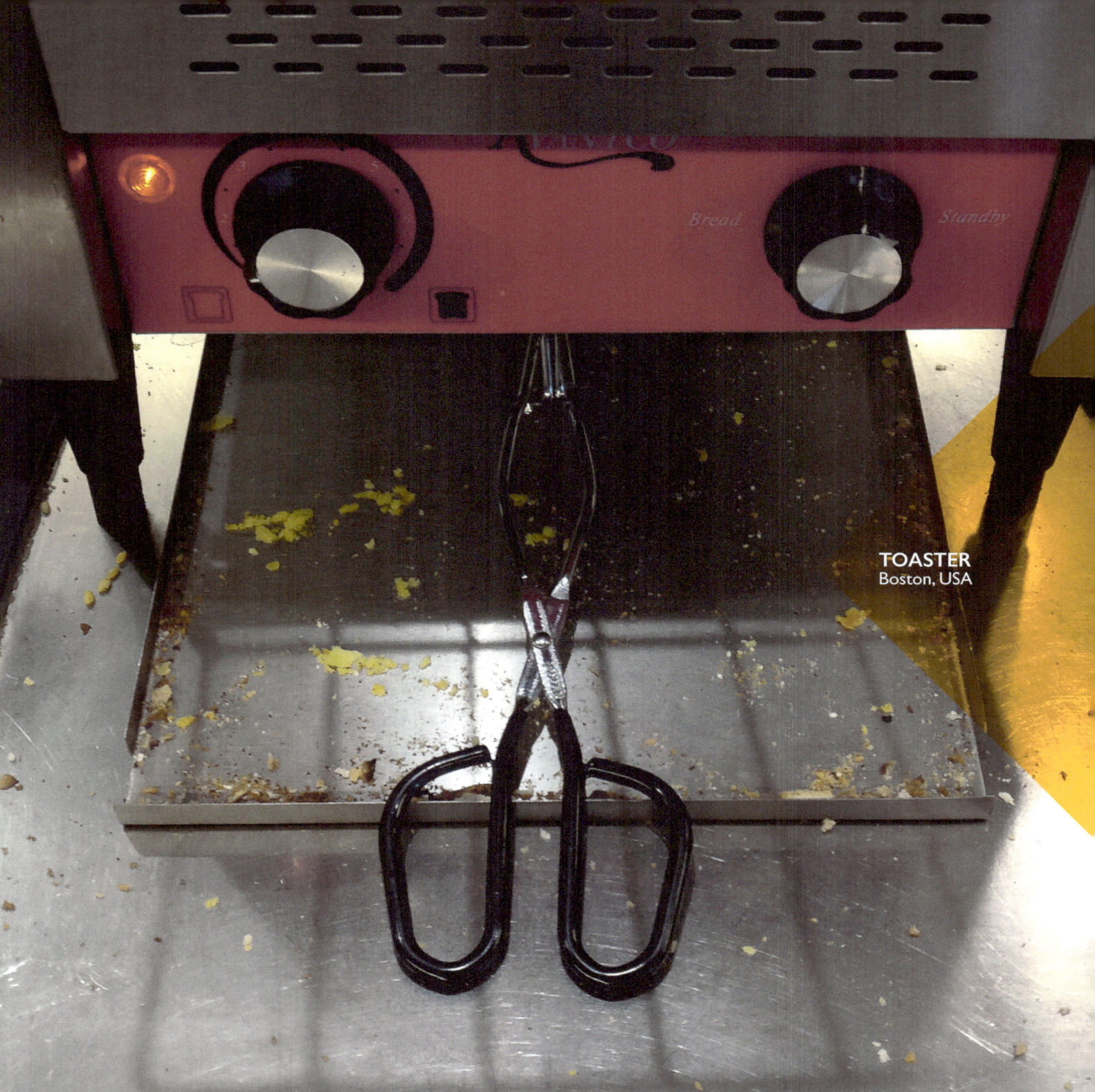

Bread

Standby

TOASTER
Boston, USA

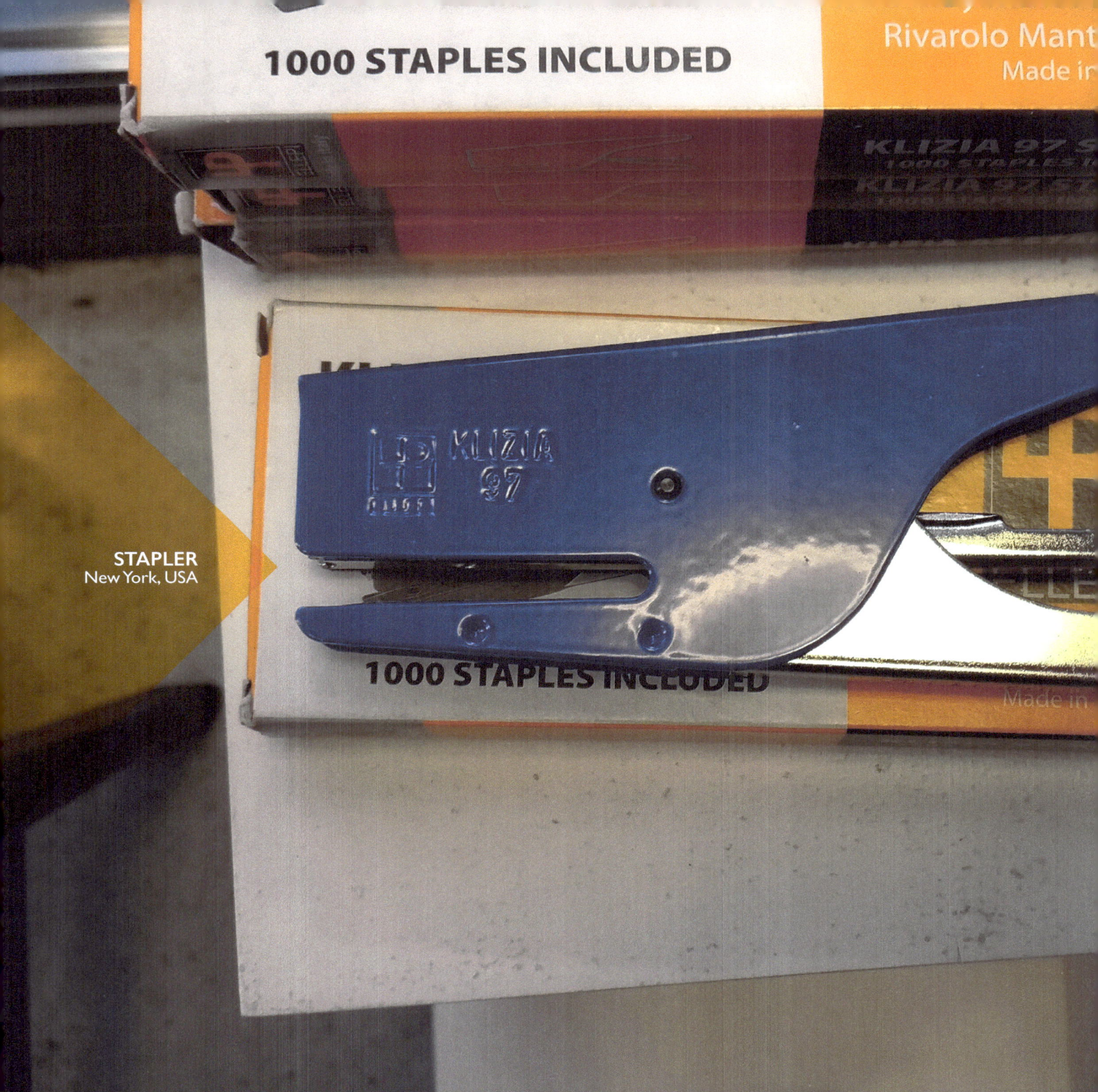

STAPLER
New York, USA

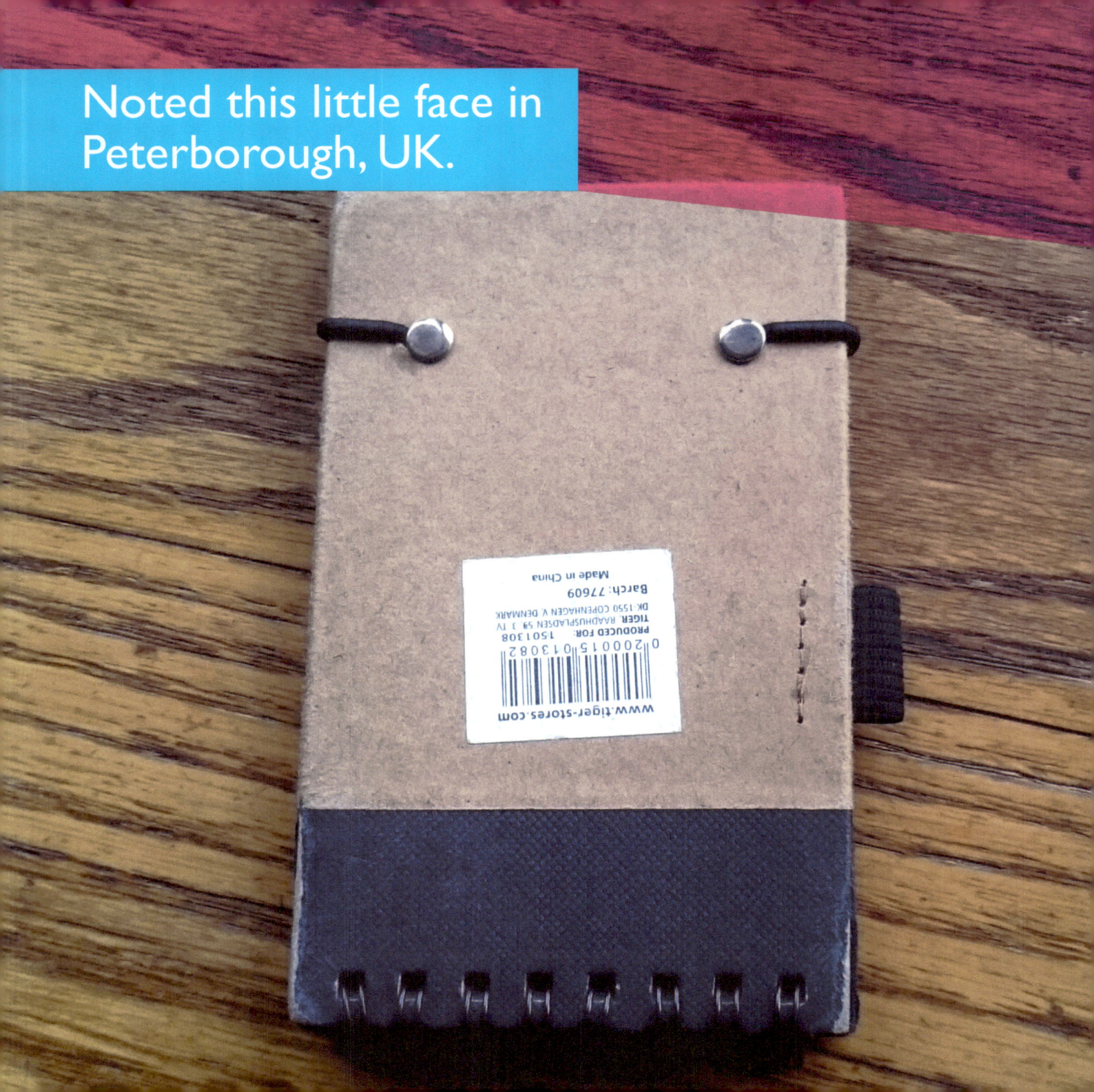

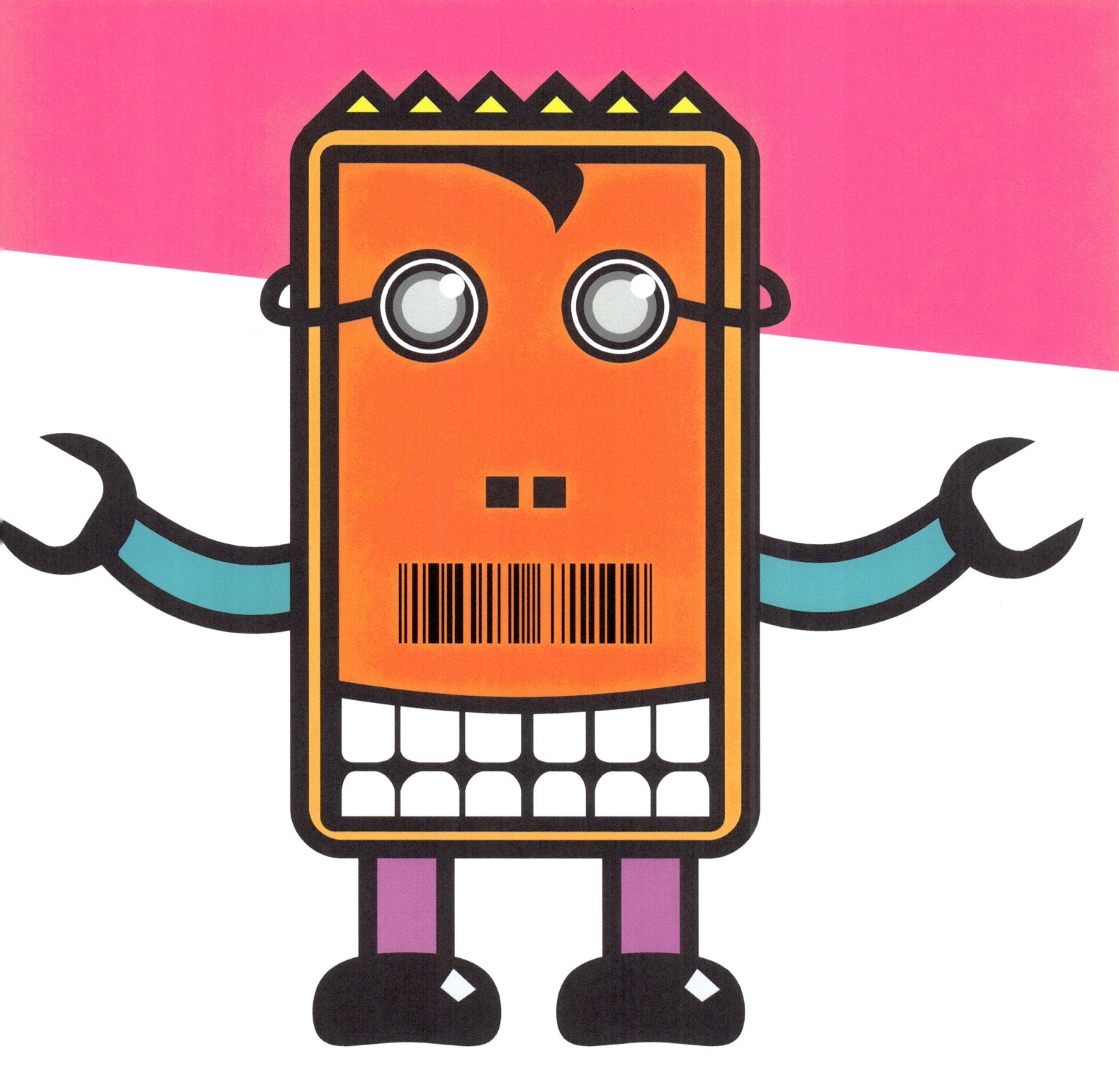

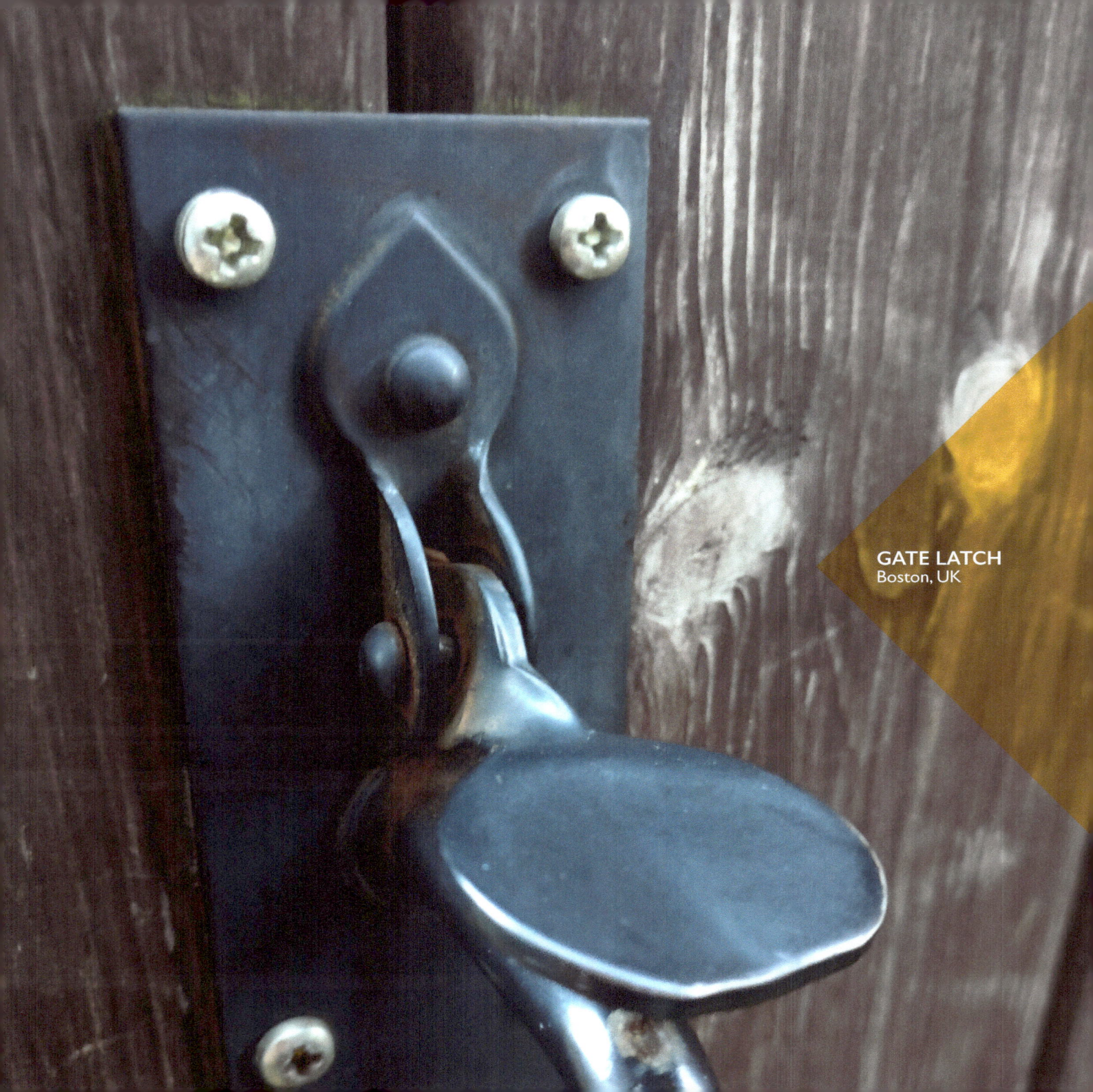

GATE LATCH
Boston, UK

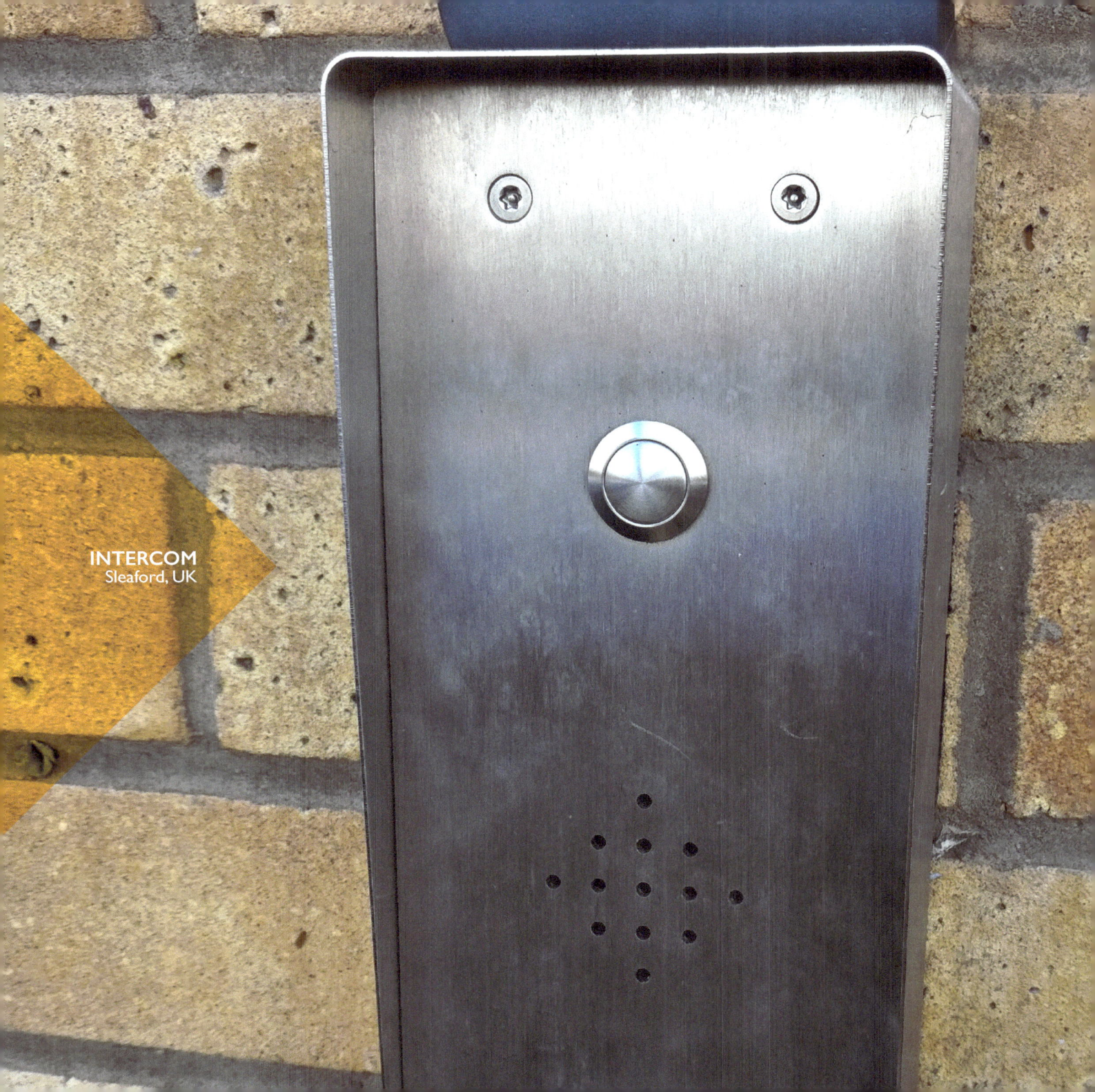

INTERCOM
Sleaford, UK

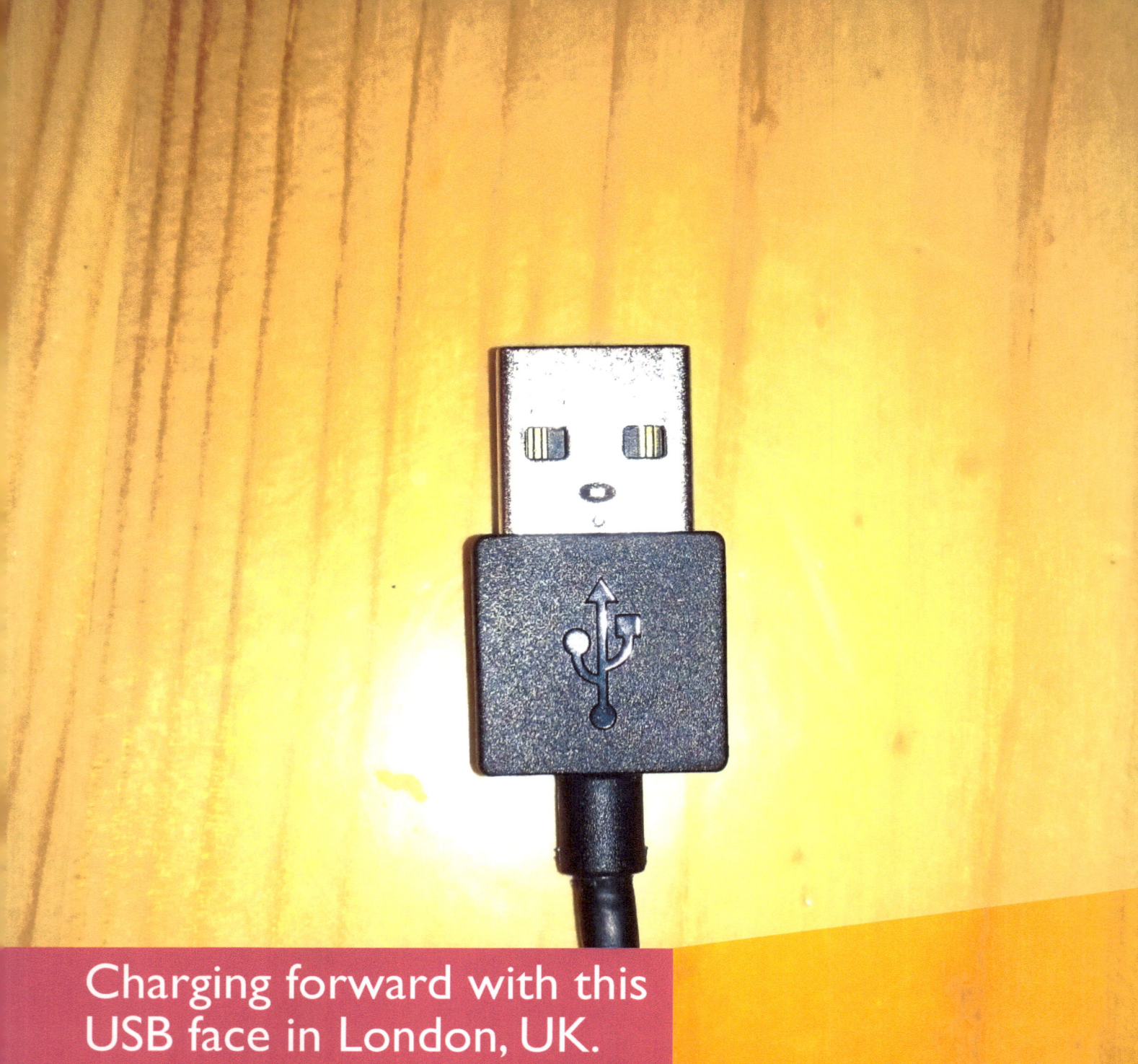

Charging forward with this USB face in London, UK.

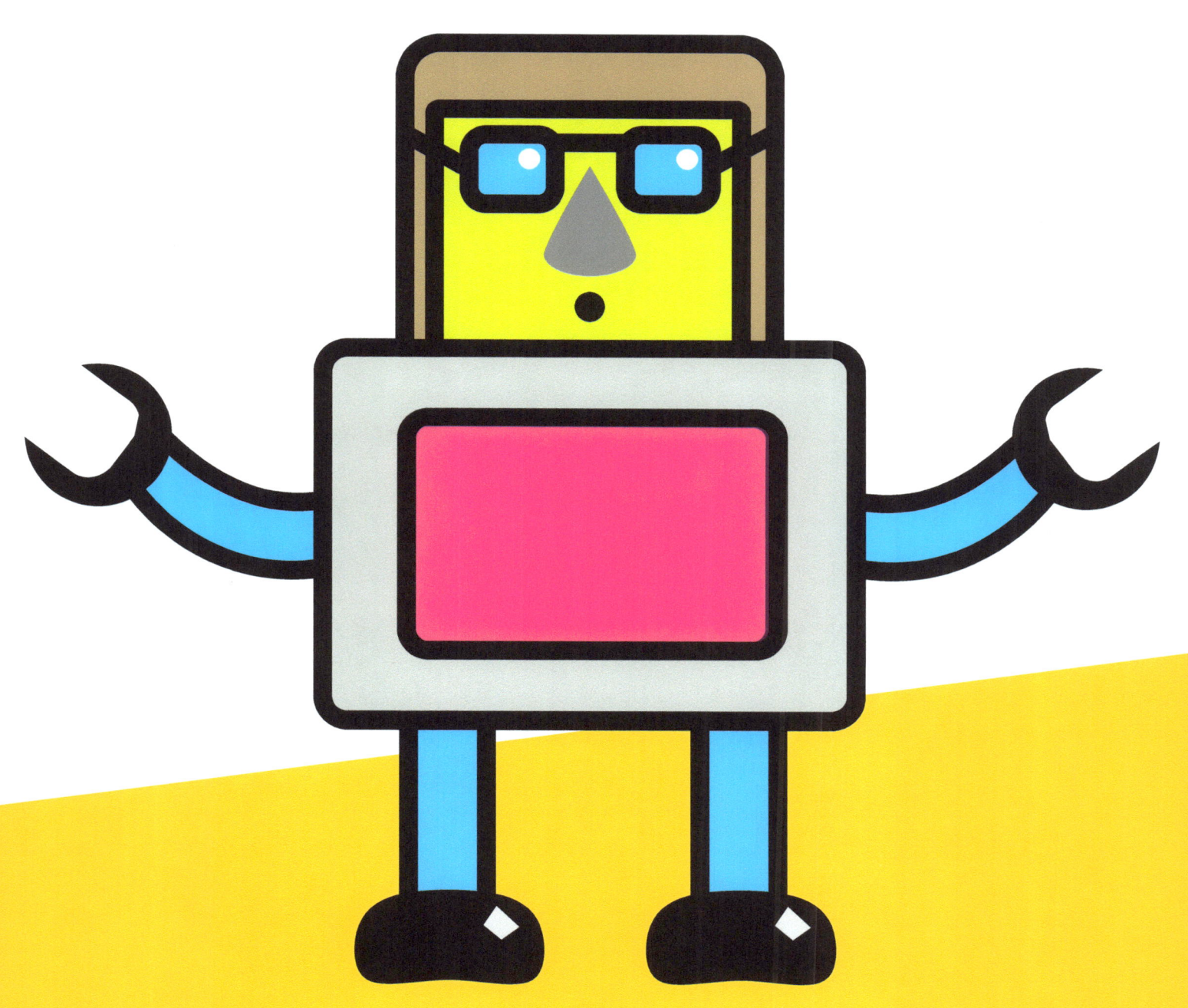

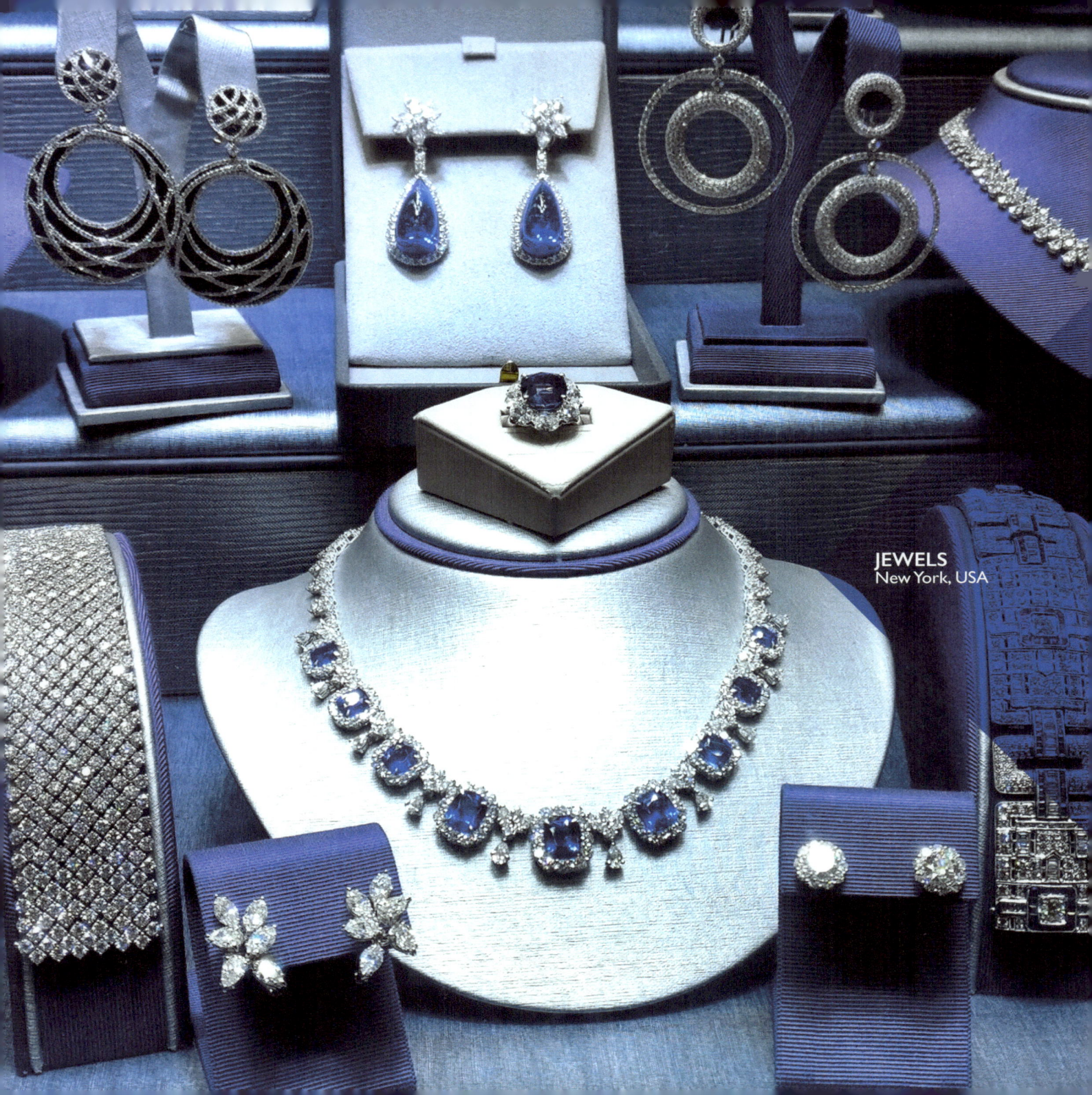

JEWELS
New York, USA

MILK CARTON
Santa Monica, USA

PUSH UP
HERE

PUSH UP
HERE

KEEP
REFRIGERATED

TO OPEN

Reduced Fat Milk Vitamin A & D
2% Milkfat

Nutrition Facts	Amount/Serving	% DV*	Amount/Serving	% DV*
Serv Size 1 Container	Total Fat 5g	8%	Potassium 460mg	13%
	Sat. Fat 3g	15%	Total Carb. 14g	5%
Calories 140 Fat Cal 45	Trans Fat 0g		Dietary Fiber 0g	0%
*Percent Daily Values (DV) are based on a 2,000-calorie diet.	Cholest. 20mg	7%	Sugars 13g	
	Sodium 150mg	6%	Protein 10g	

Vitamin A 10% • Vitamin C 4% • Calcium 35%
Iron 0% • • Vitamin D 25%

INGREDIENTS: REDUCED FAT MILK, SKIM MILK,
VITAMIN A PALMITATE, VITAMIN D3.
DISTRIBUTED BY: DEAN FOODS COMPANY
DALLAS, TEXAS 75204
www.dairypure.com
FAT REDUCED FROM 8g TO 5g.
2% MILKFAT

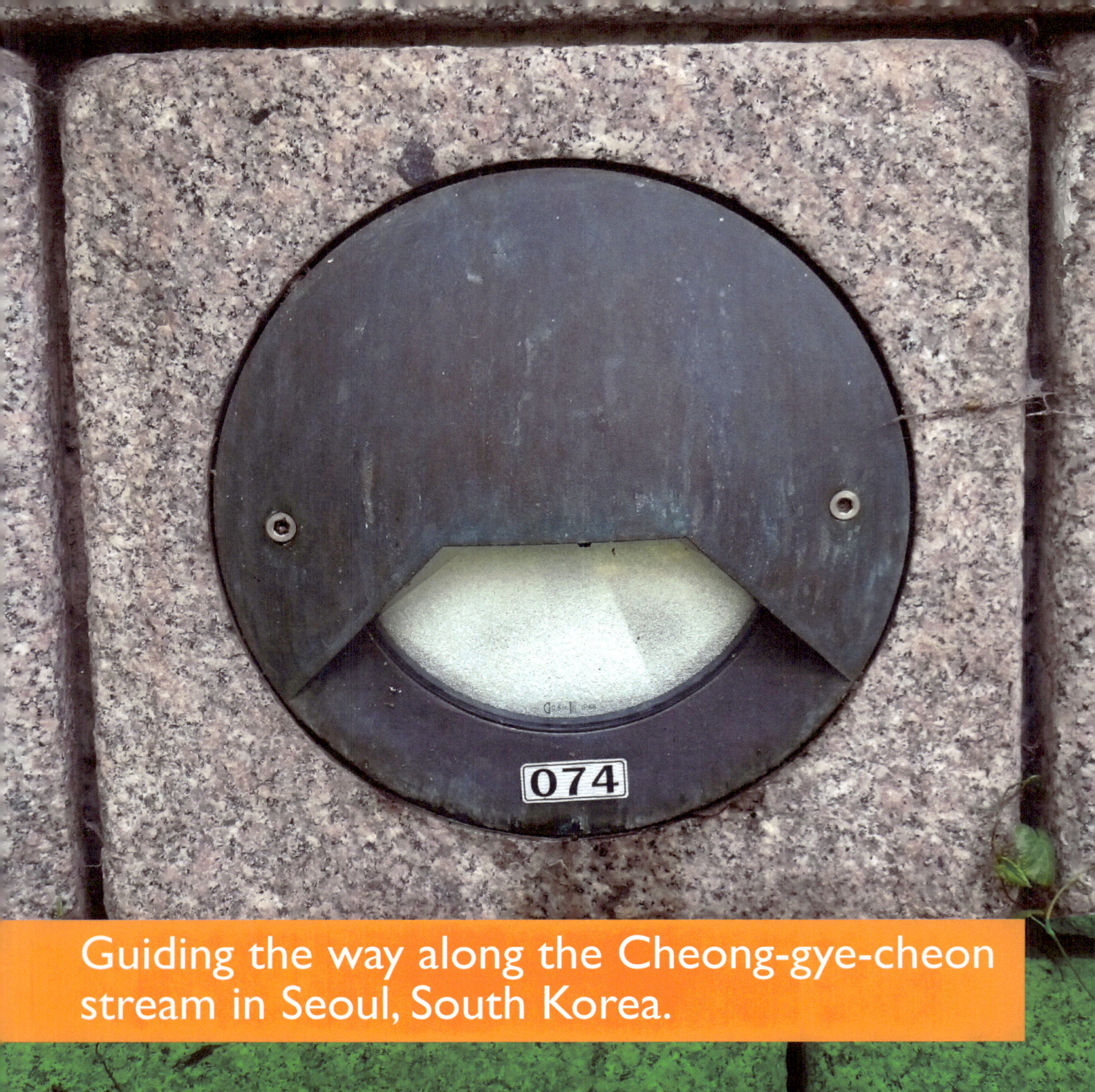

Guiding the way along the Cheong-gye-cheon stream in Seoul, South Korea.

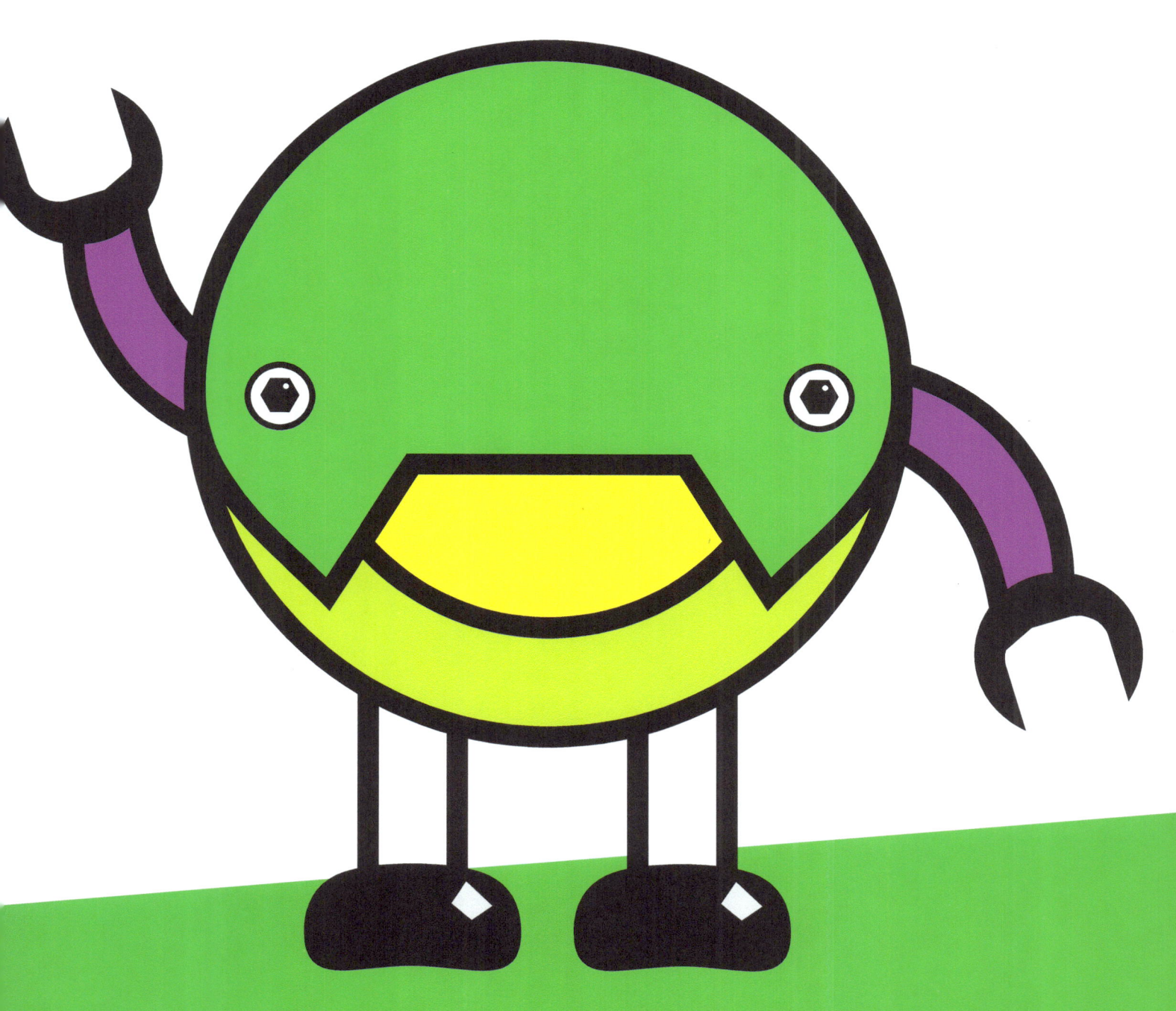

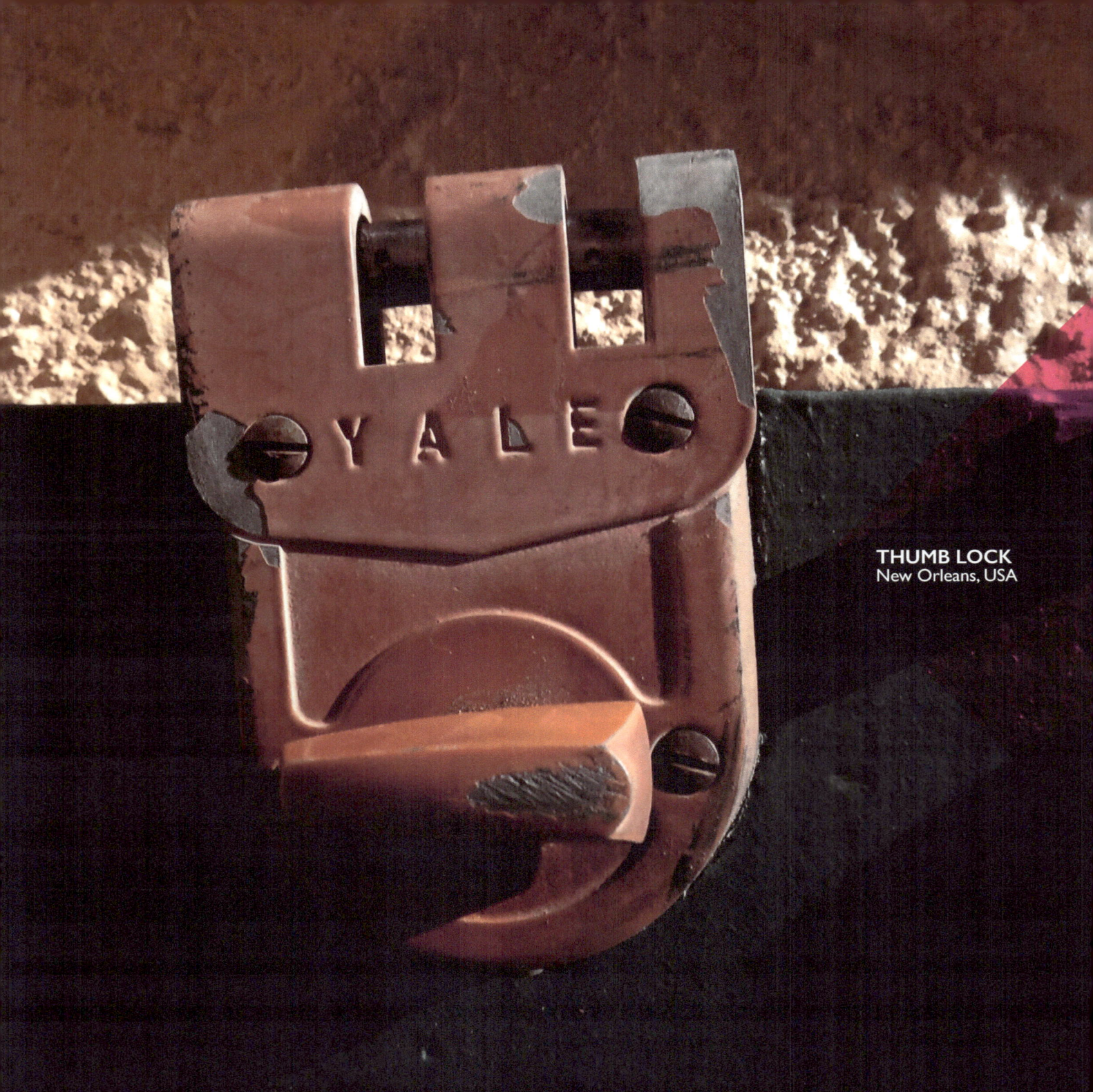

THUMB LOCK
New Orleans, USA

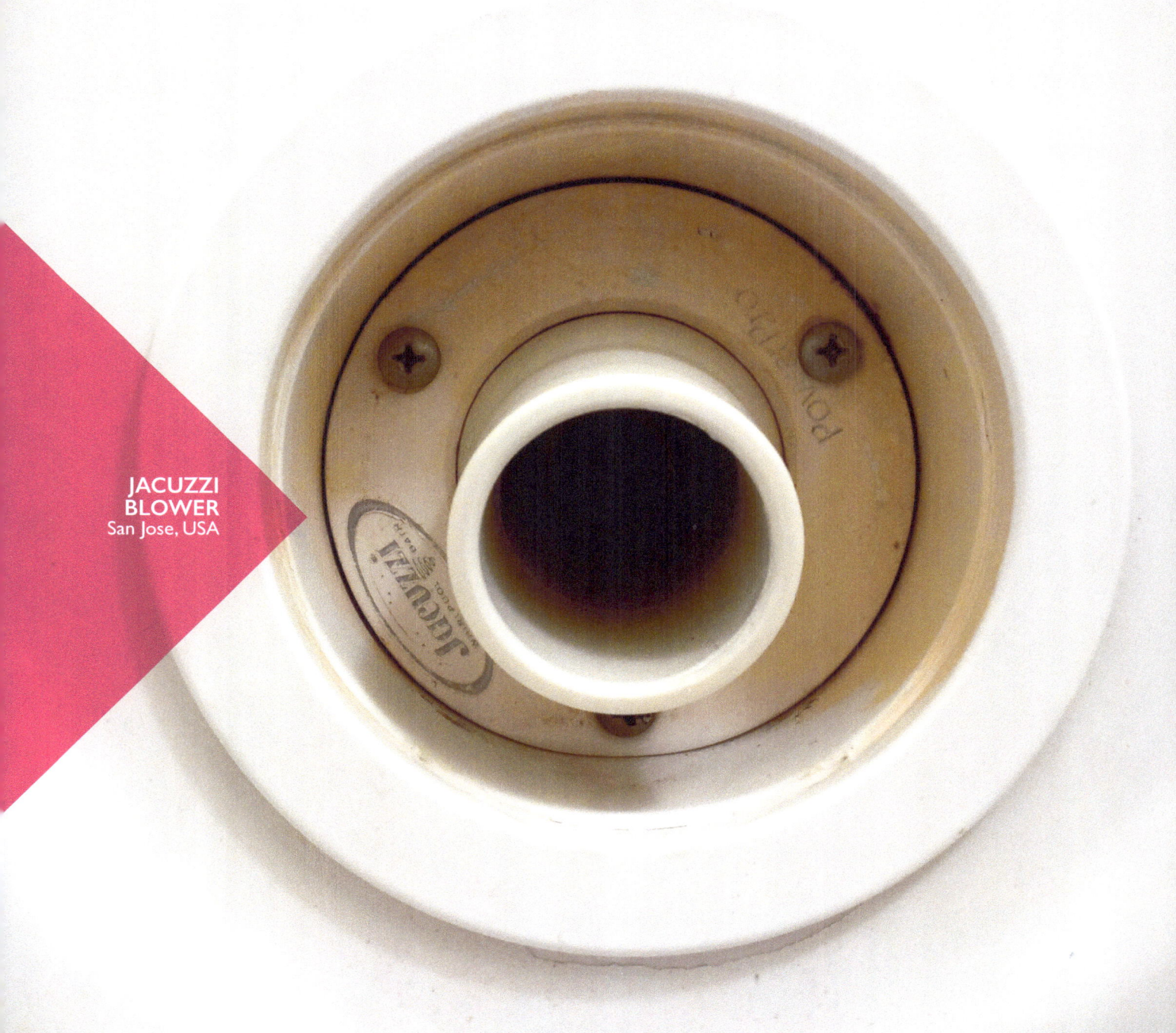

**JACUZZI
BLOWER**
San Jose, USA

Temp.

Spin

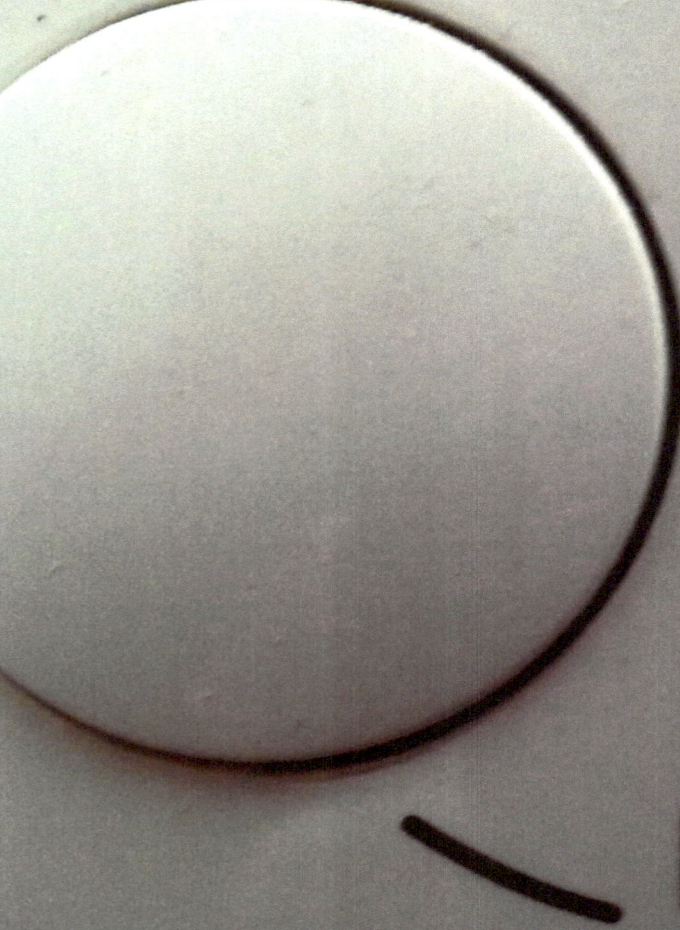

Washing machine buttons
in Boston, UK

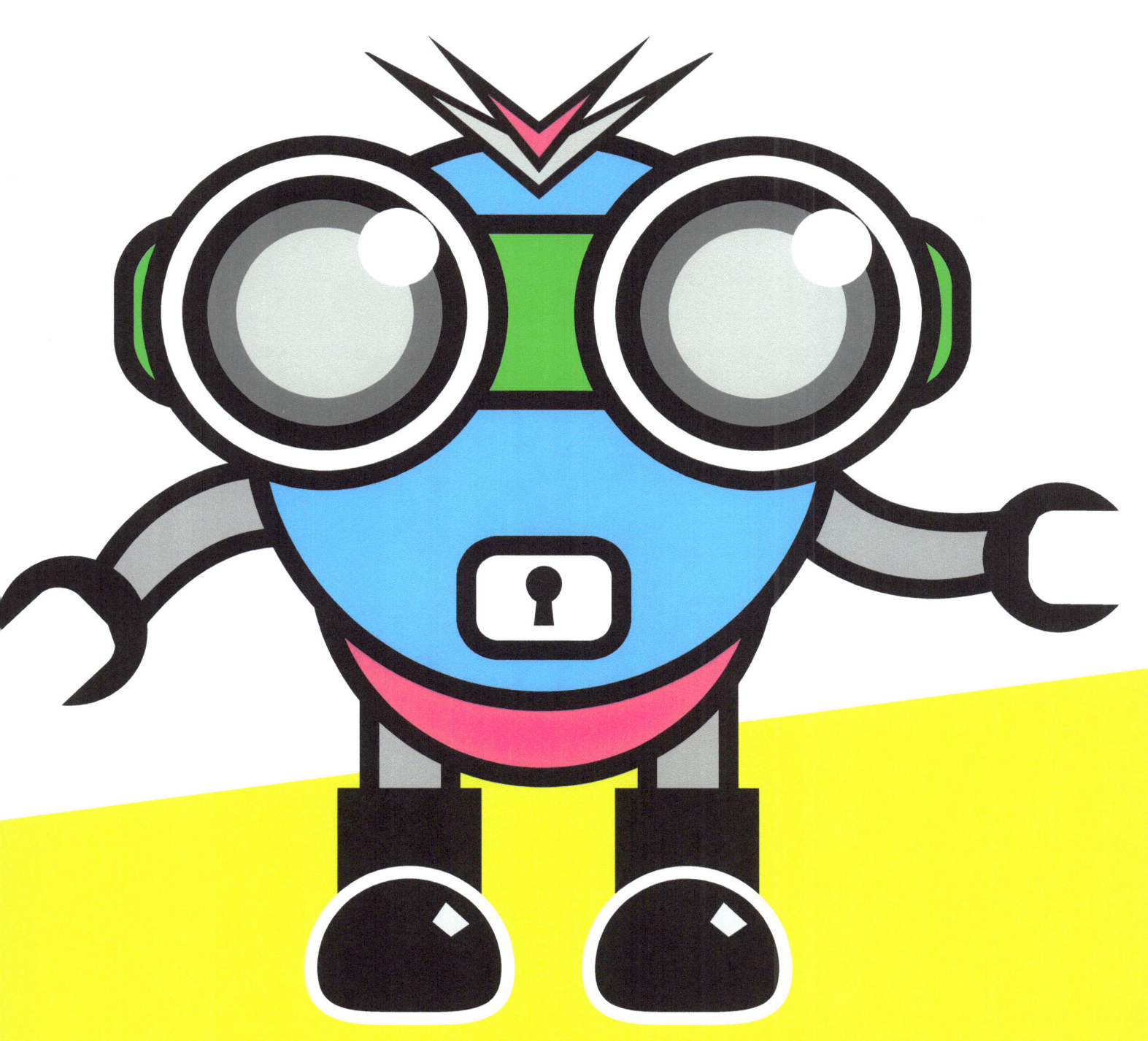

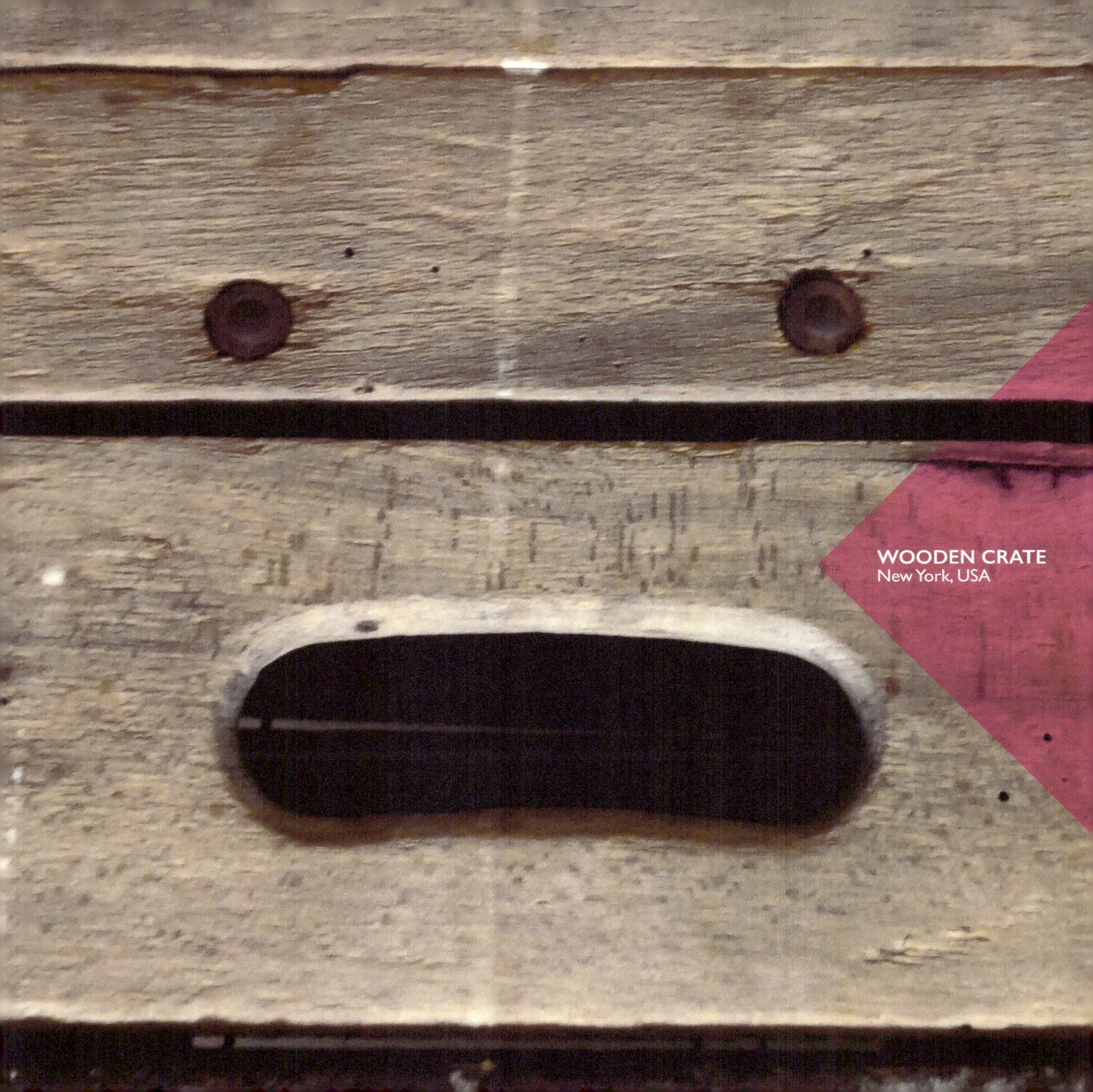

WOODEN CRATE
New York, USA

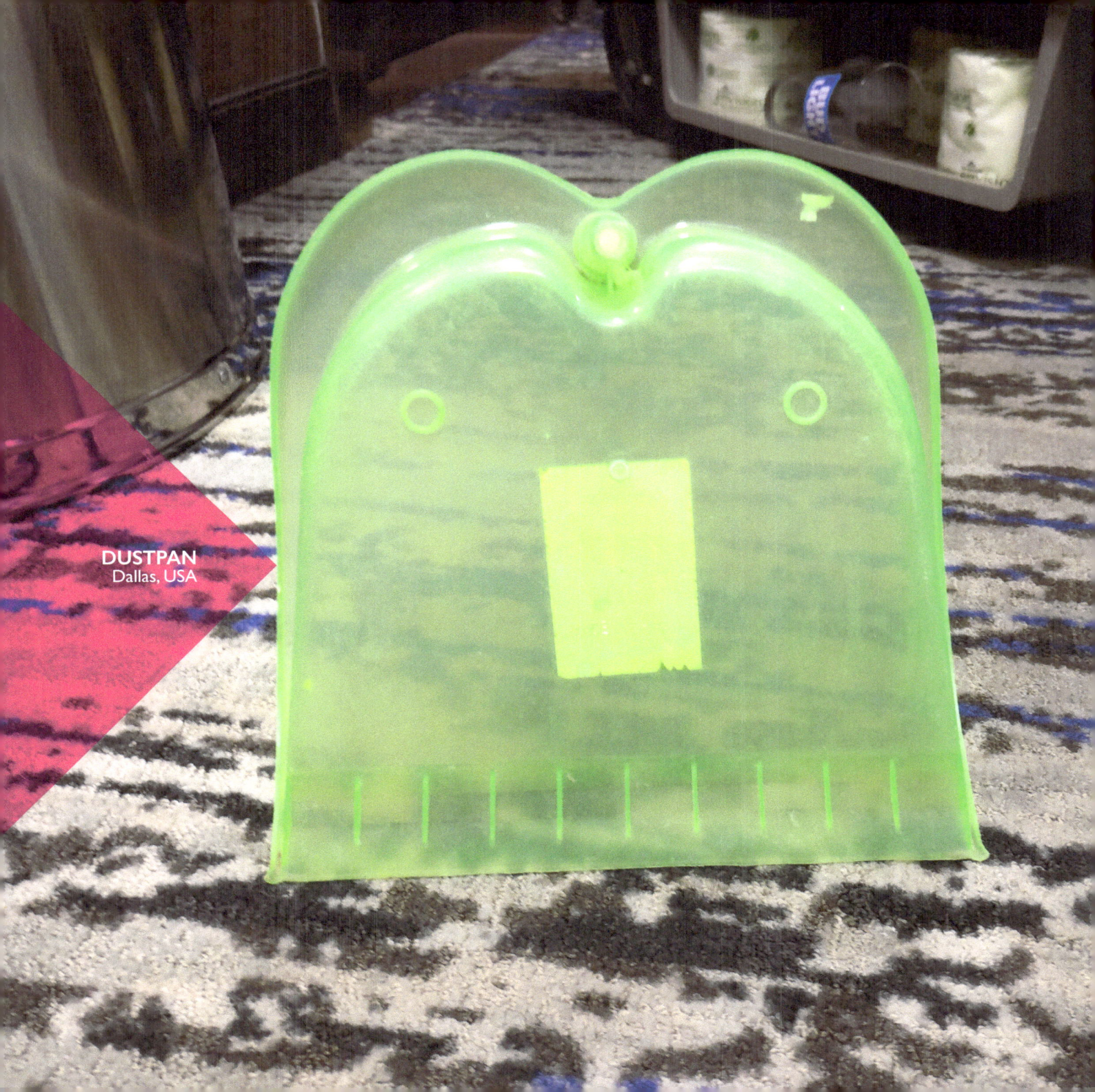

DUSTPAN
Dallas, USA

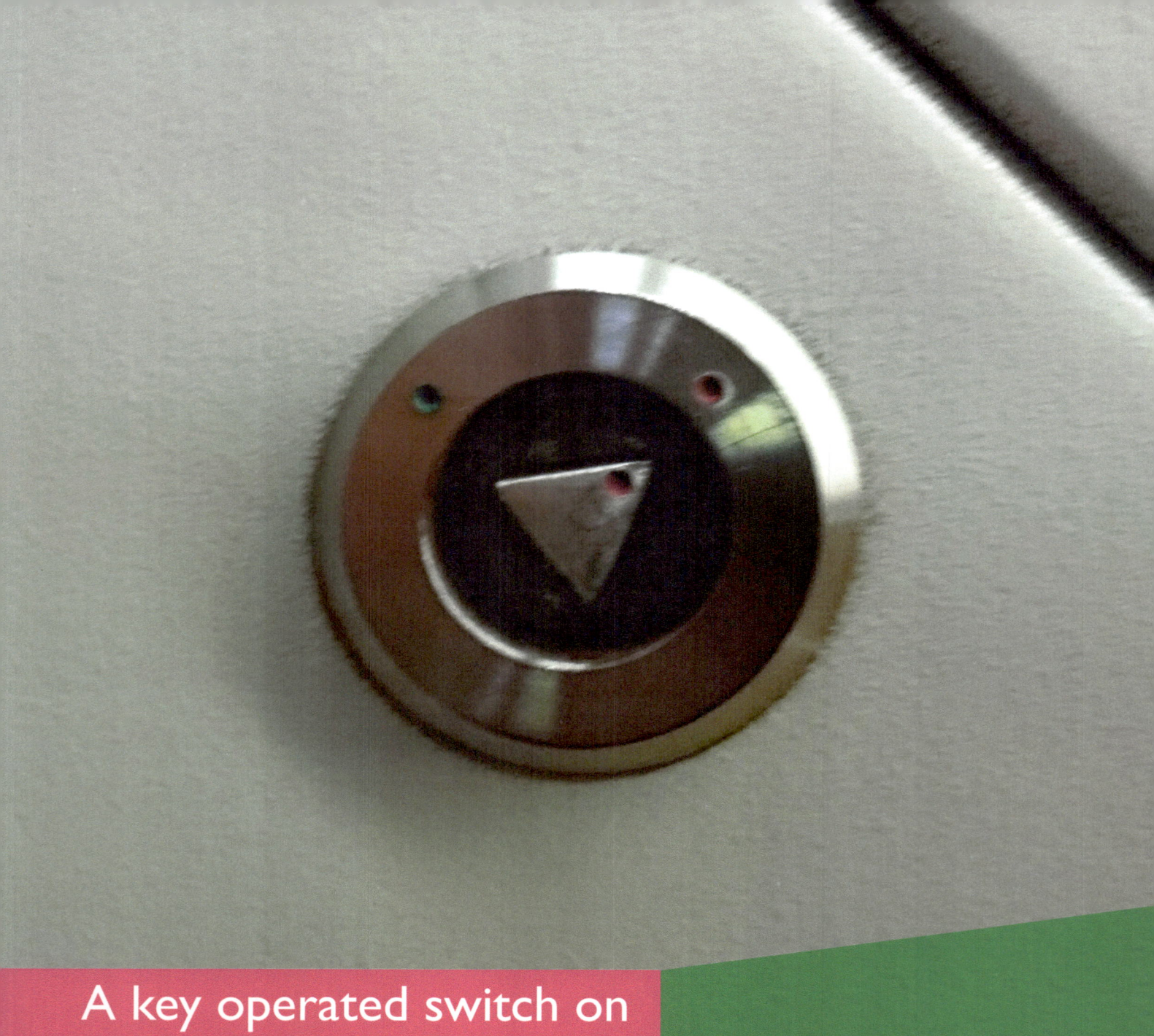

A key operated switch on a train in Beijing, China

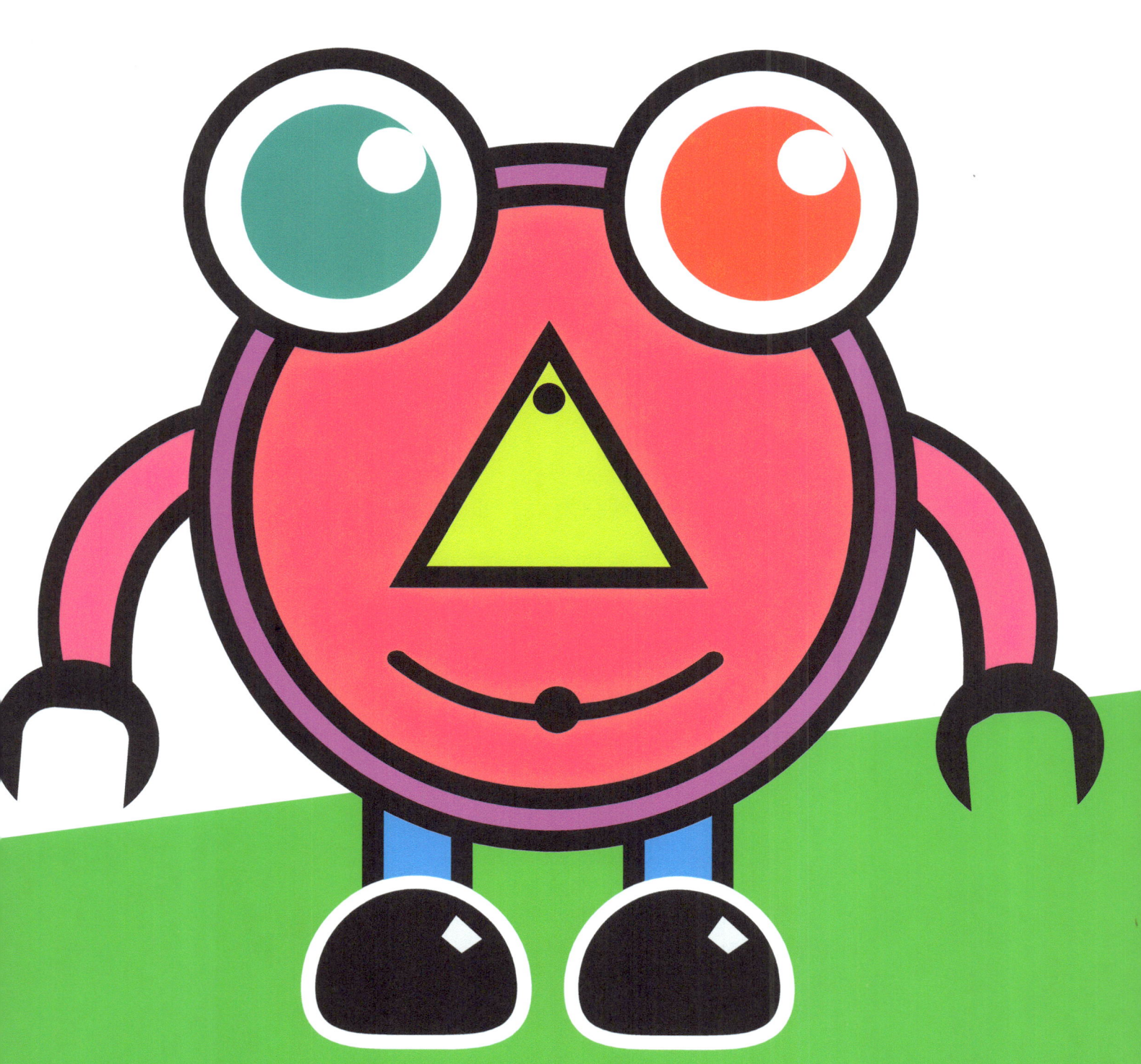

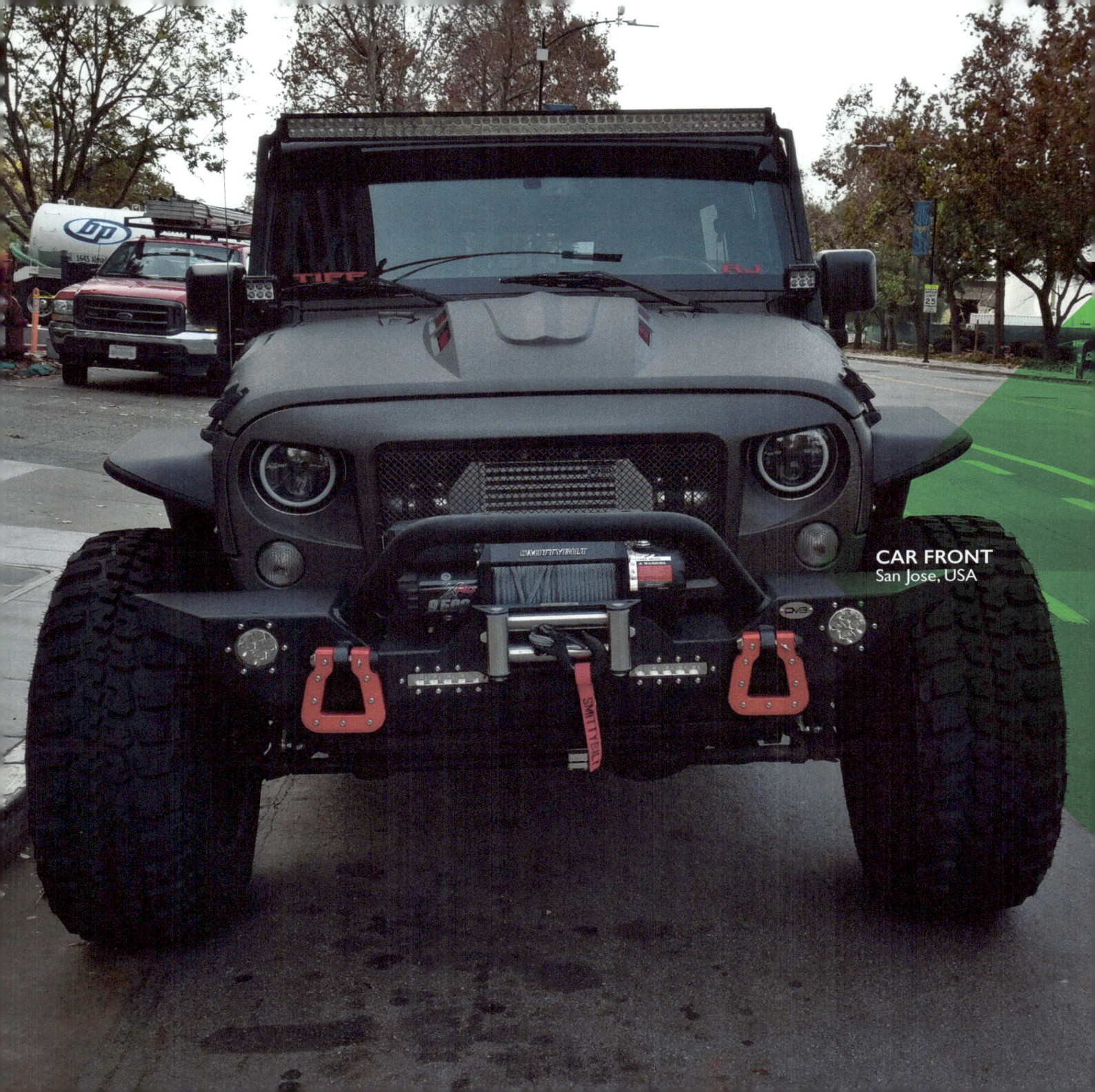

CAR FRONT
San Jose, USA

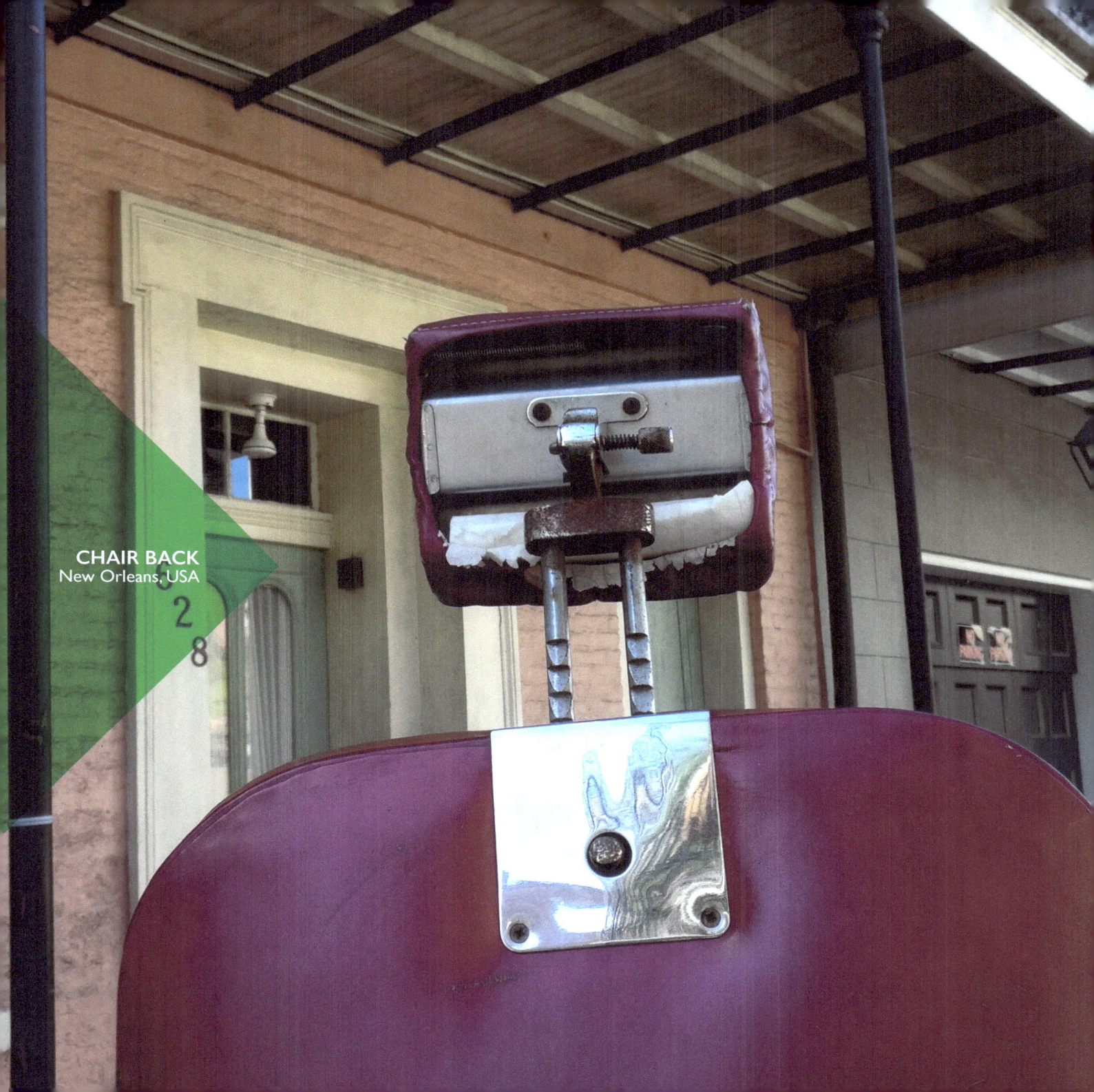

CHAIR BACK
New Orleans, USA

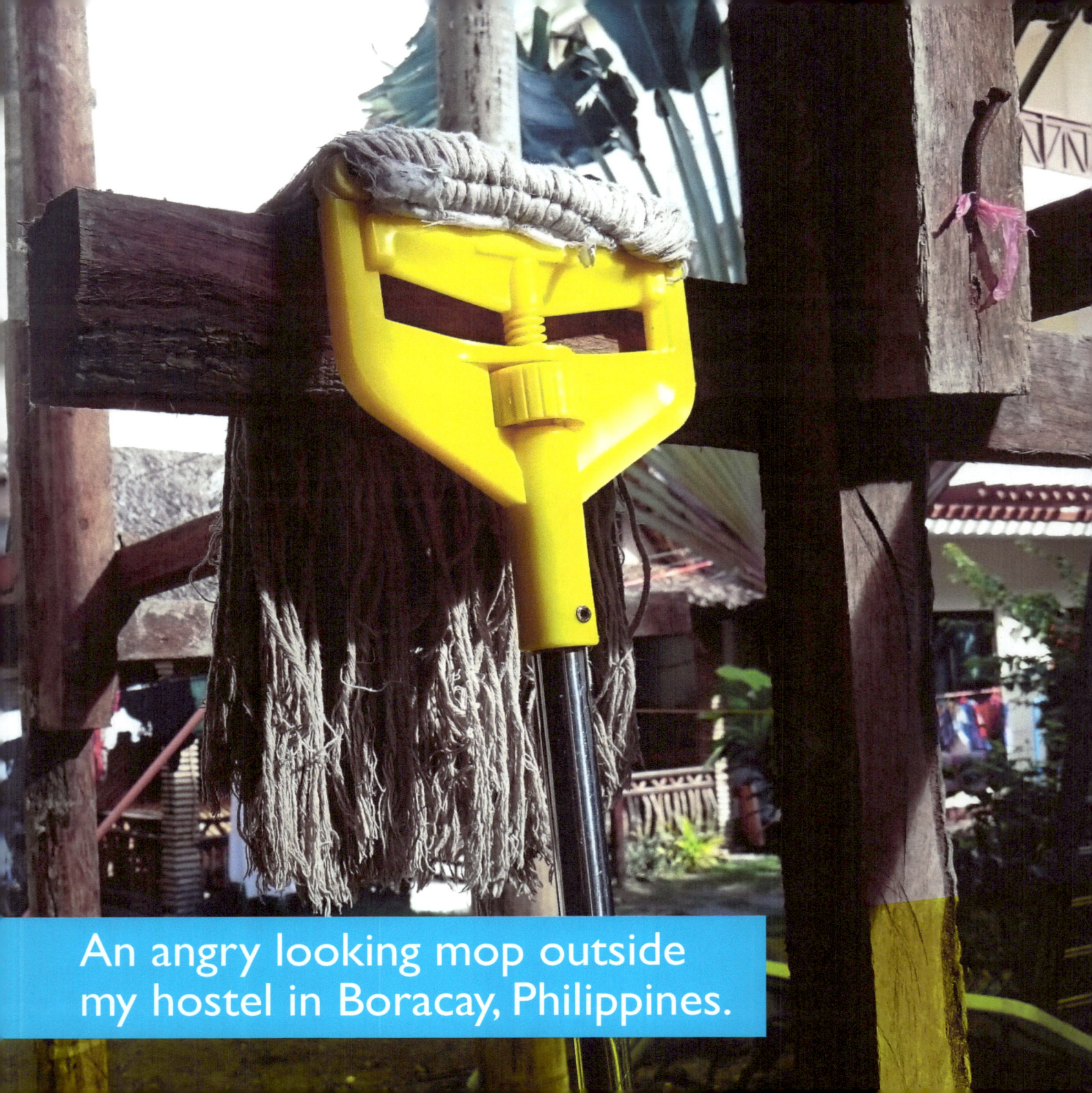

An angry looking mop outside my hostel in Boracay, Philippines.

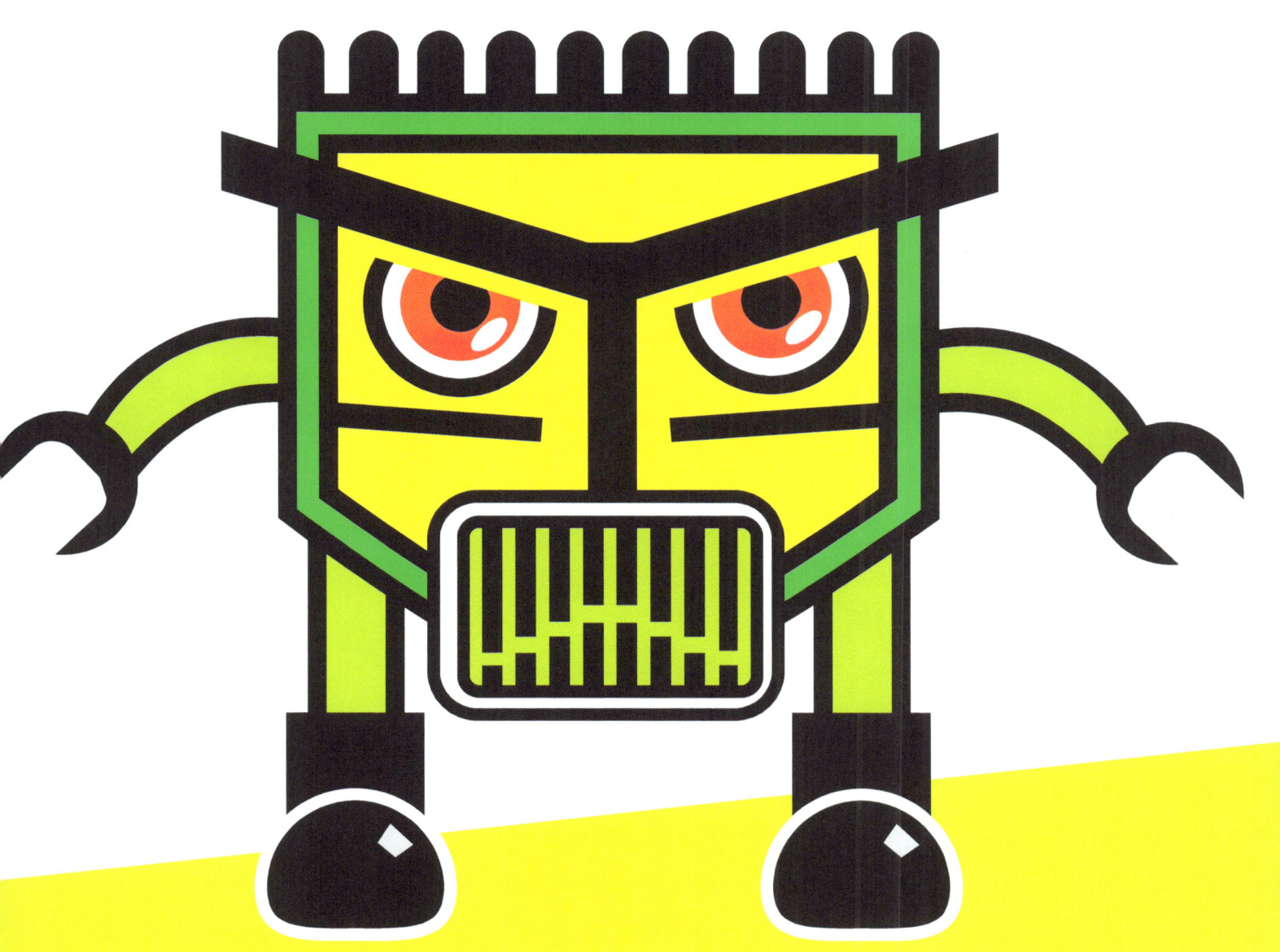

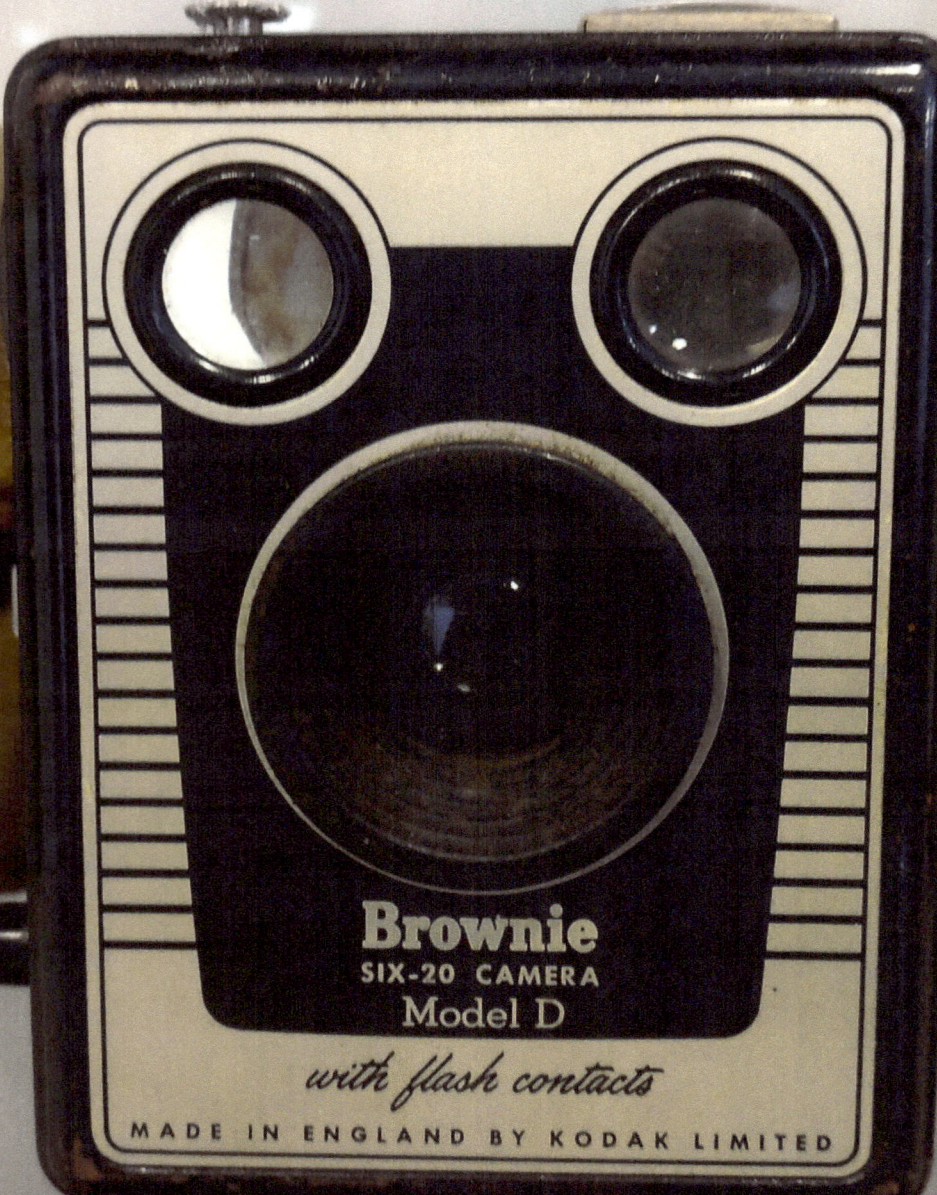

CAMERA
Boston, UK

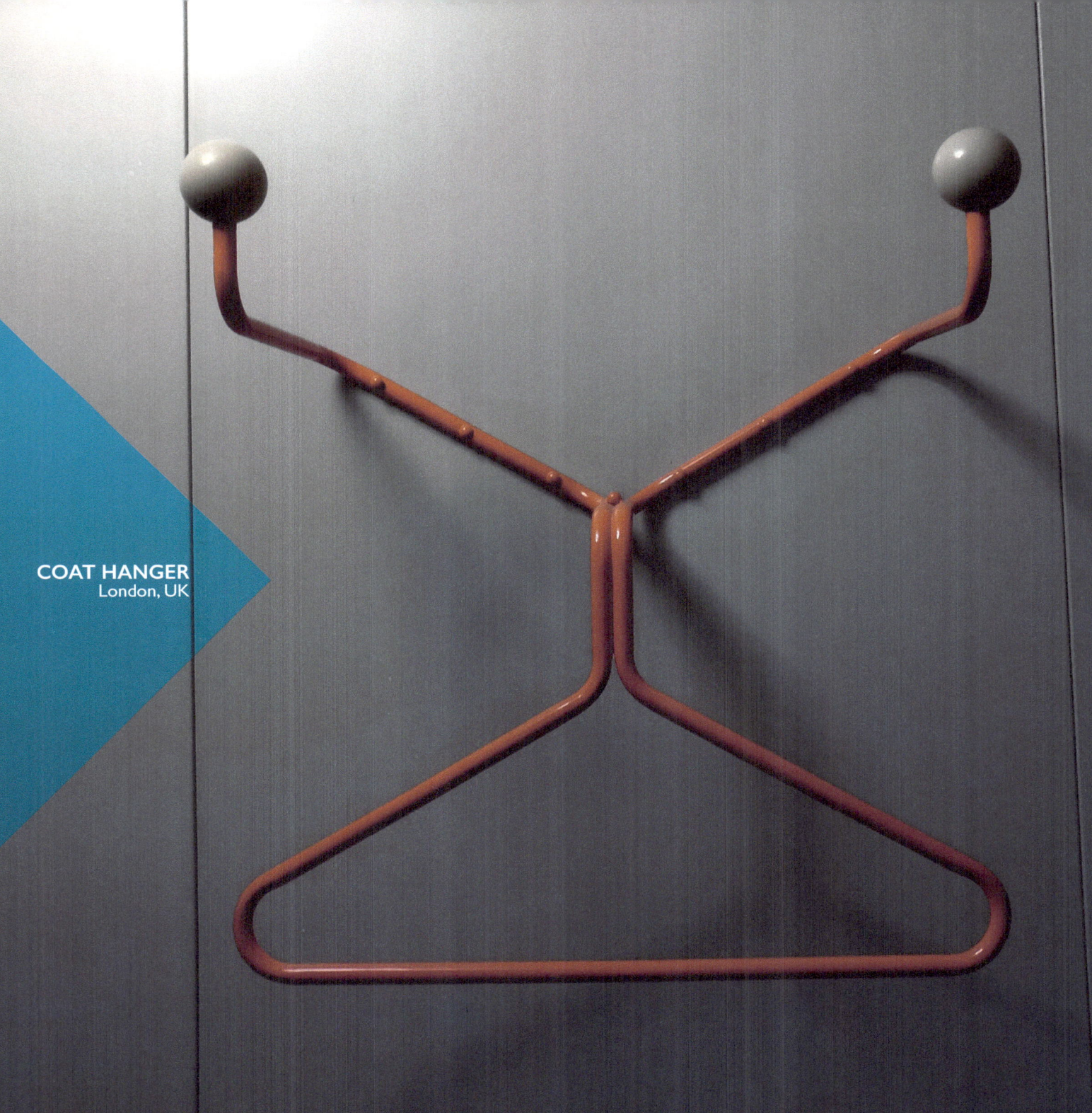

COAT HANGER
London, UK

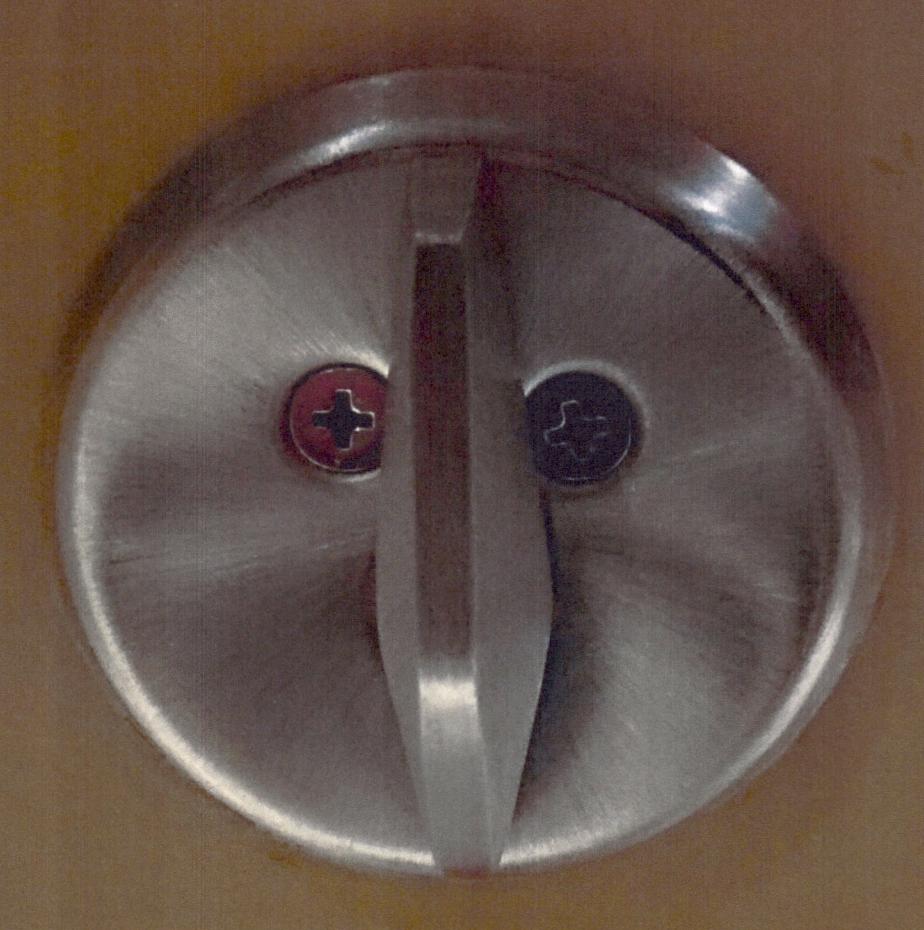

This nosey lock on a door in Boracay, Philippines.

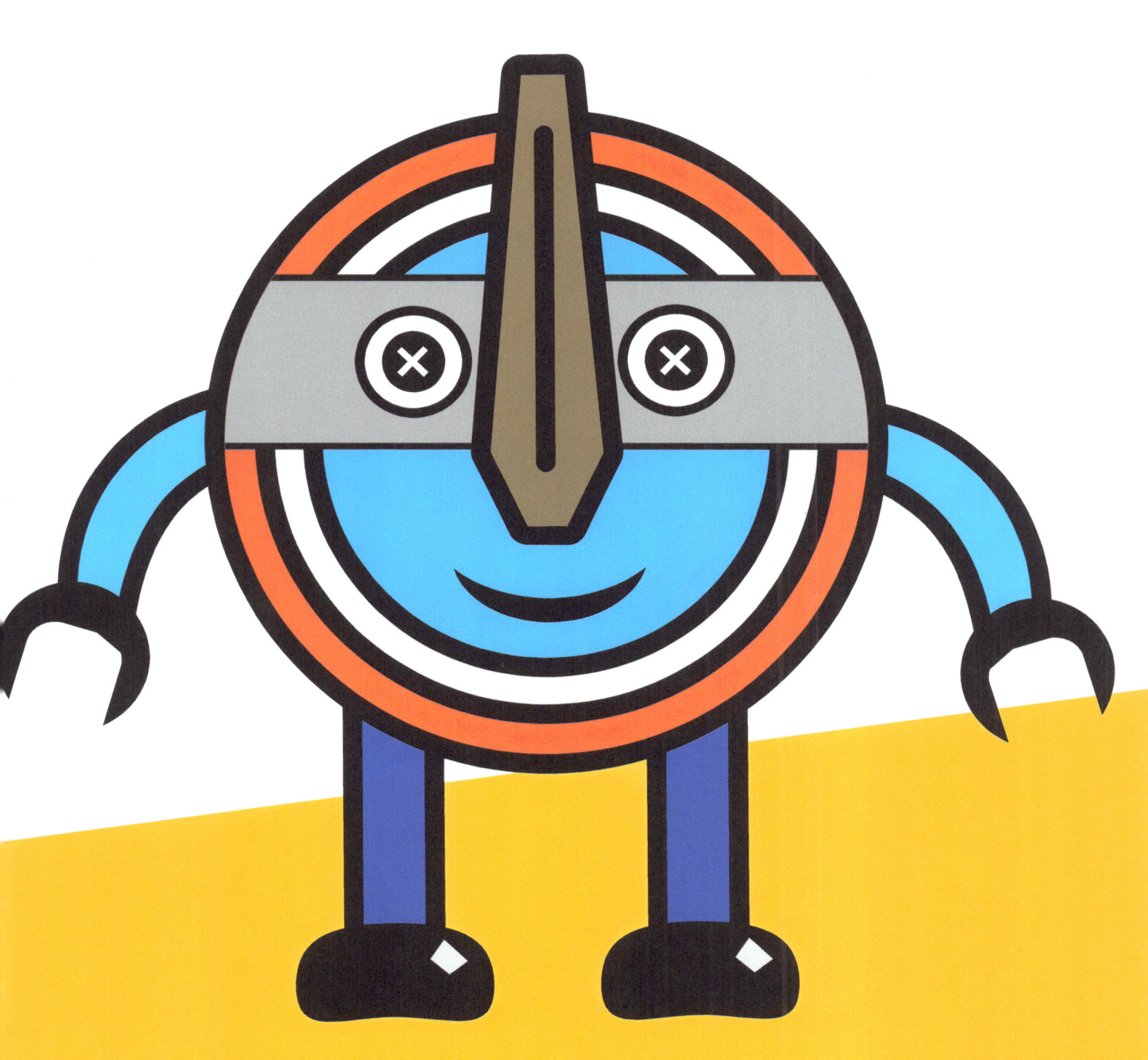

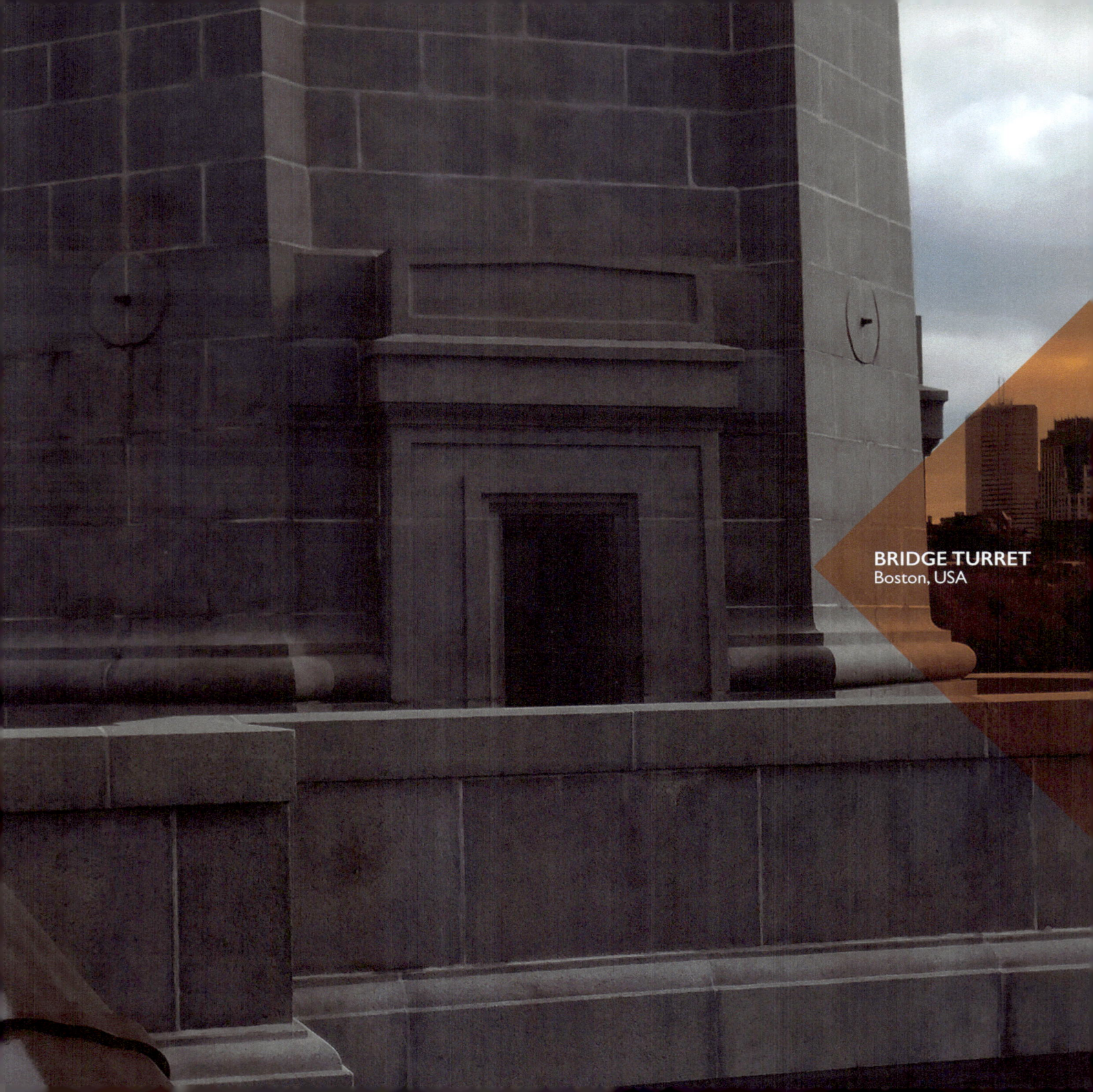

BRIDGE TURRET
Boston, USA

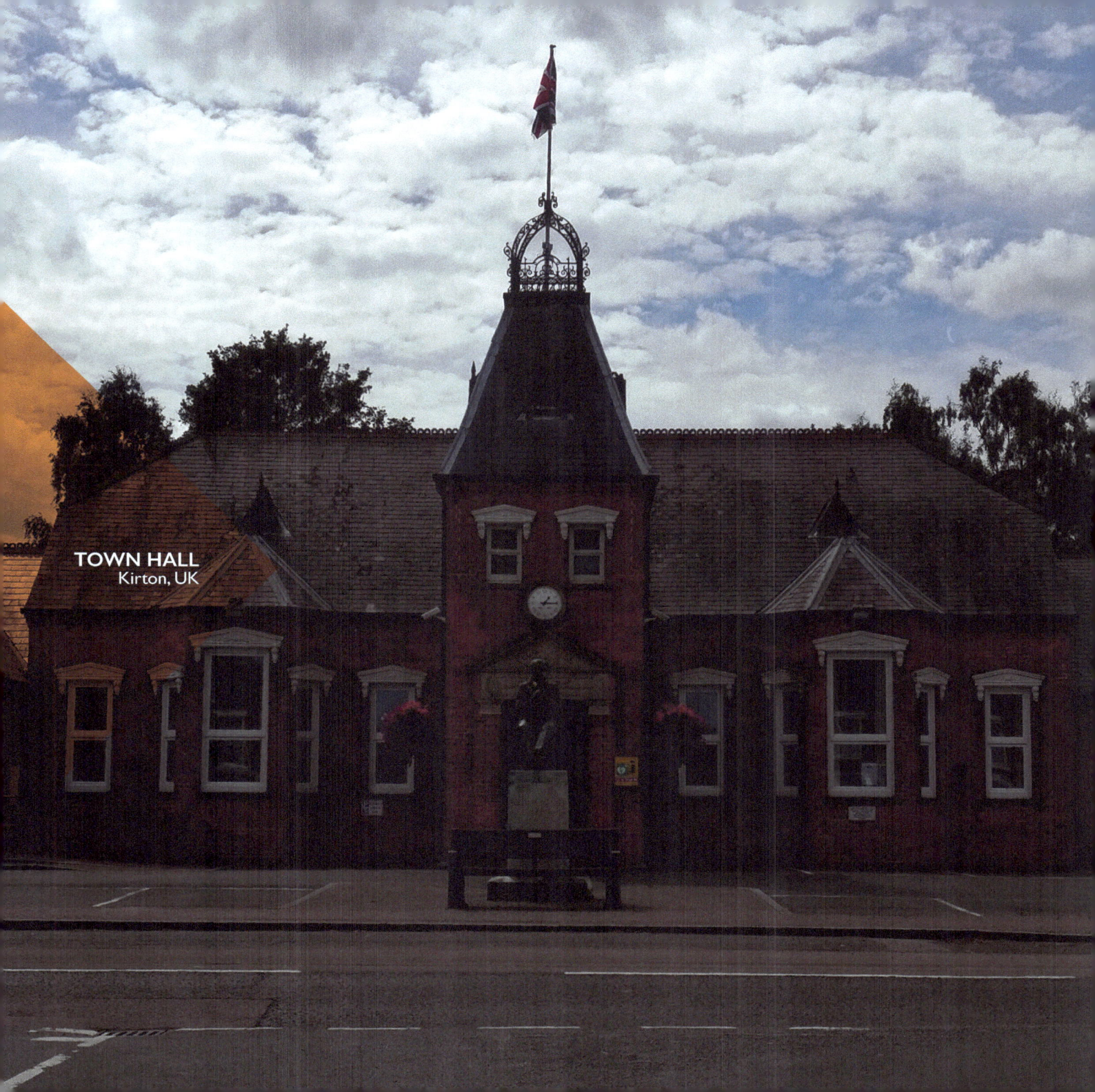

TOWN HALL
Kirton, UK

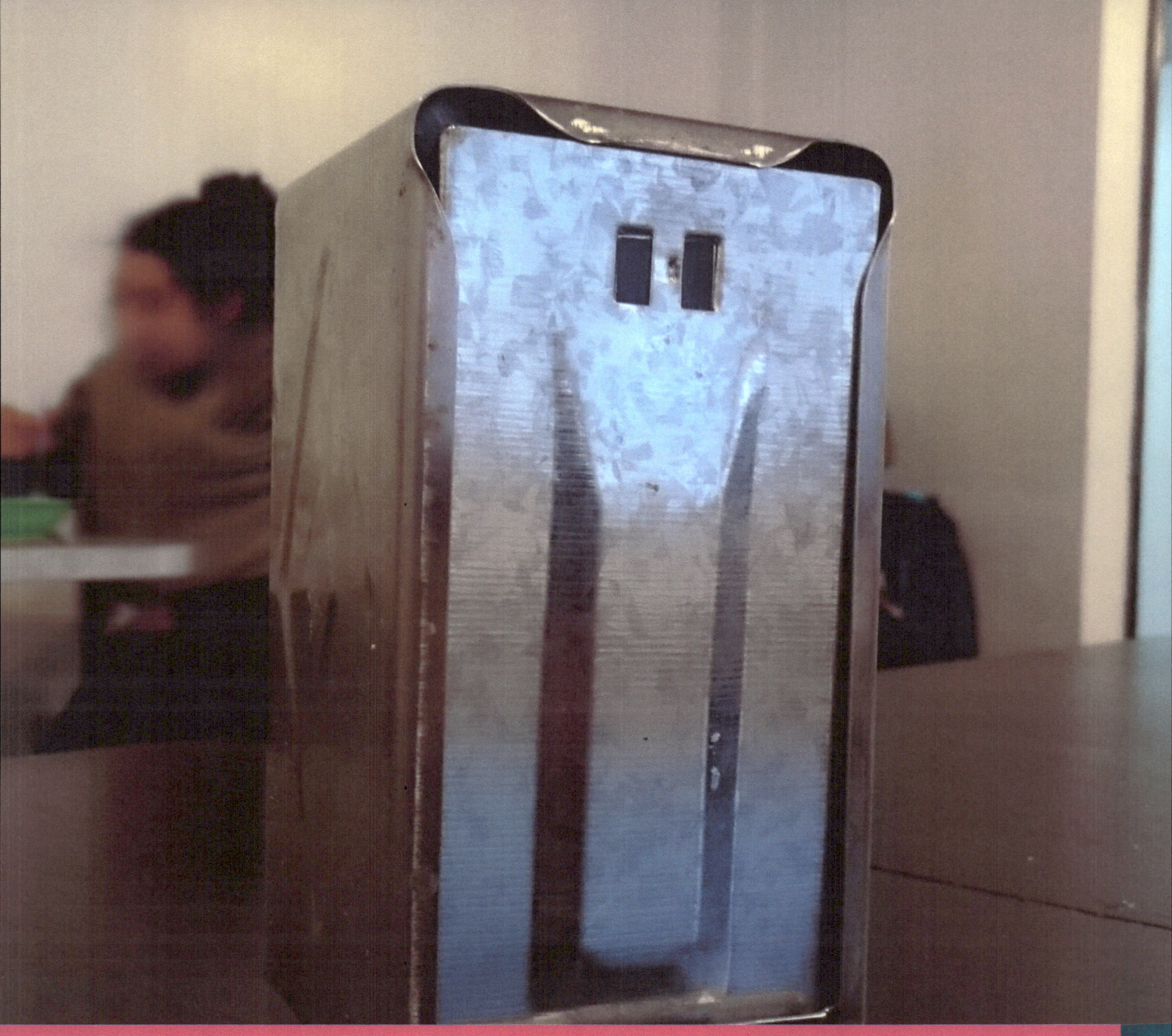

Vancouver, Canada a napkin holder stared back.

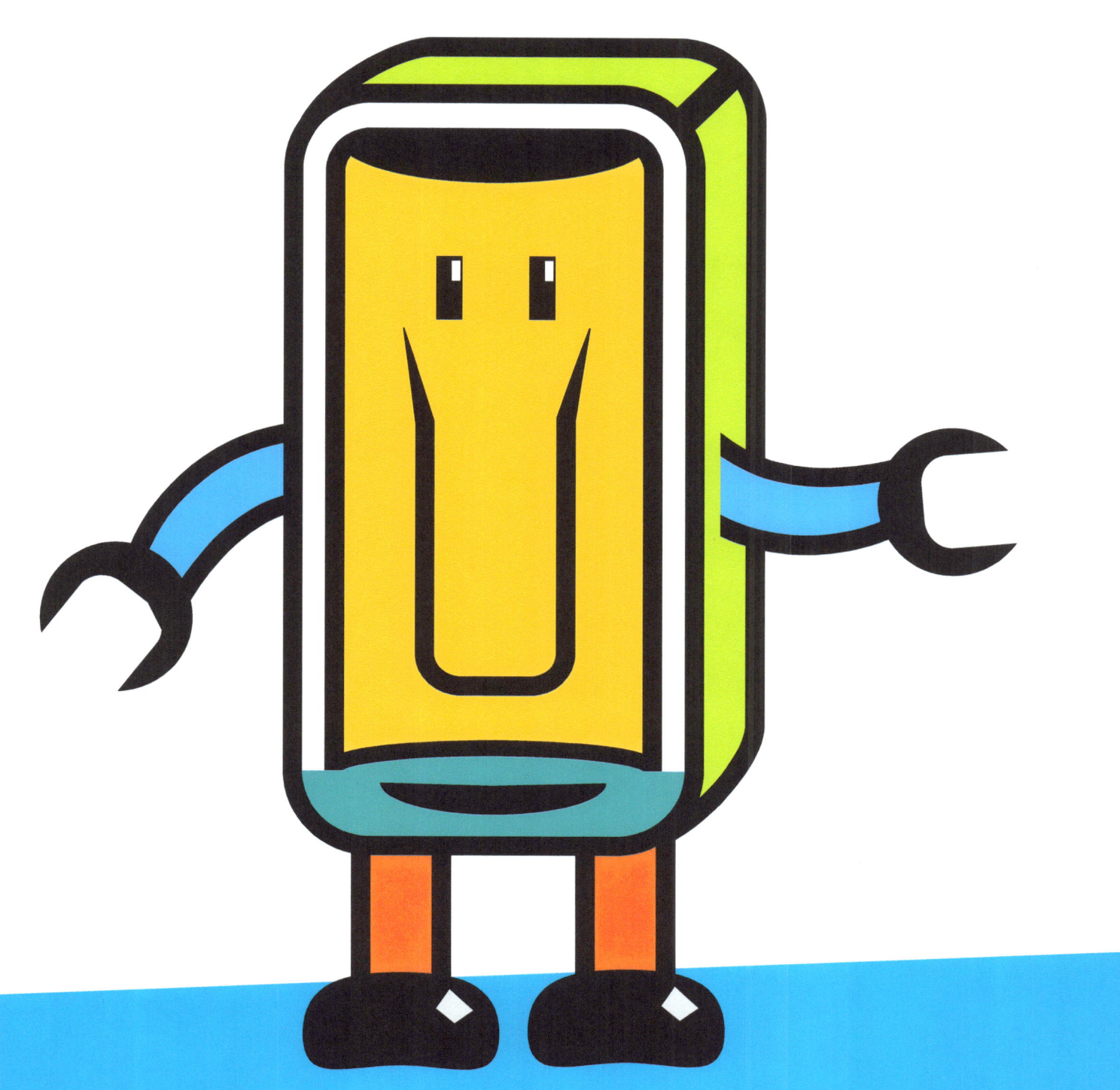

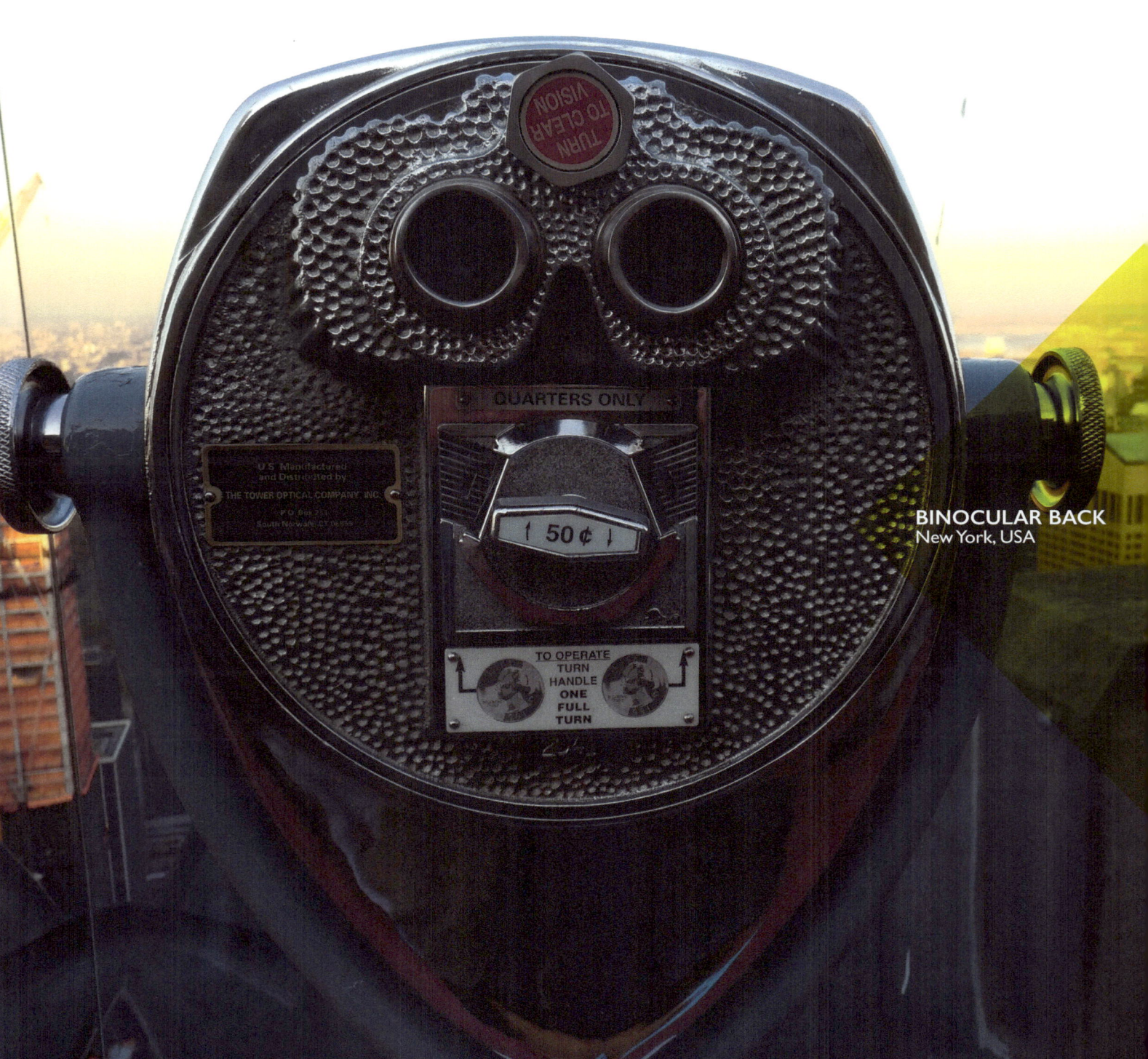

BINOCULAR BACK
New York, USA

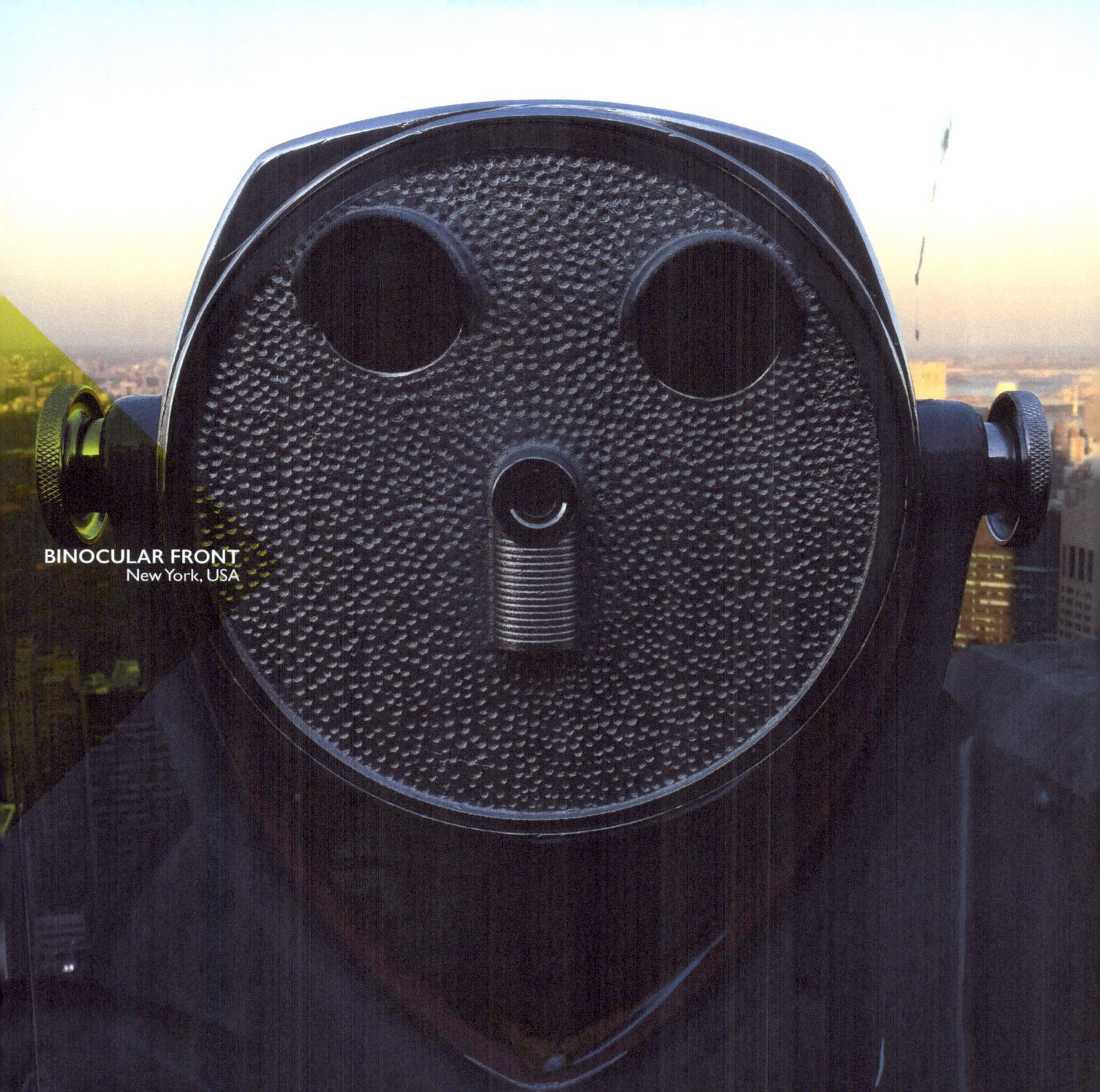

BINOCULAR FRONT
New York, USA

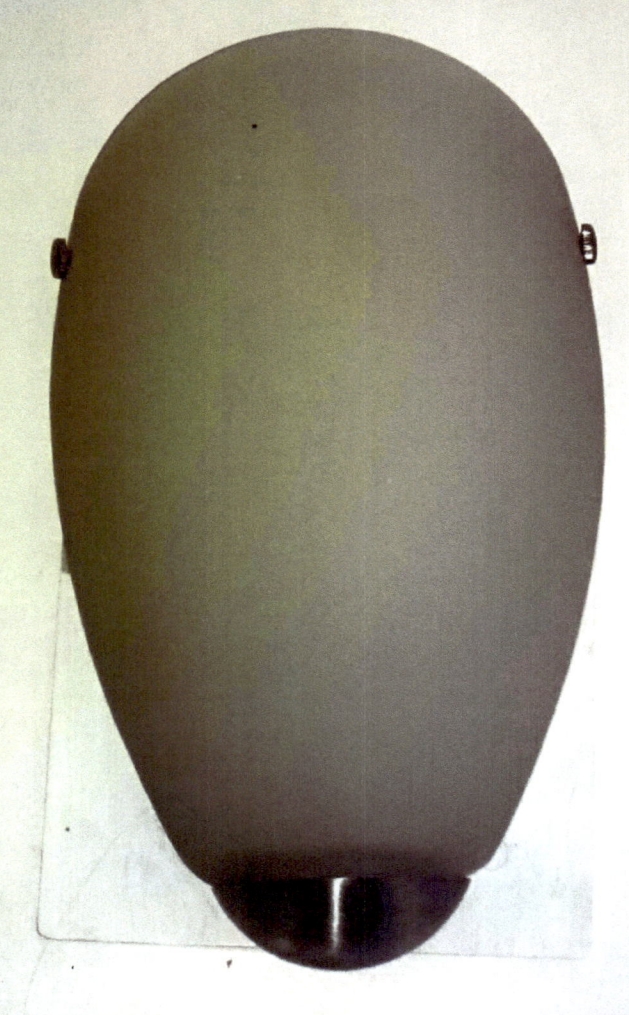

It lit the way to finding this face in Vancouver, Canada.

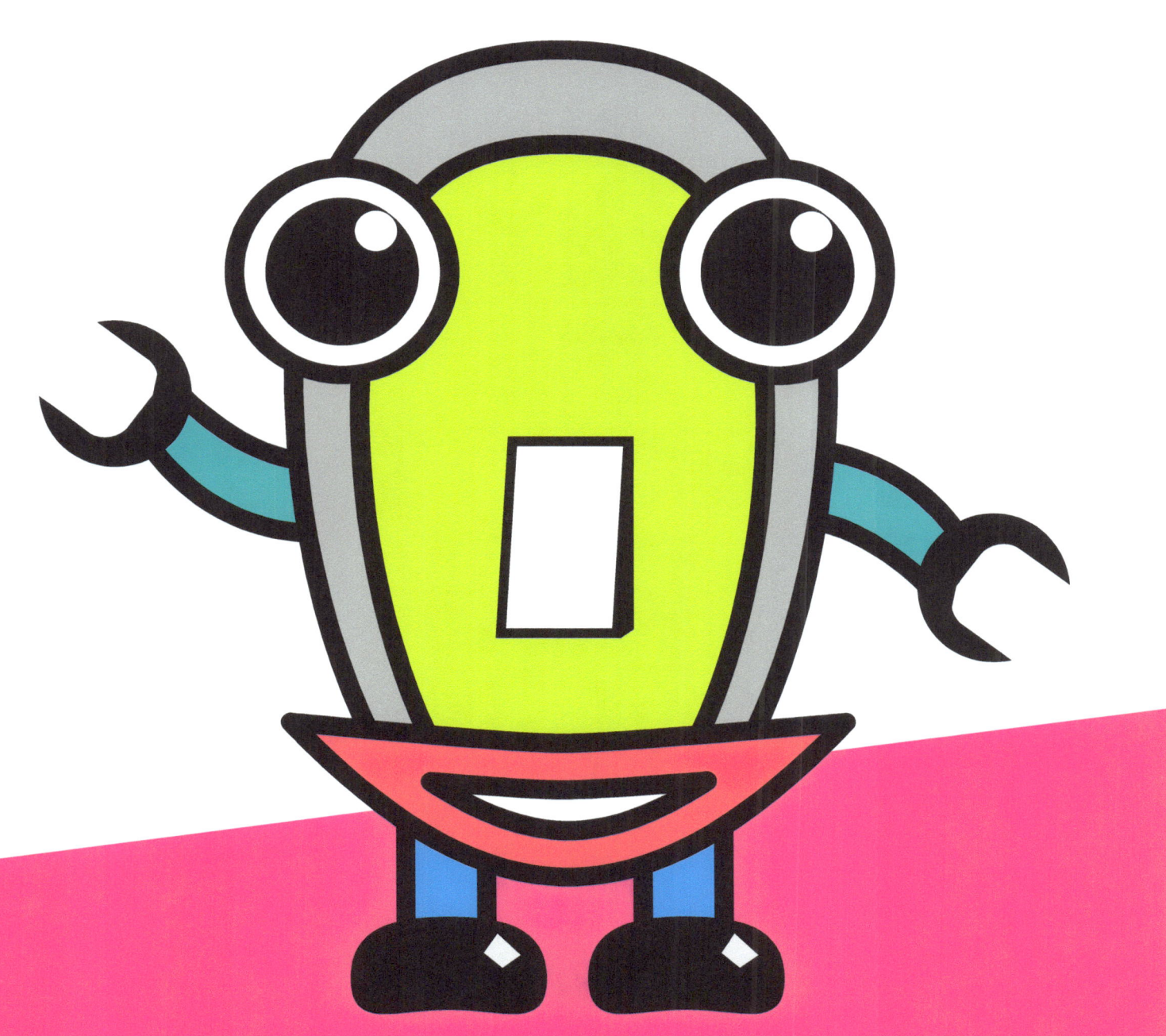

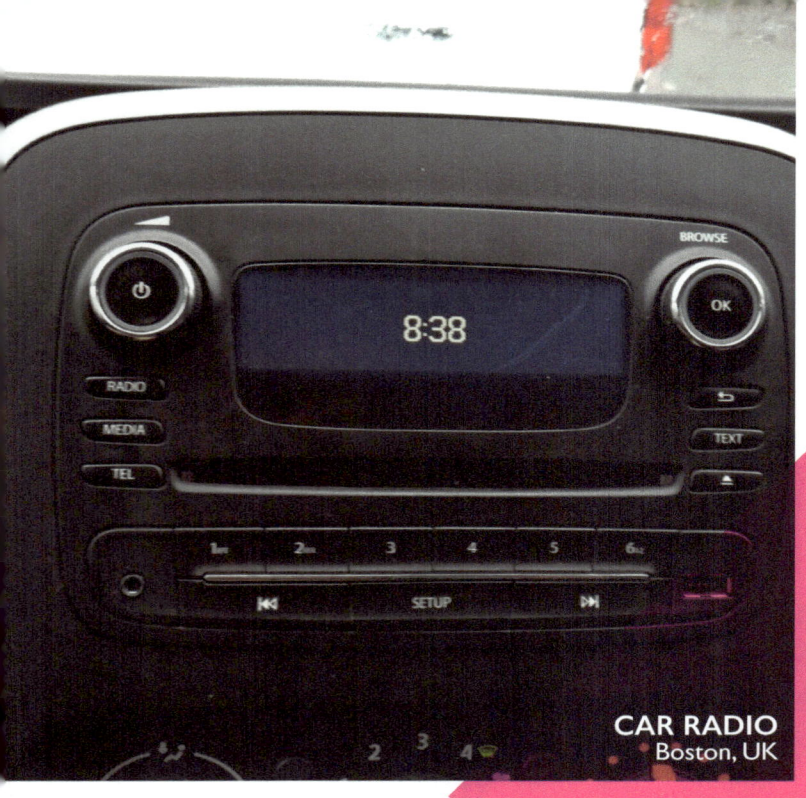

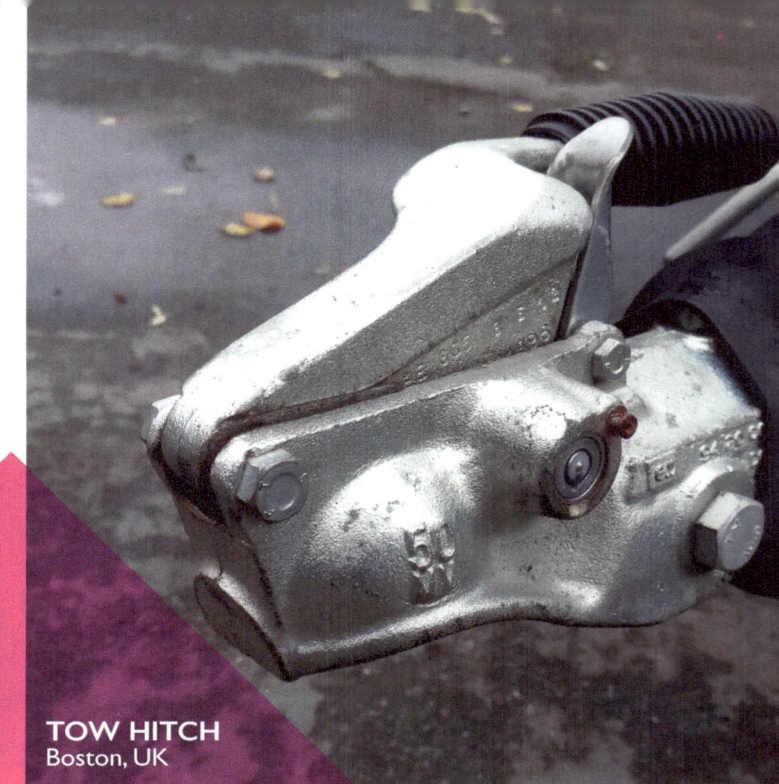

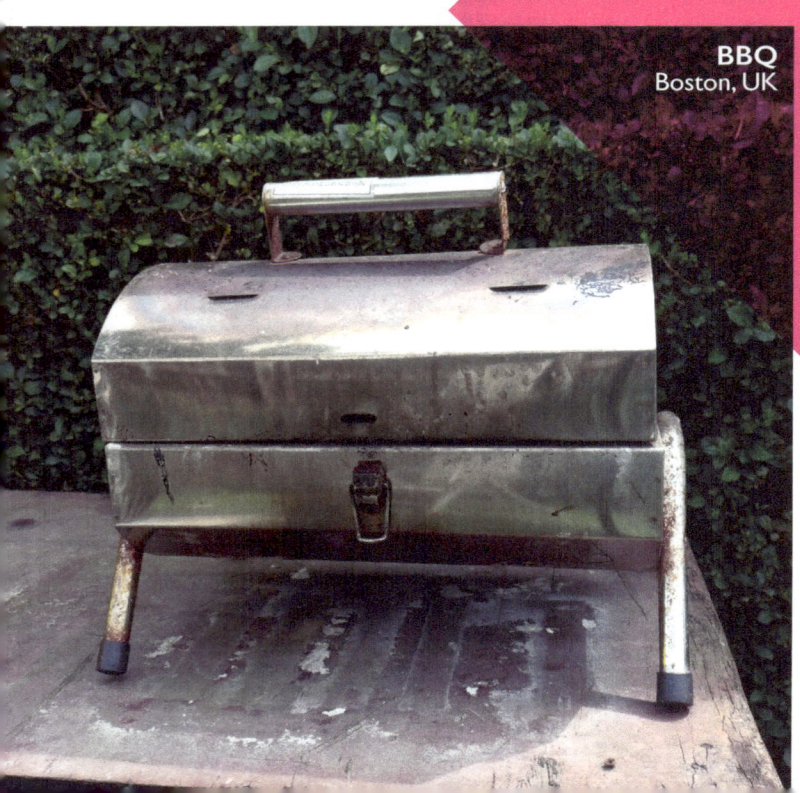

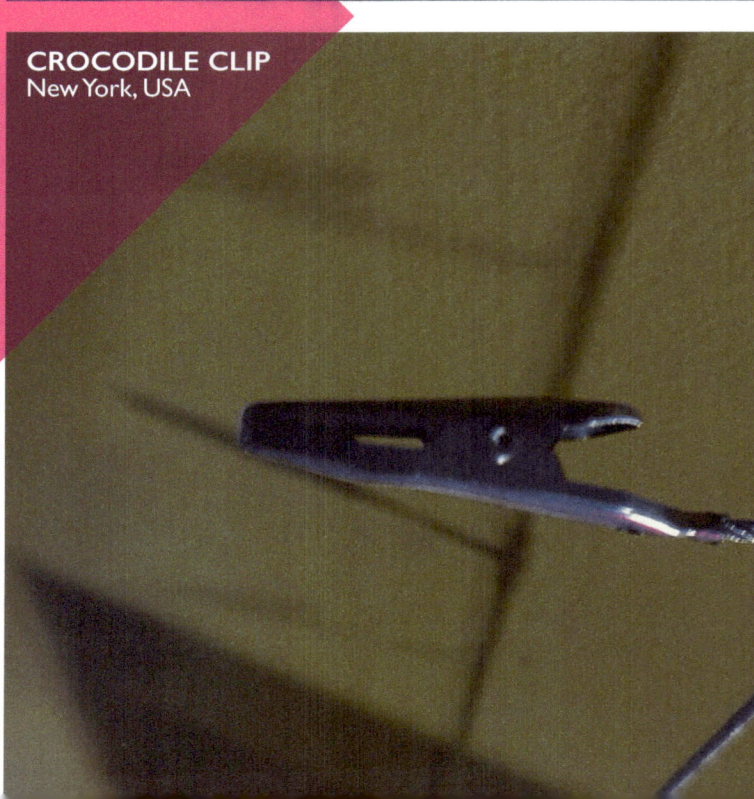

CAR RADIO
Boston, UK

TOW HITCH
Boston, UK

BBQ
Boston, UK

CROCODILE CLIP
New York, USA

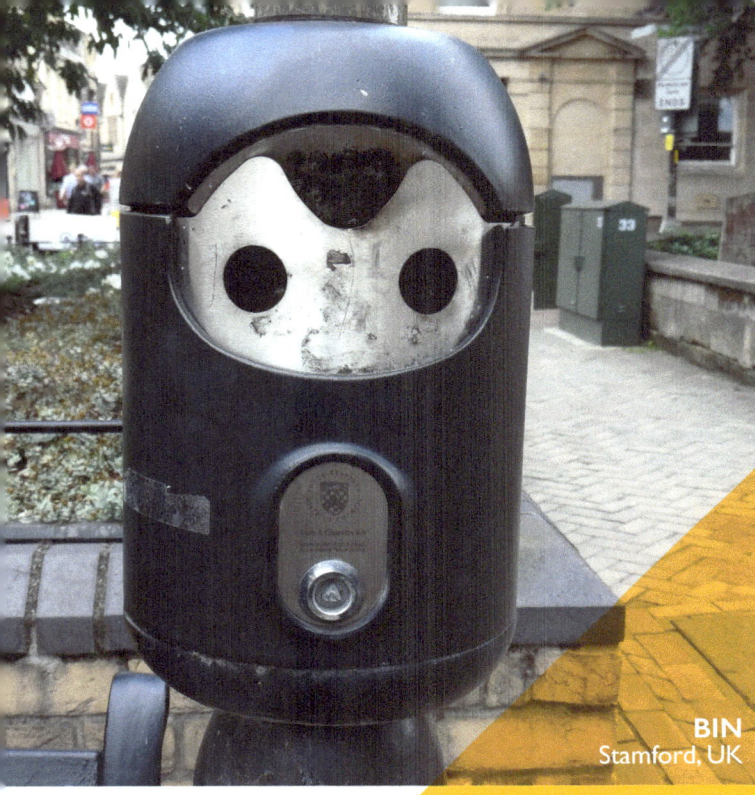

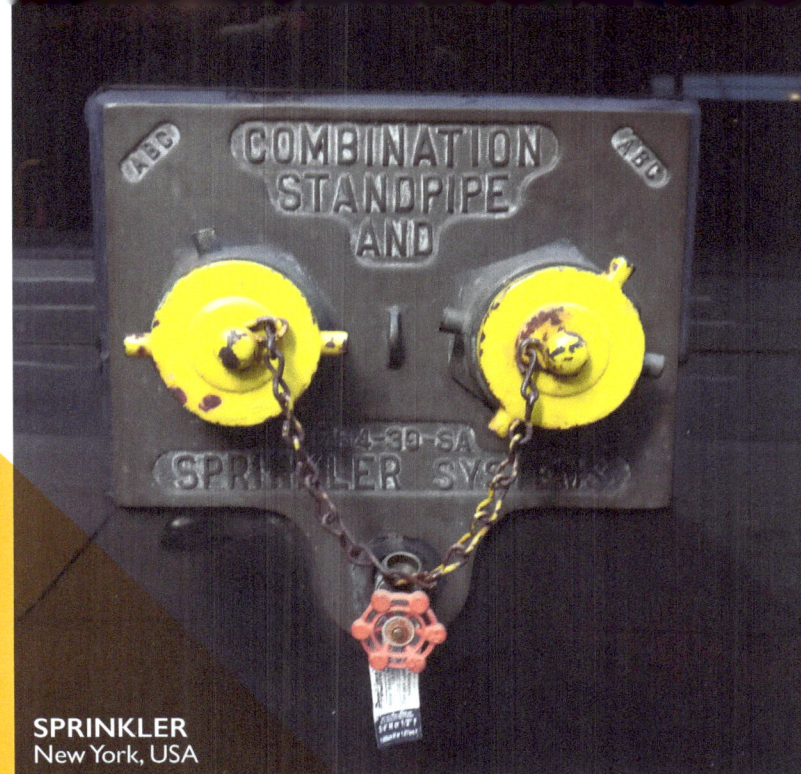

BIN
Stamford, UK

SPRINKLER
New York, USA

COFFEE CUP
Vancouver, Canada

DOOR LOCK
Manila, Philippines

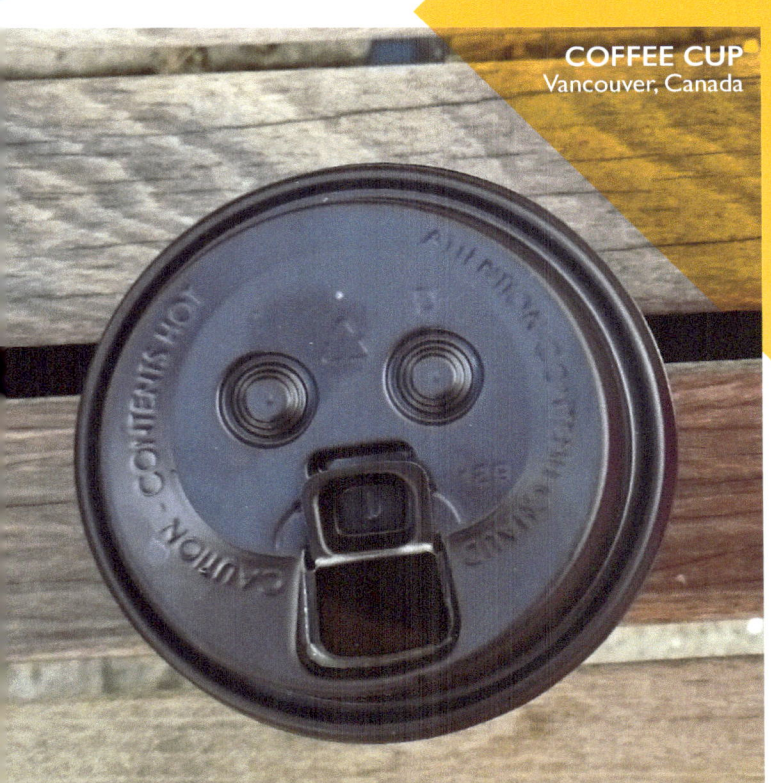

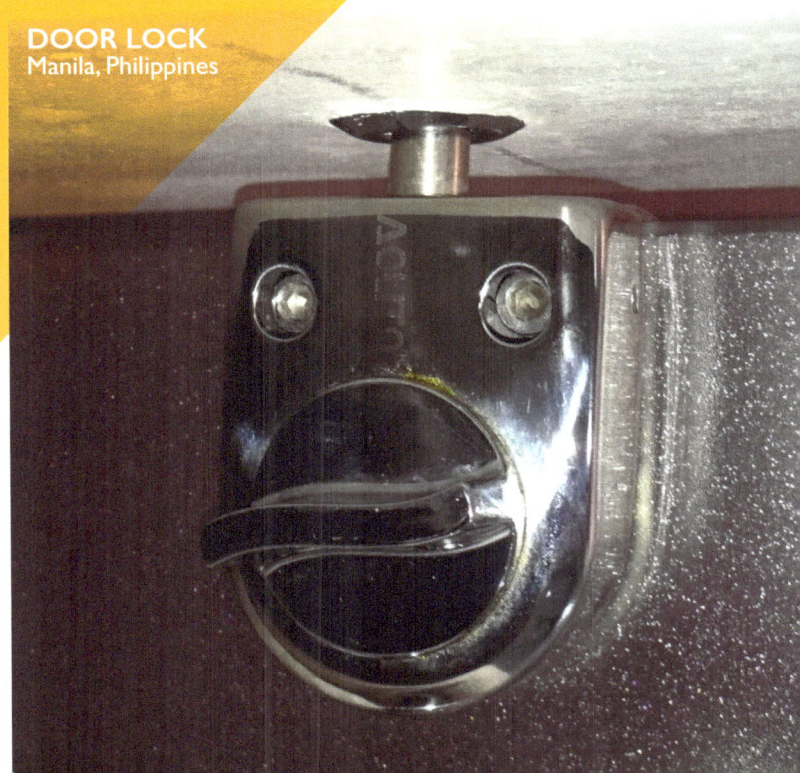

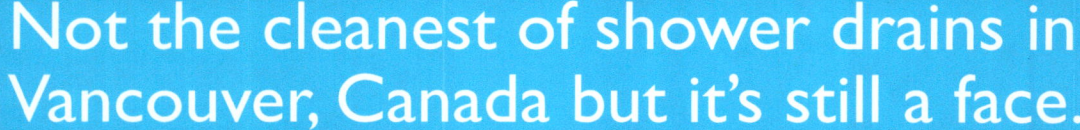
Not the cleanest of shower drains in Vancouver, Canada but it's still a face.

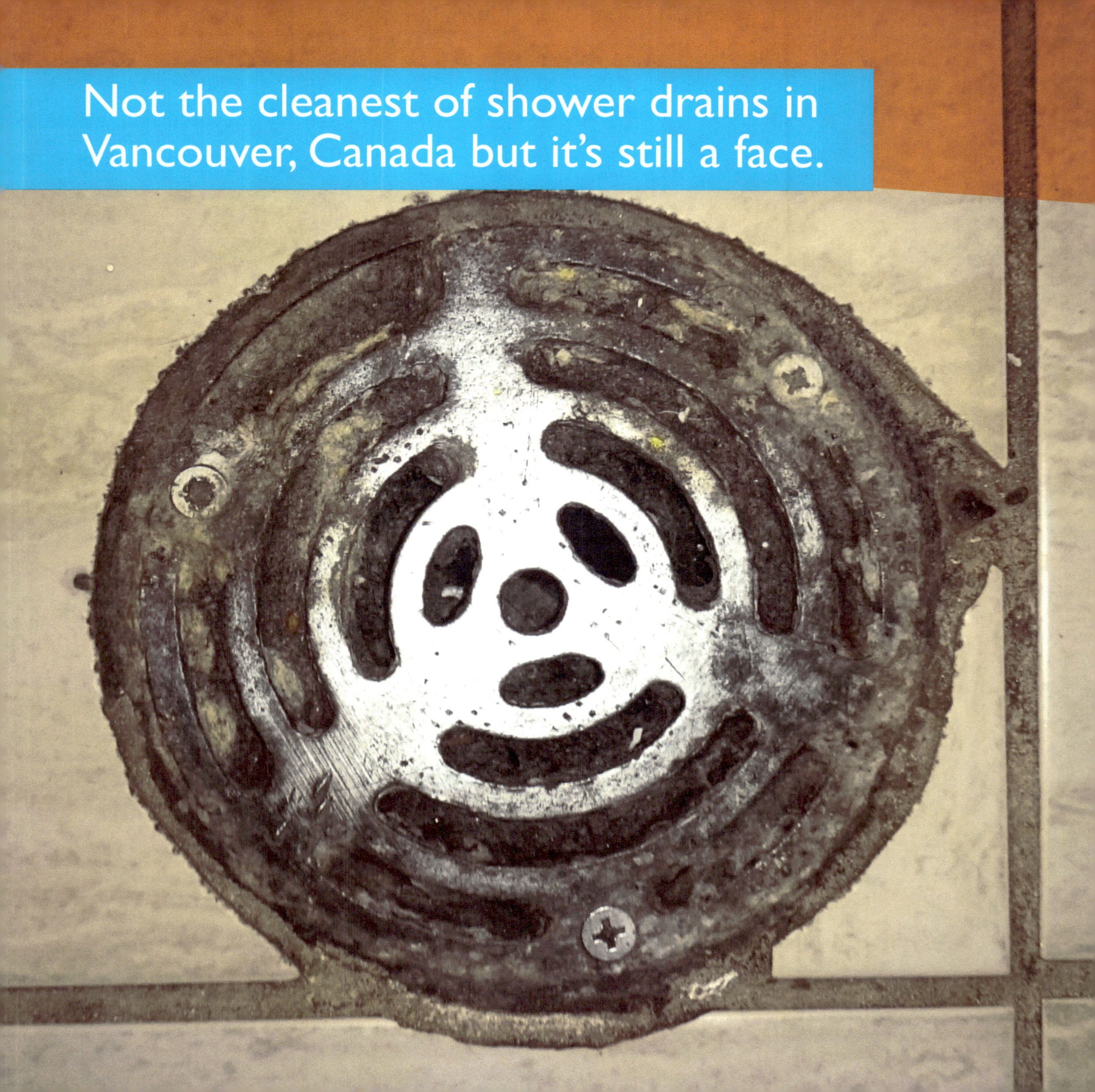

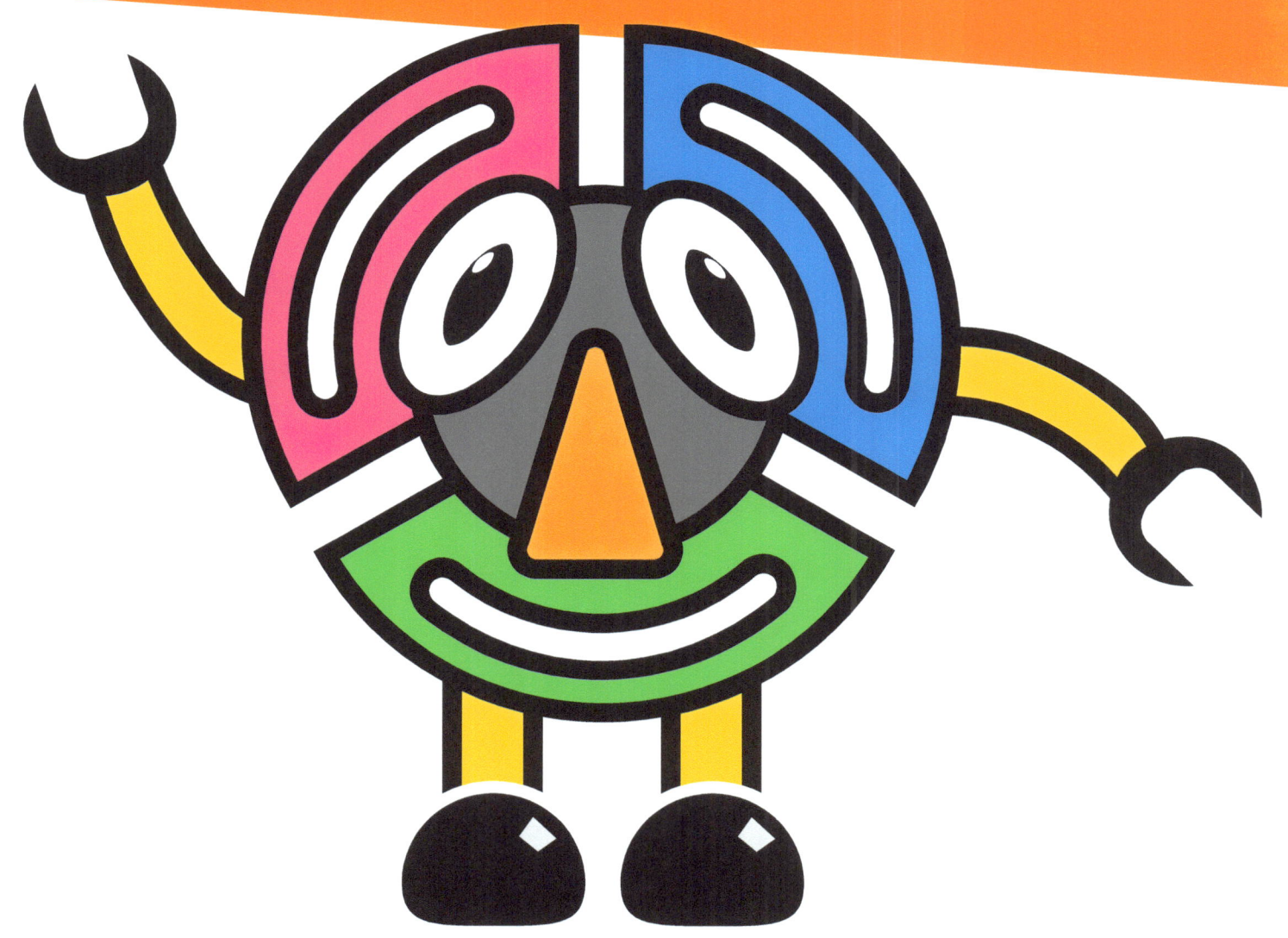

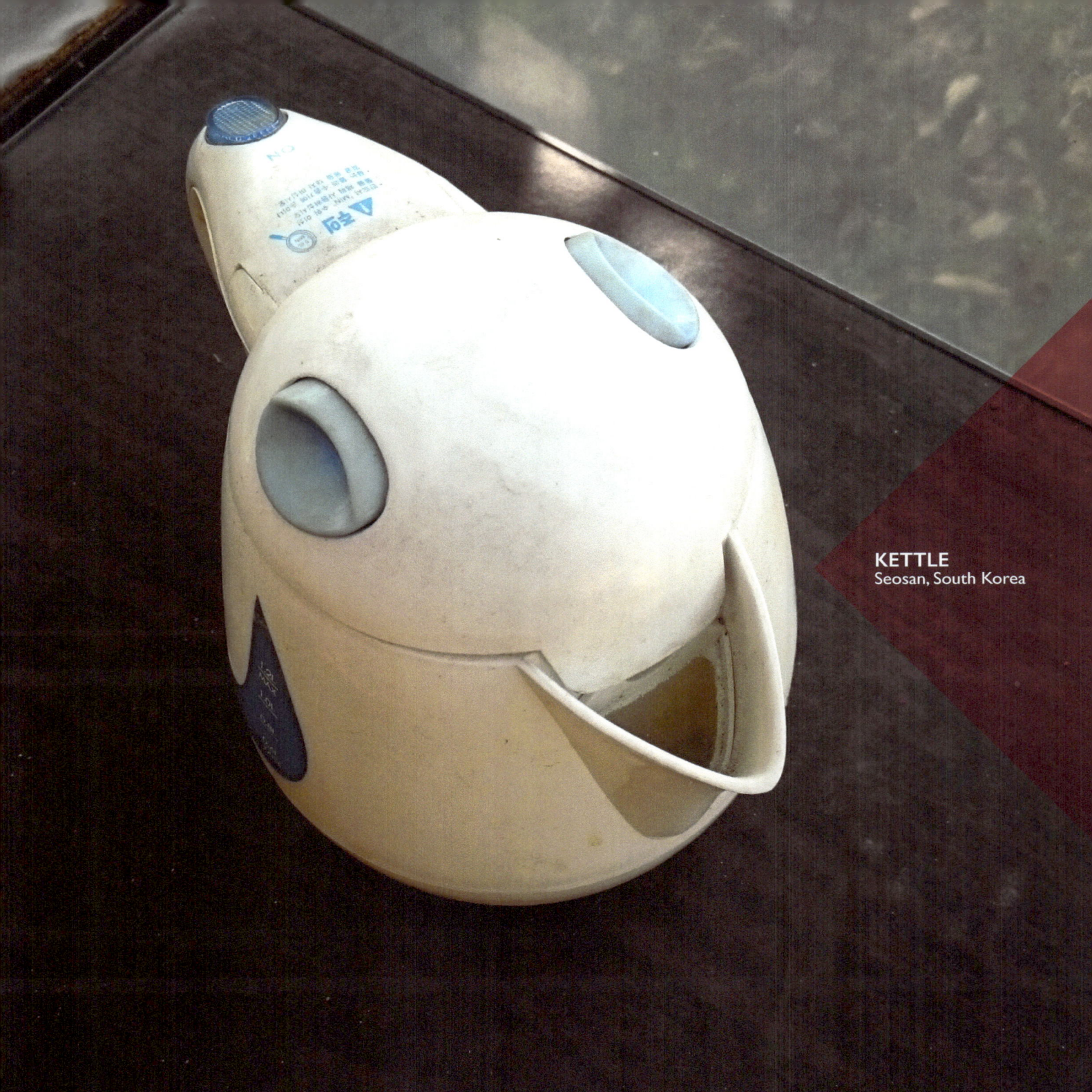

KETTLE
Seosan, South Korea

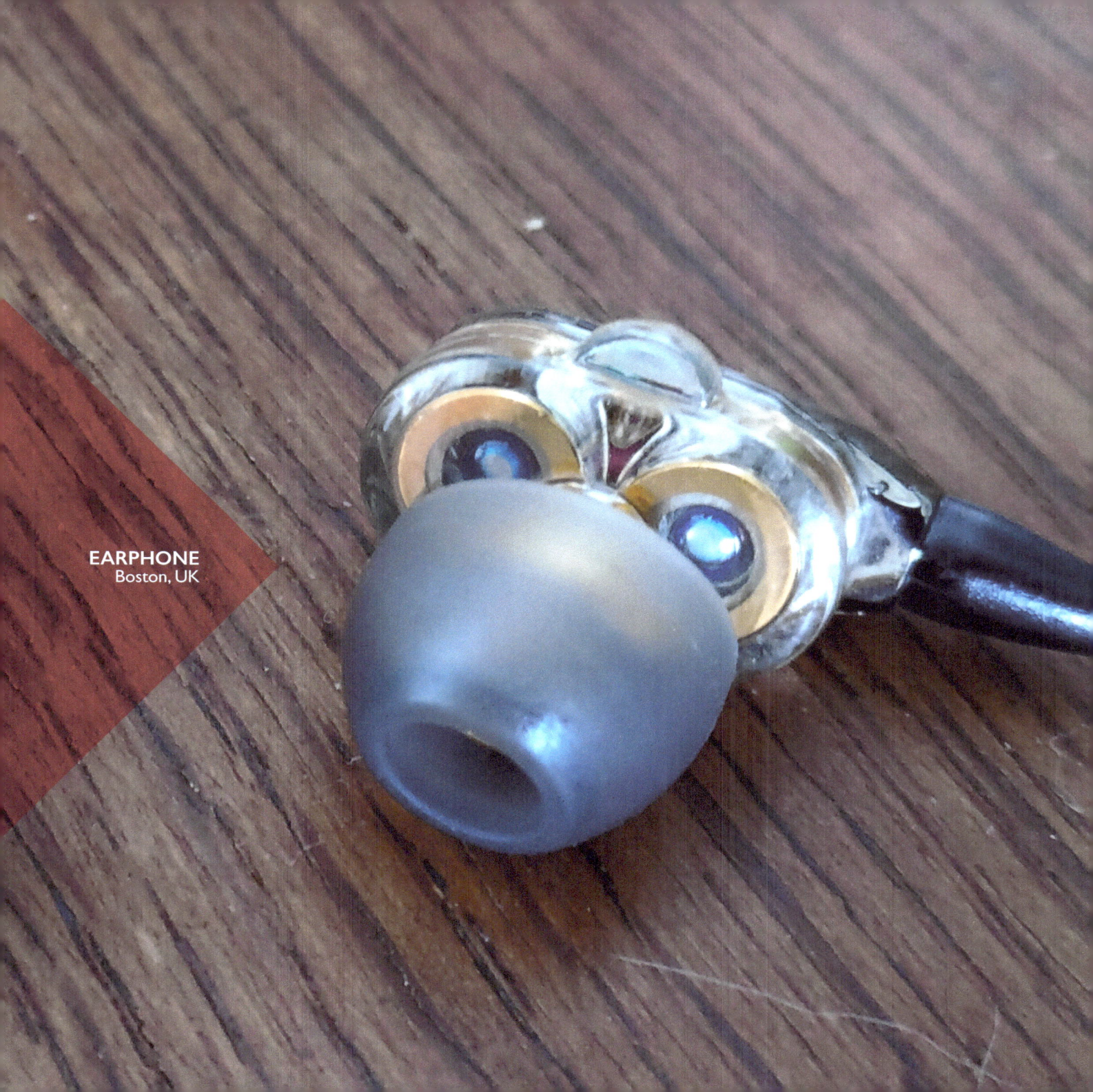

EARPHONE
Boston, UK

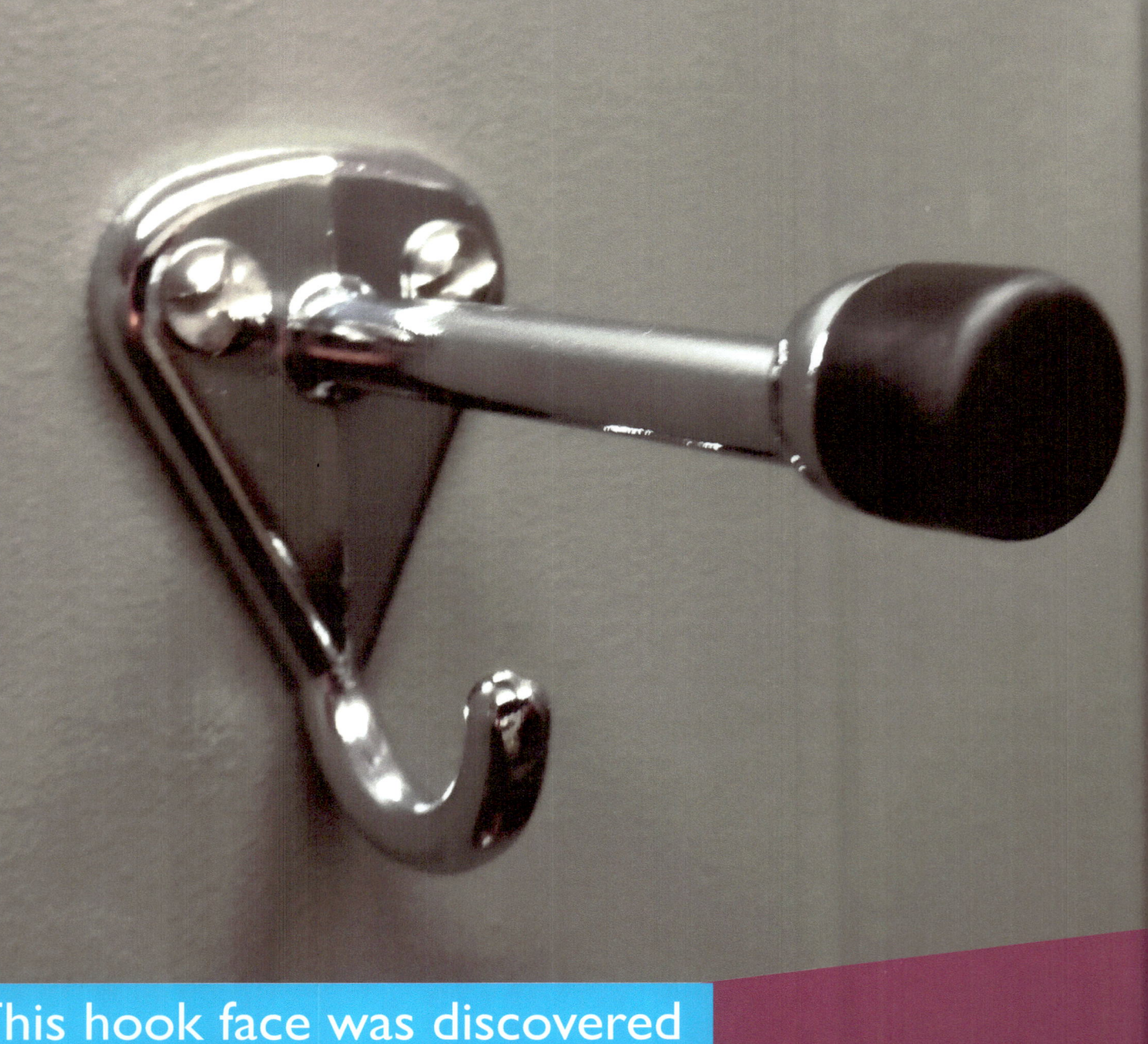

This hook face was discovered in Albany, USA.

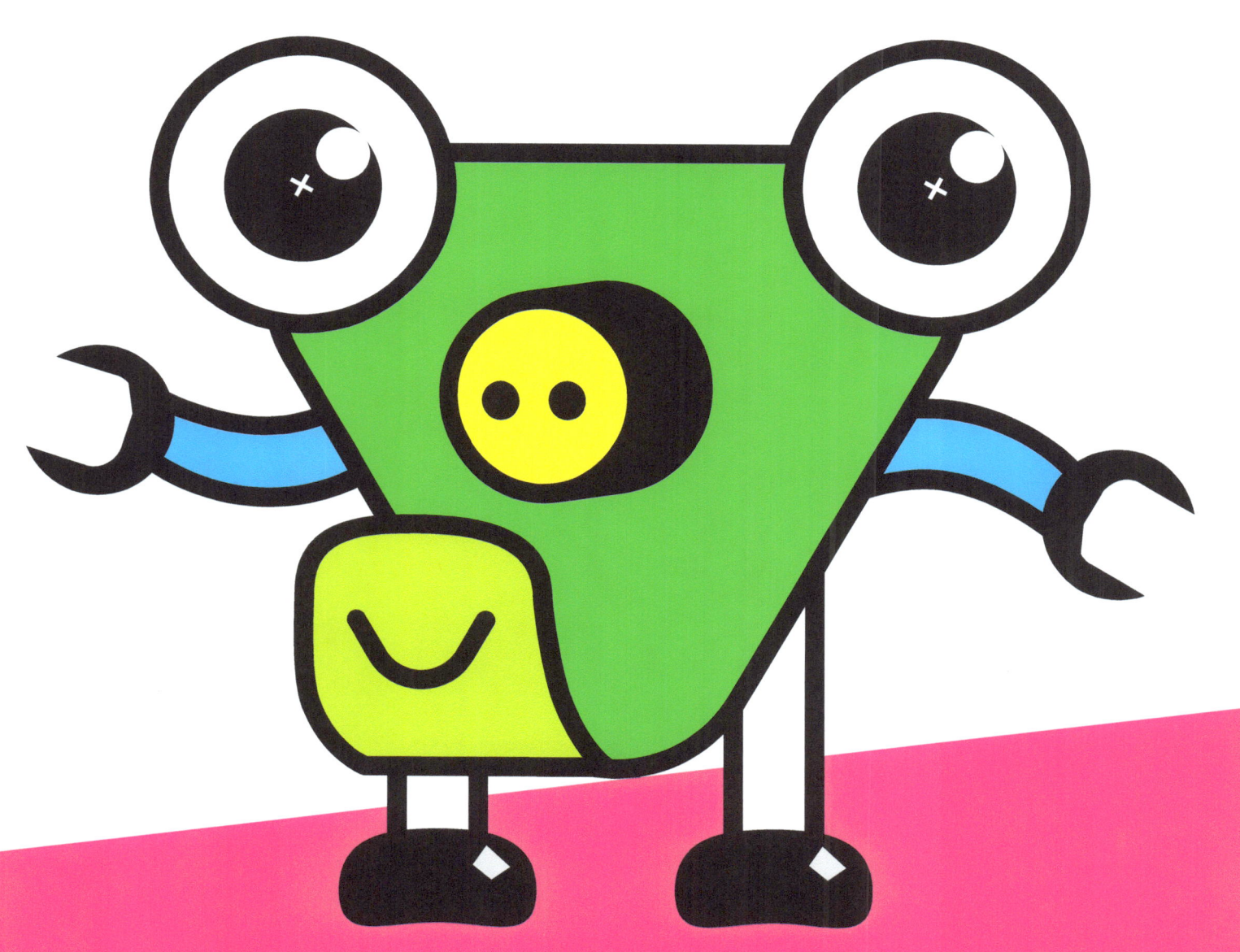

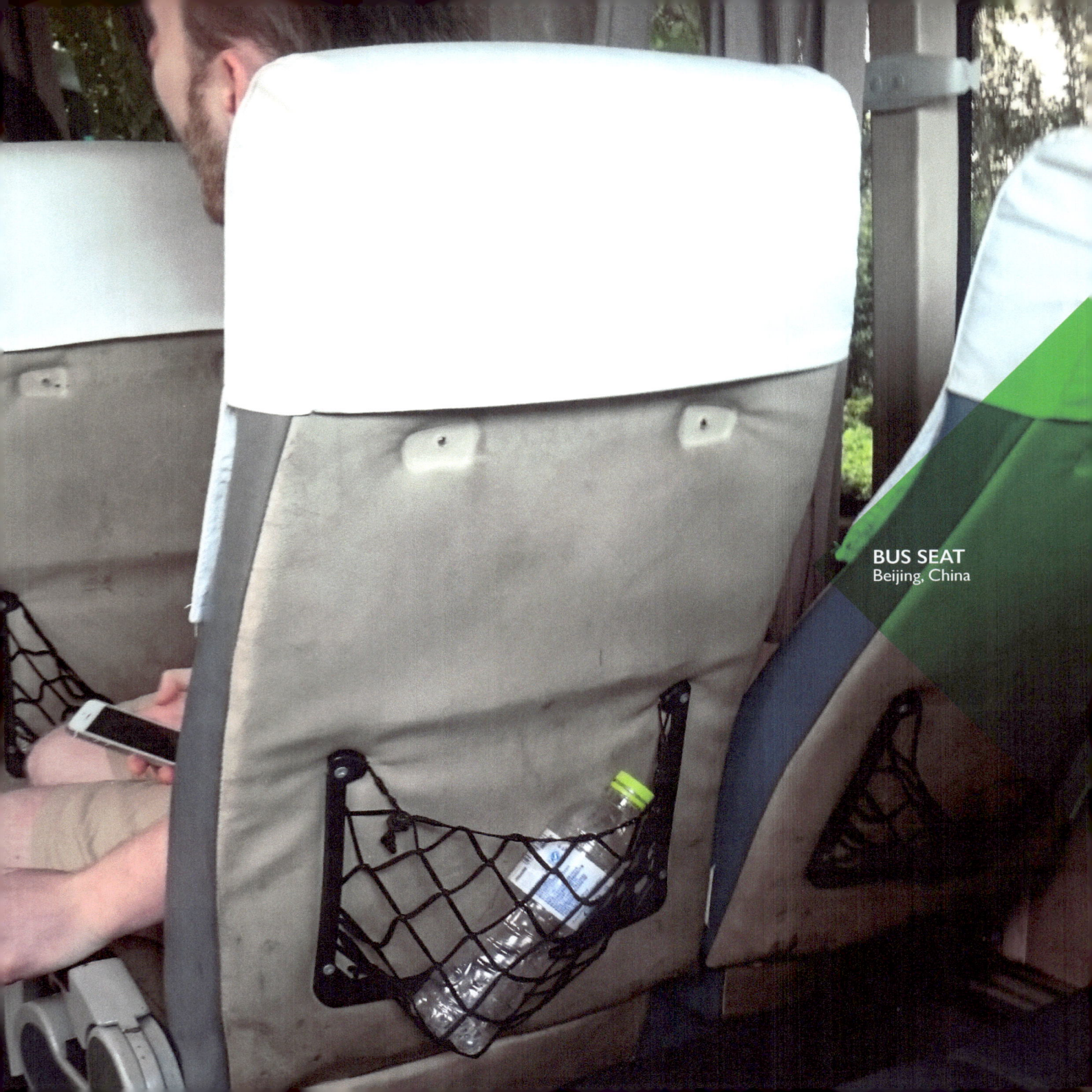

BUS SEAT
Beijing, China

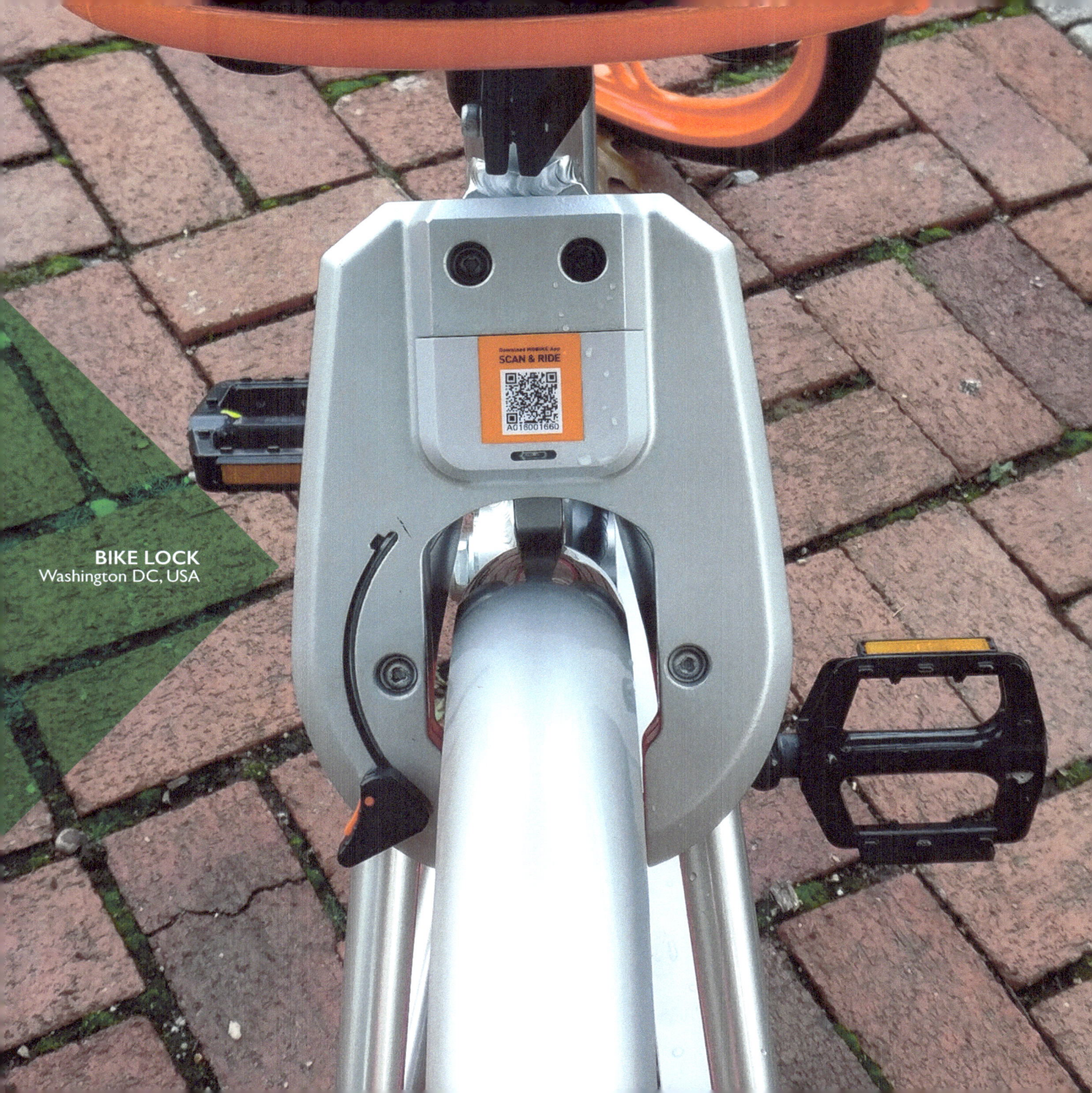

BIKE LOCK
Washington DC, USA

SCAN & RIDE
Download MOBIKE App
A018001660

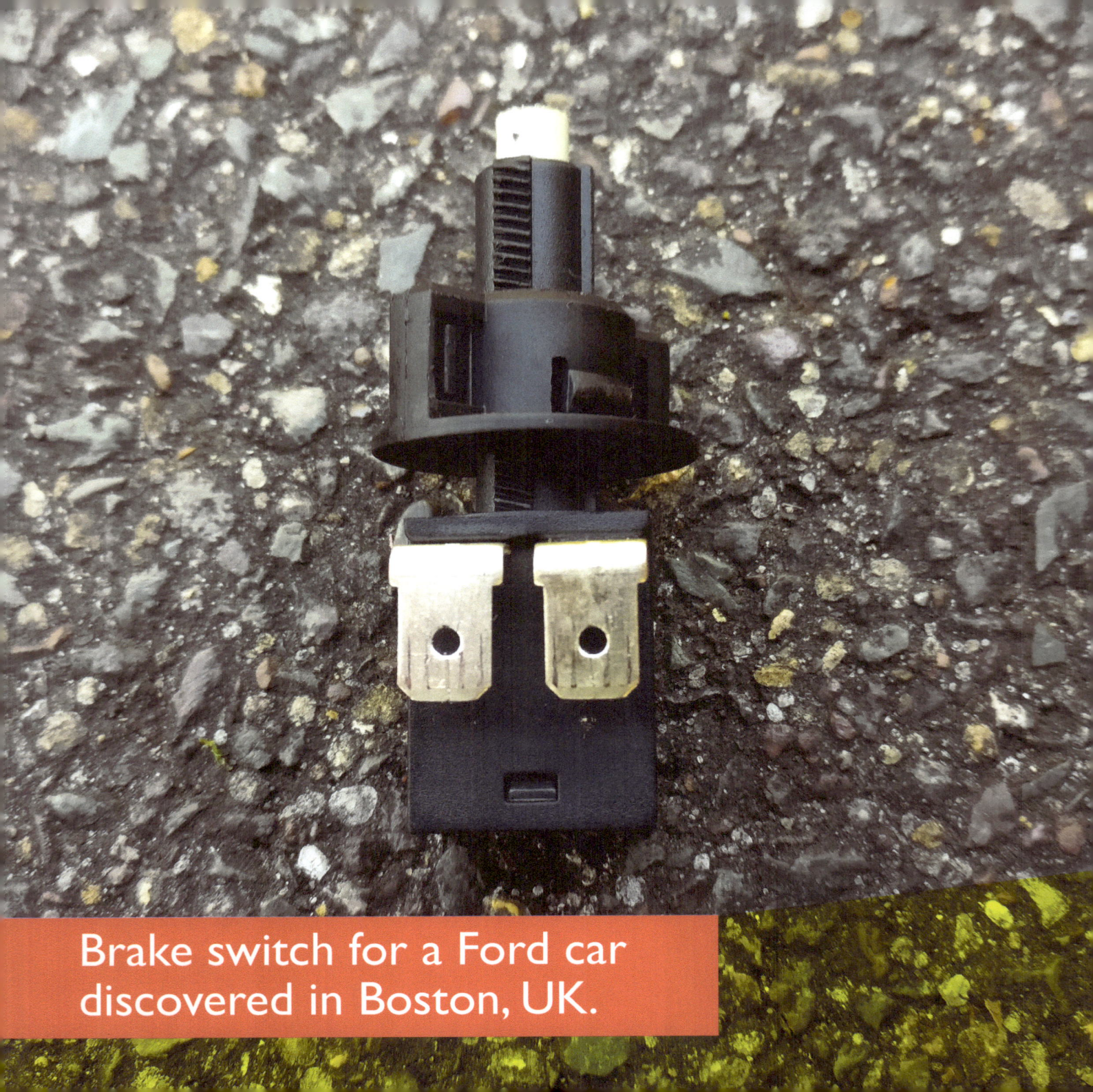

Brake switch for a Ford car discovered in Boston, UK.

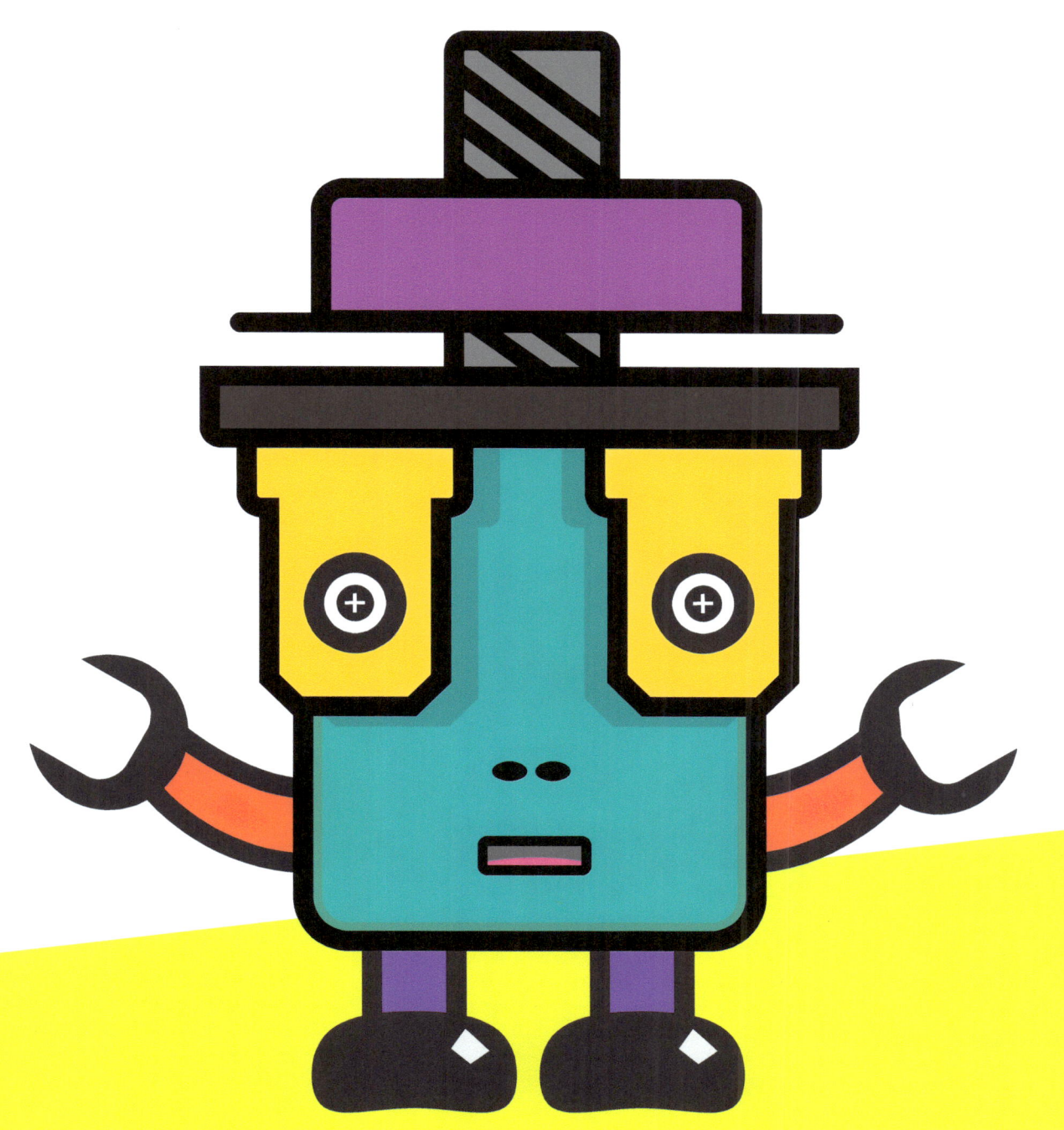

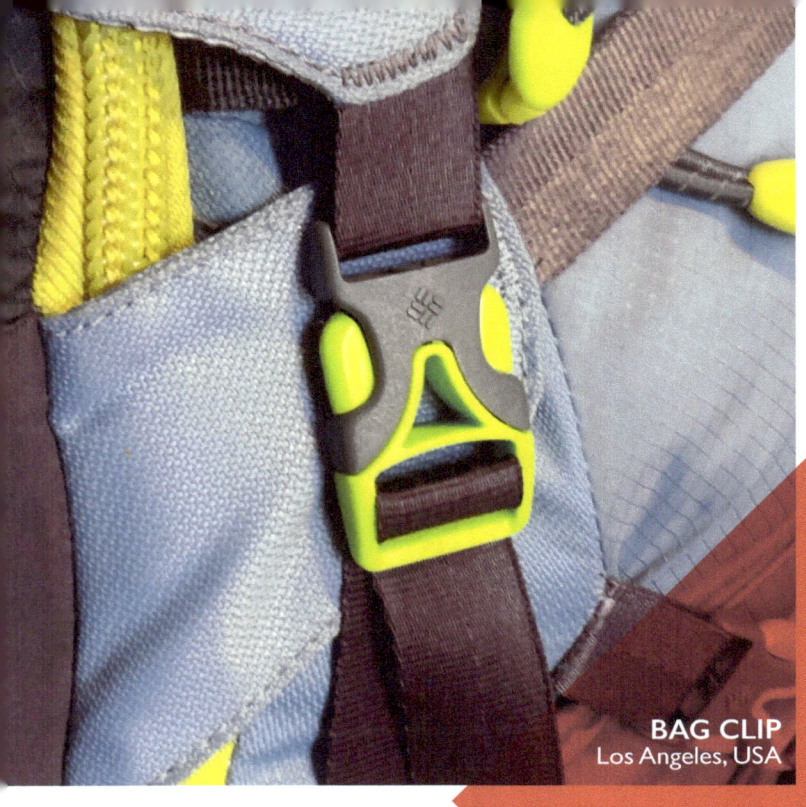

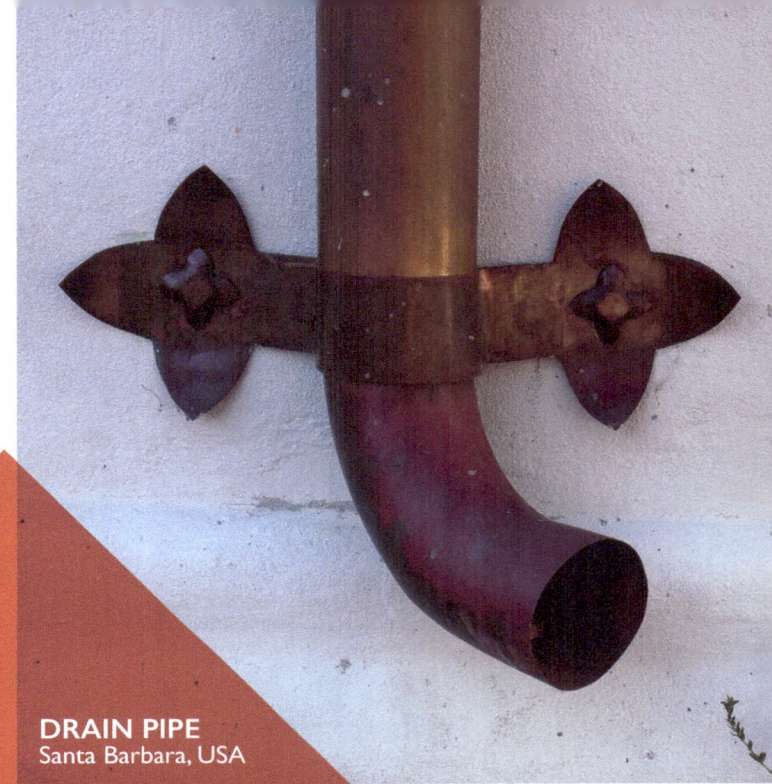

BAG CLIP
Los Angeles, USA

DRAIN PIPE
Santa Barbara, USA

POLE CONDUIT
Frome, UK

FENCE POST
Geneva, USA

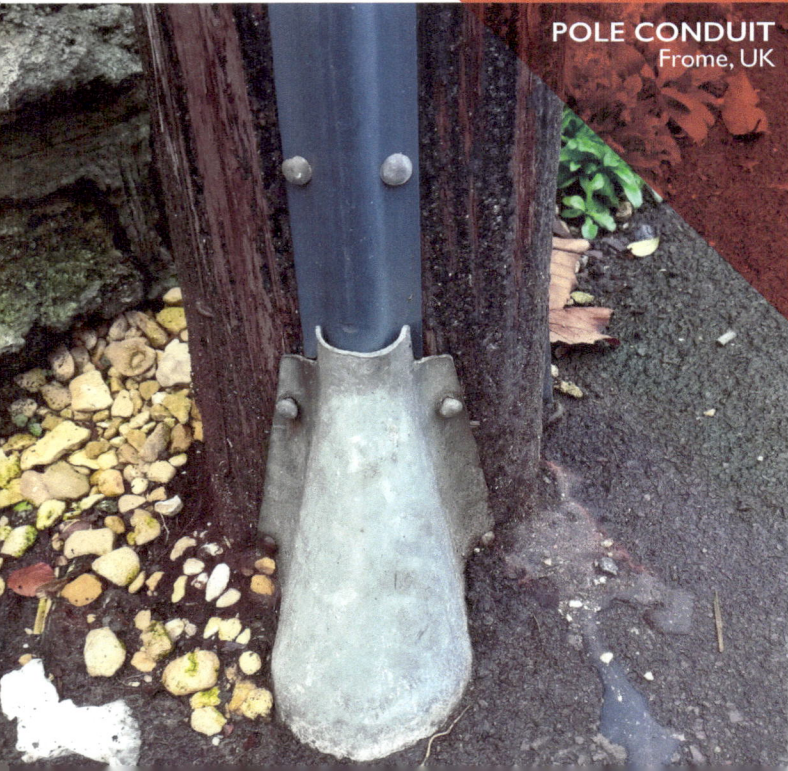

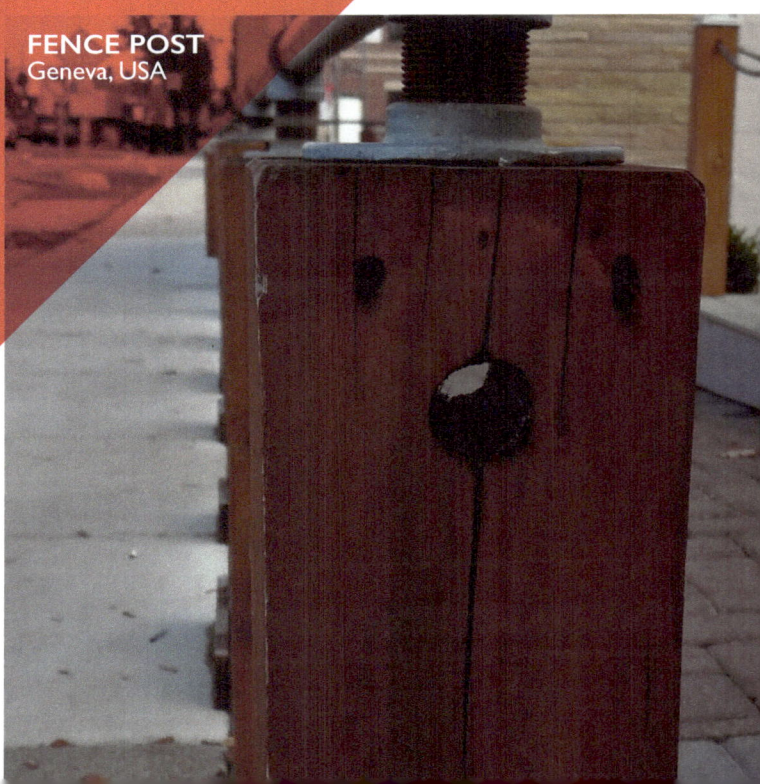

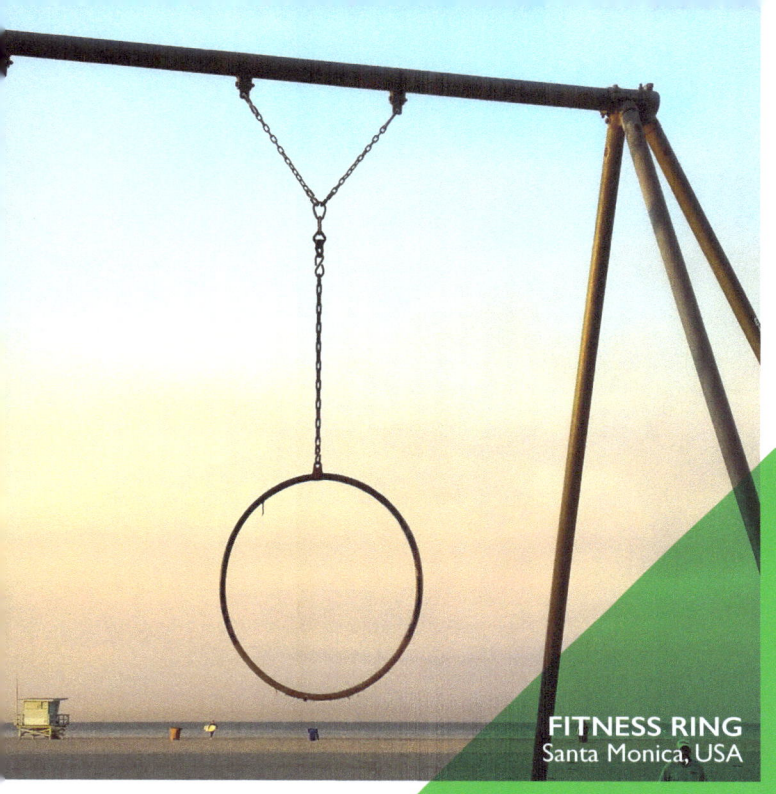

FITNESS RING
Santa Monica, USA

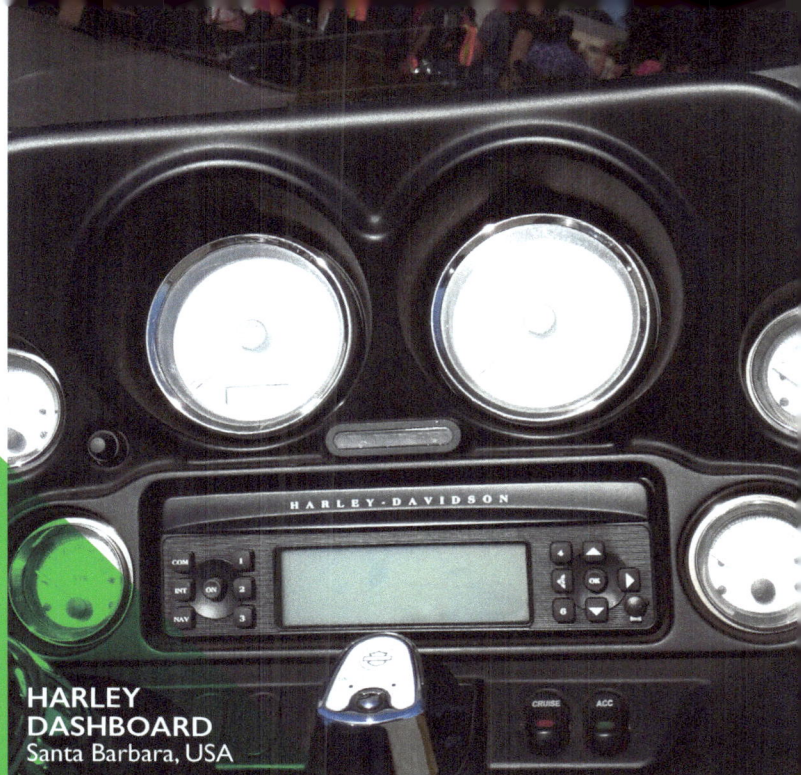

HARLEY DASHBOARD
Santa Barbara, USA

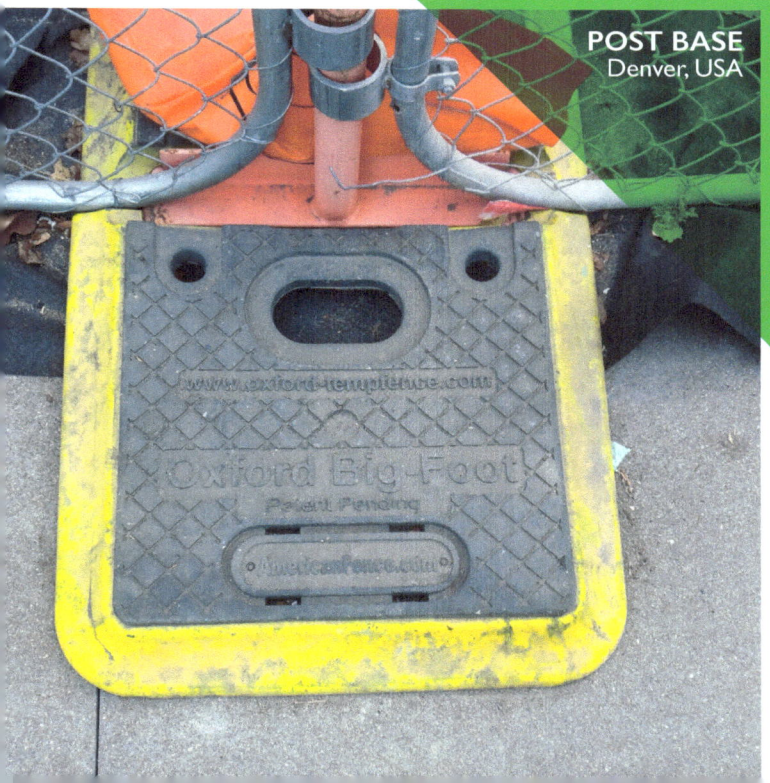

POST BASE
Denver, USA

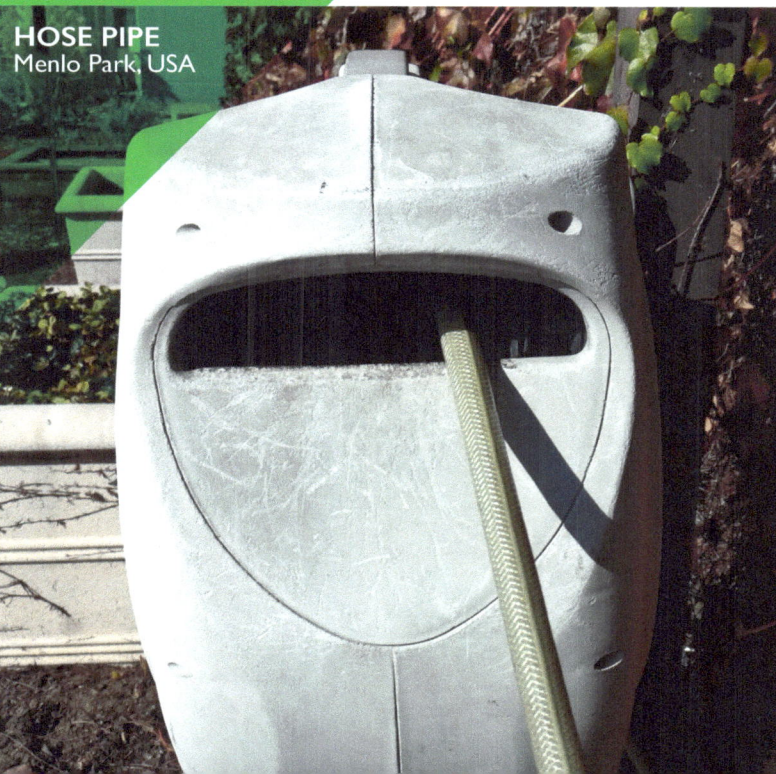

HOSE PIPE
Menlo Park, USA

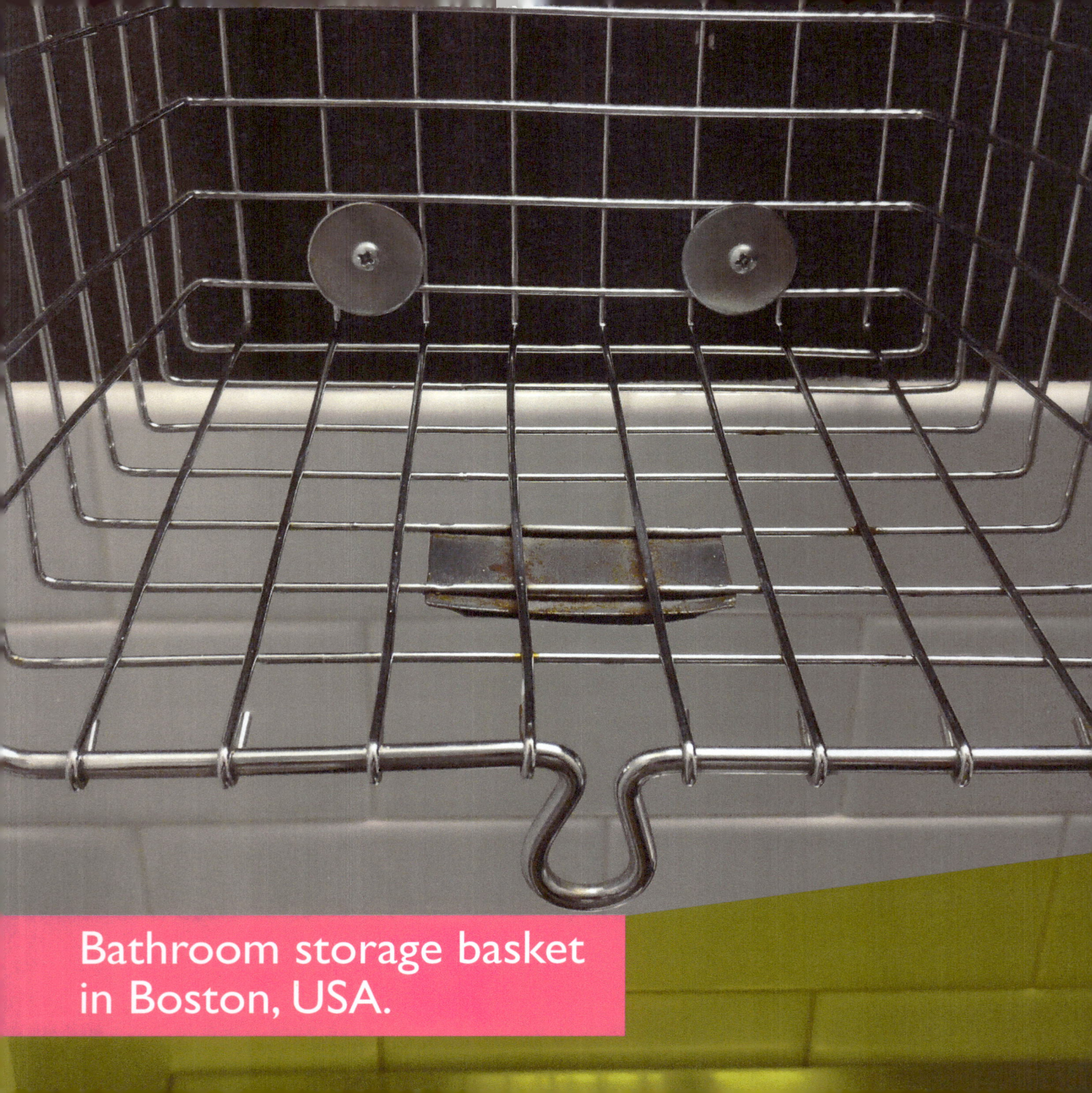

Bathroom storage basket
in Boston, USA.

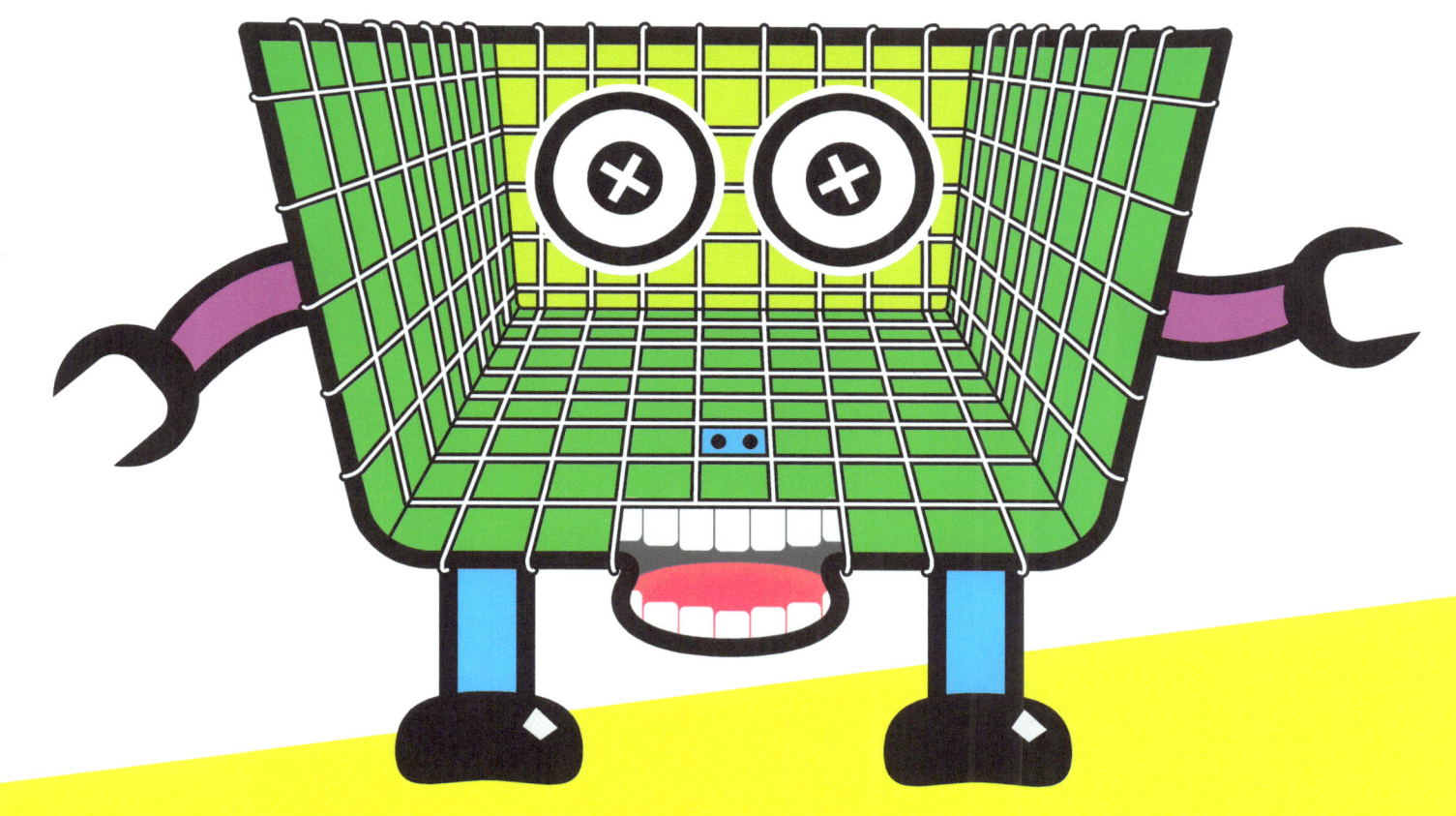

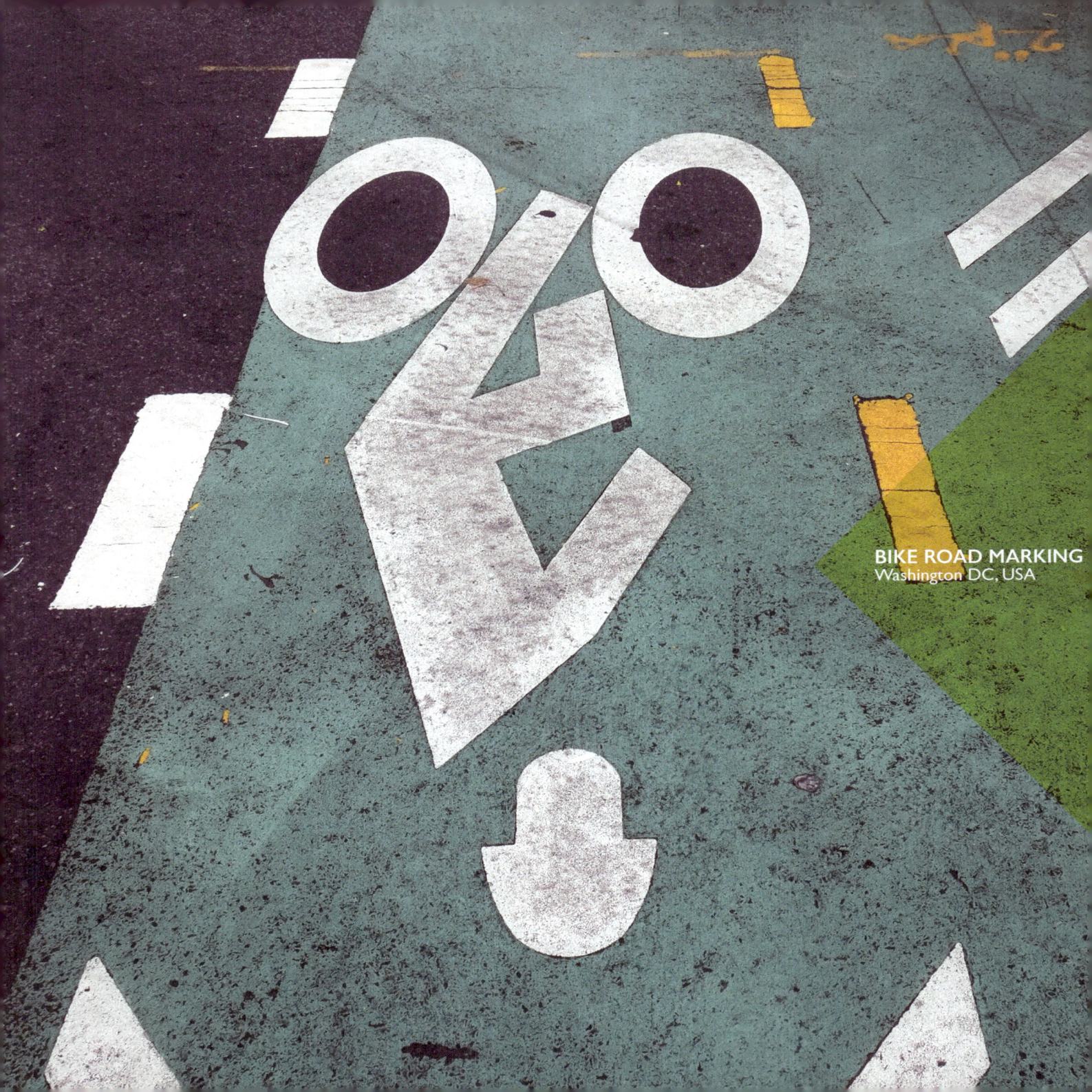

BIKE ROAD MARKING
Washington DC, USA

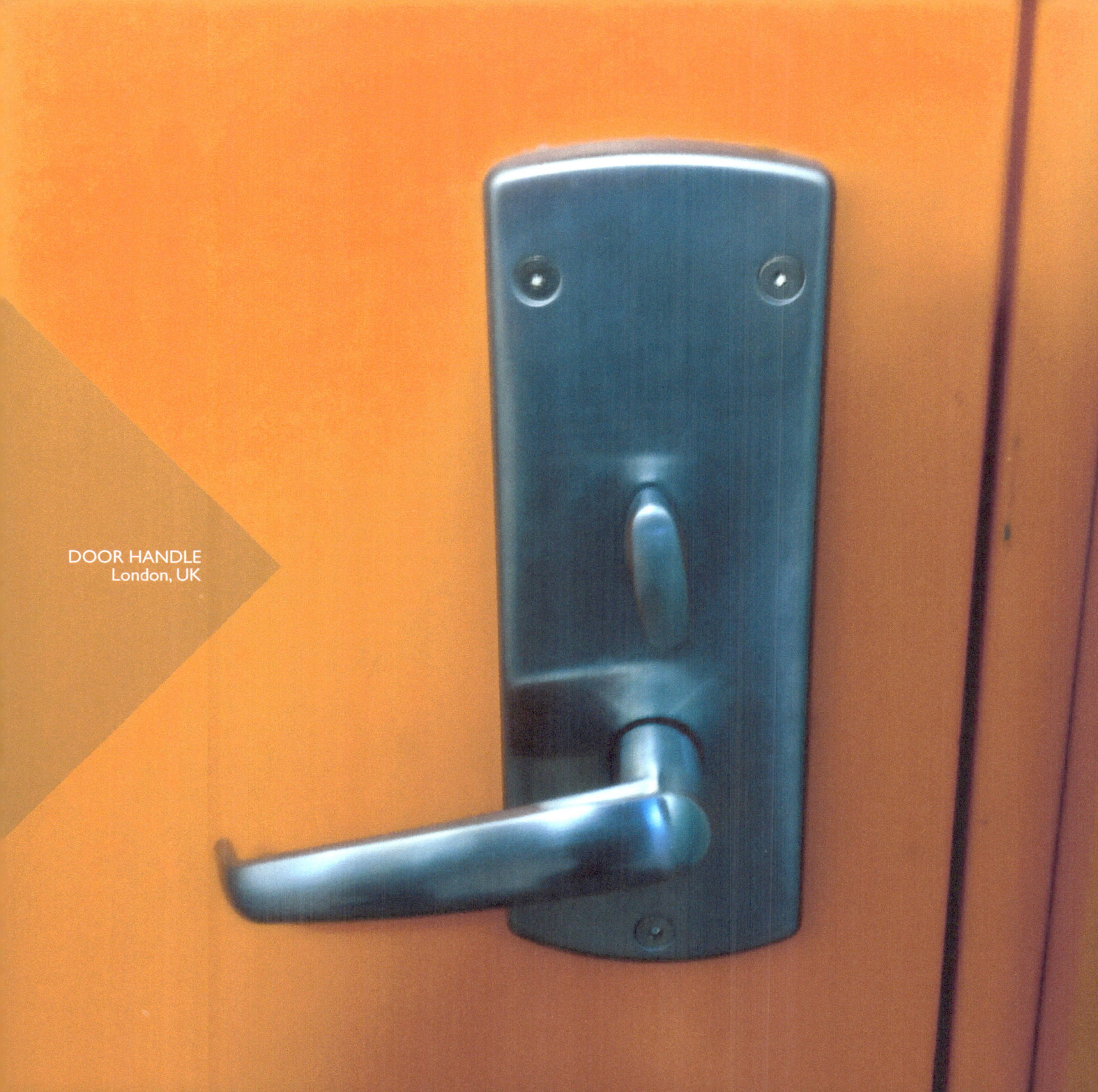

DOOR HANDLE
London, UK

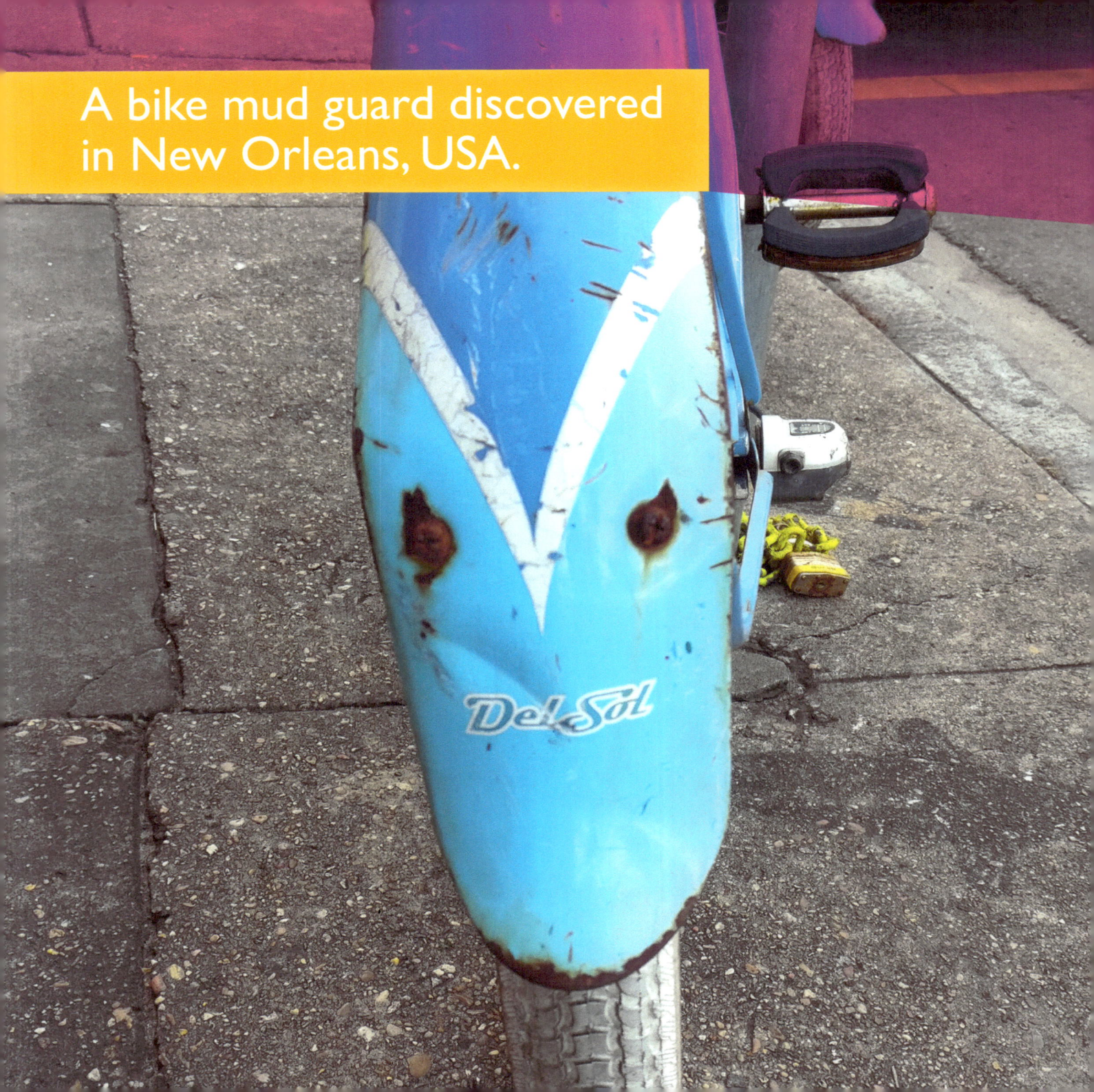

A bike mud guard discovered in New Orleans, USA.

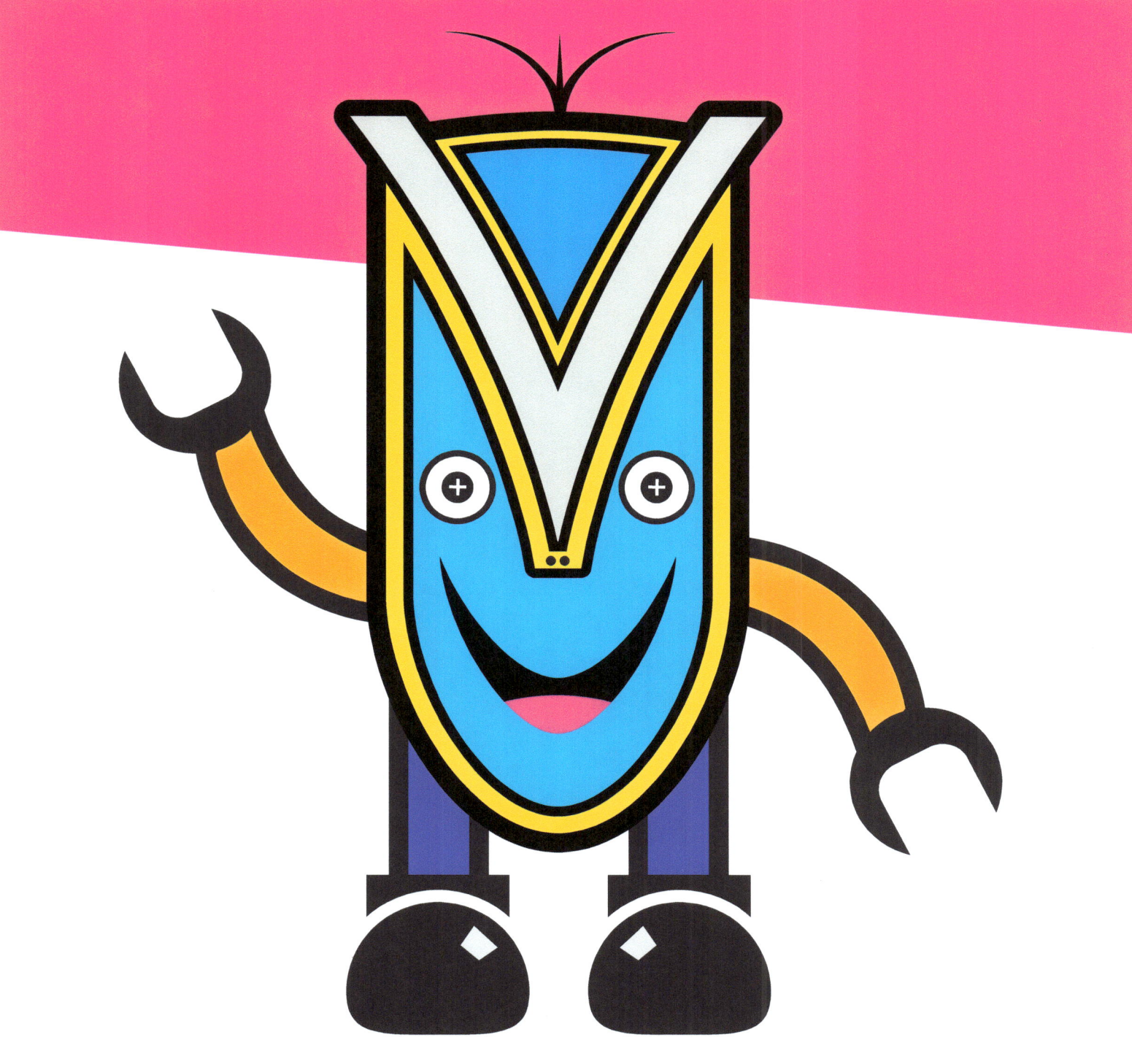

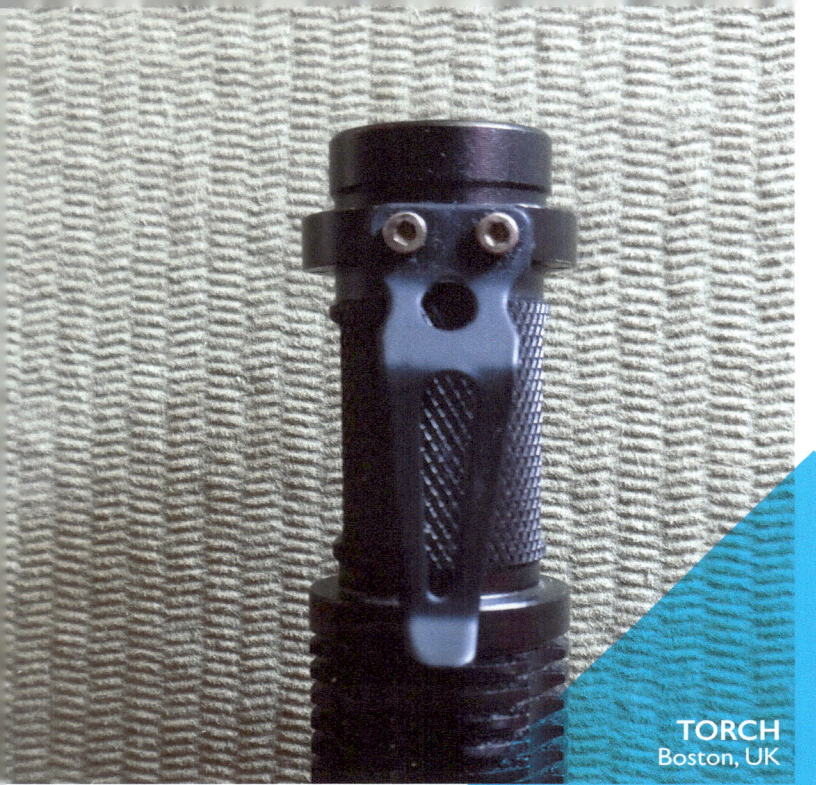

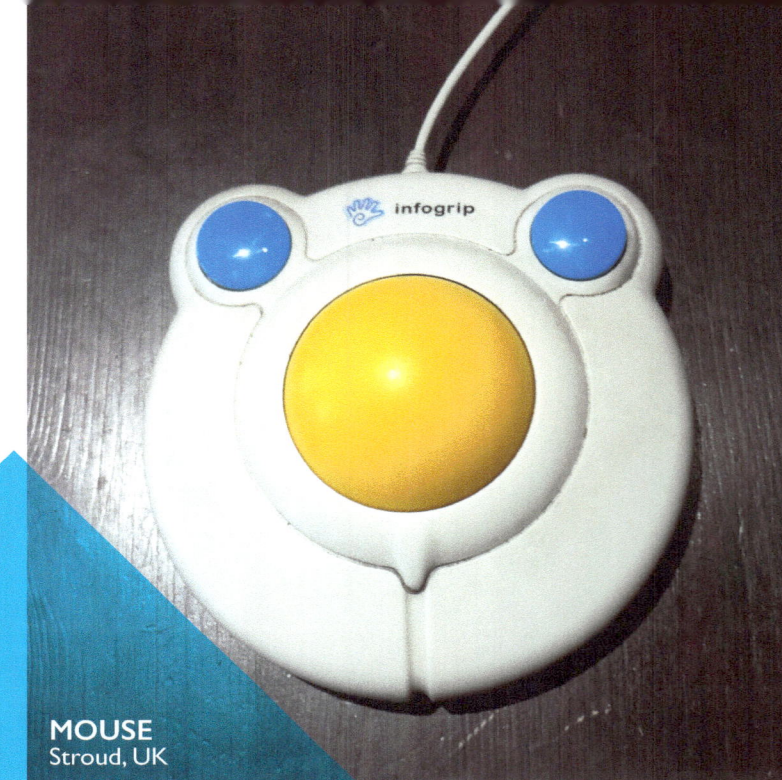

TORCH
Boston, UK

MOUSE
Stroud, UK

BOLT LOCK
Boston, UK

CAR DOOR
Boston, UK

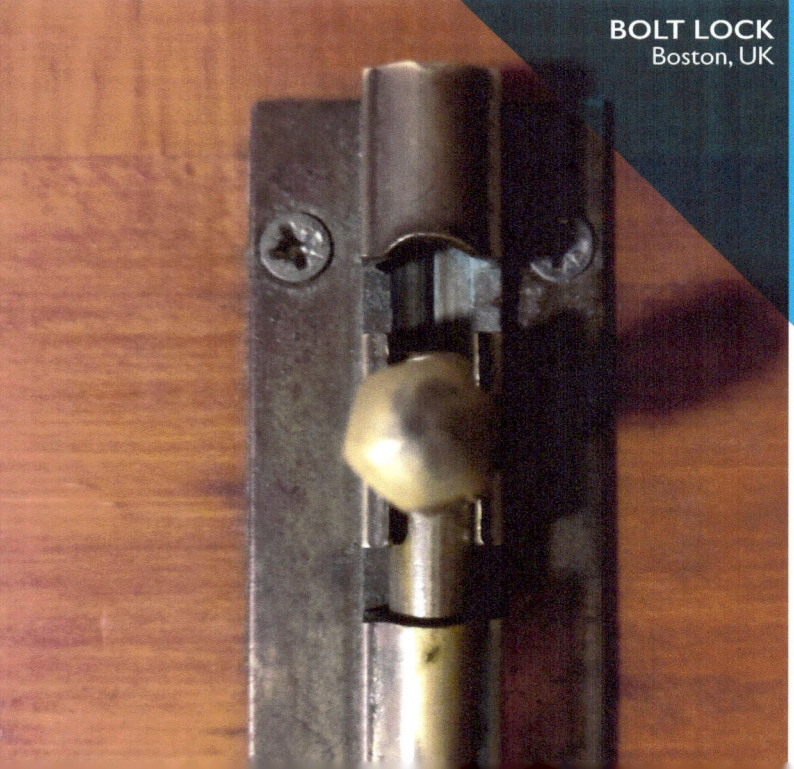

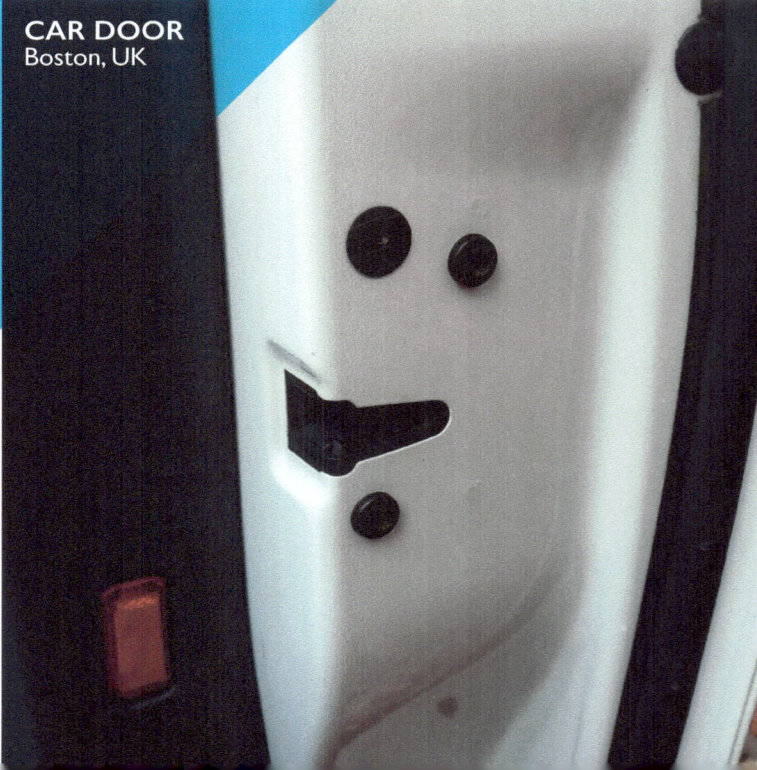

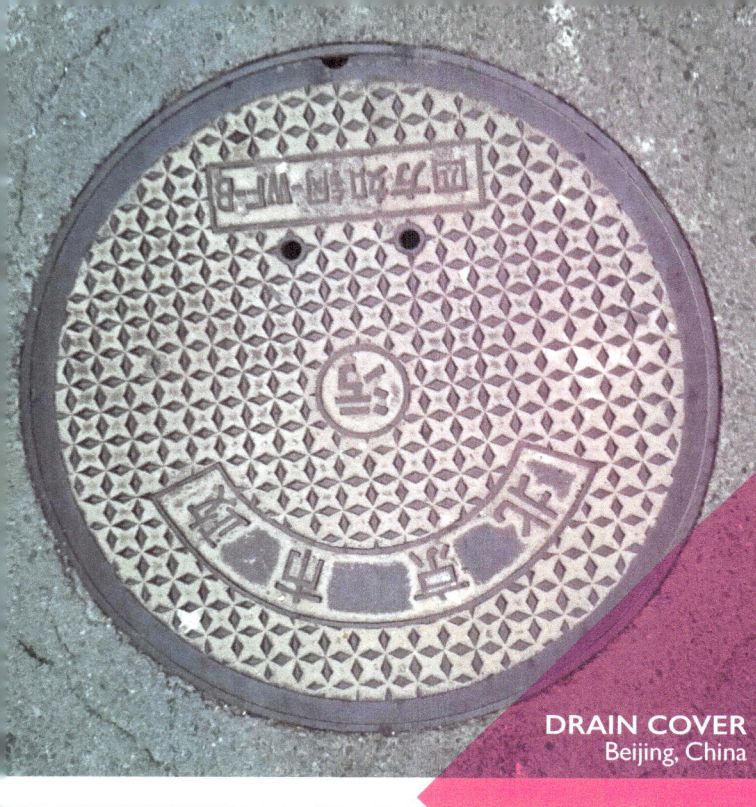

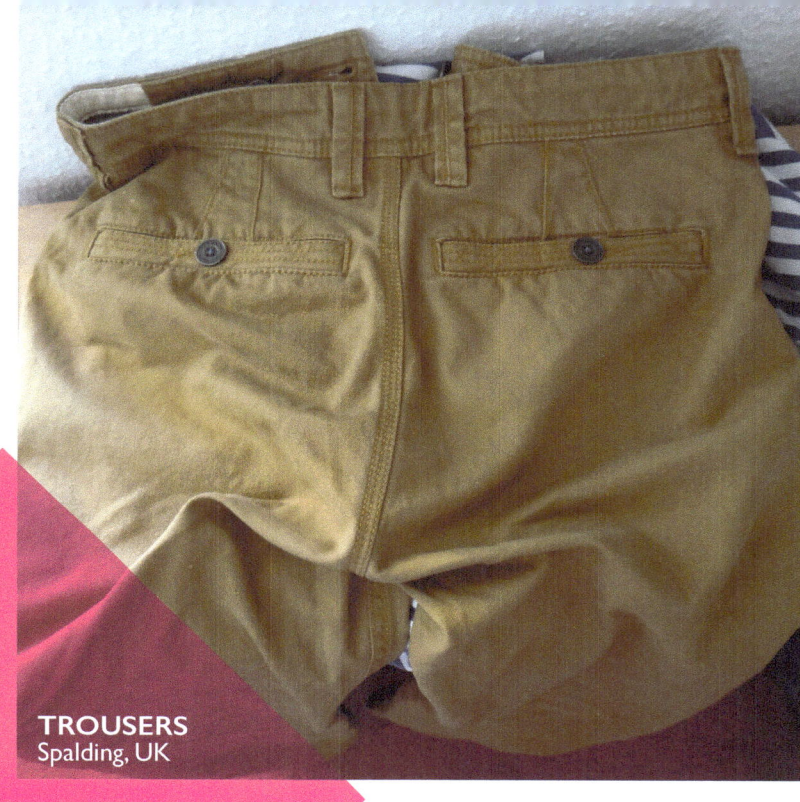

DRAIN COVER
Beijing, China

TROUSERS
Spalding, UK

ARROW HOLDER
Boston, UK

FENCE RAILING
St Petersburg, Russia

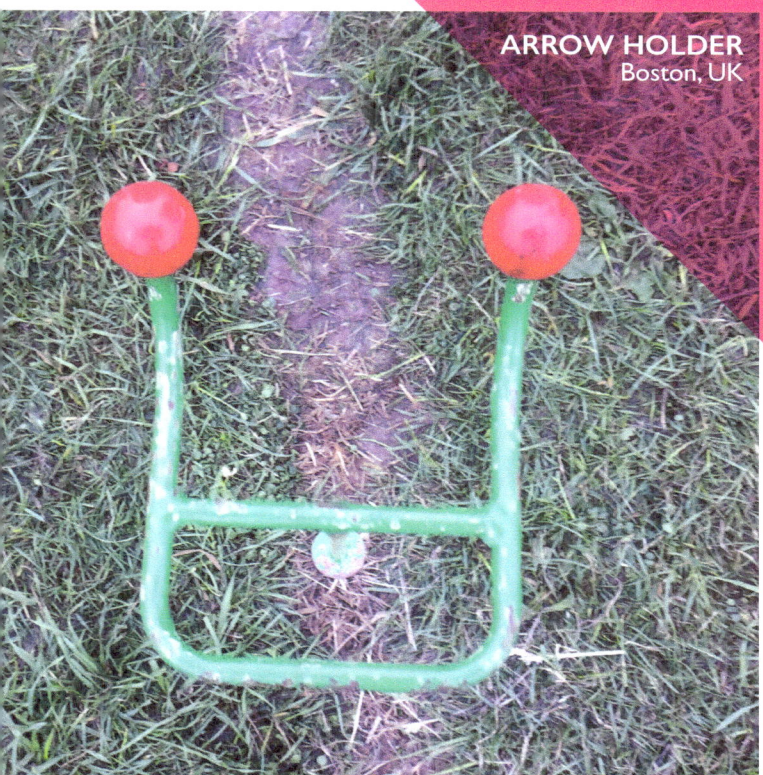

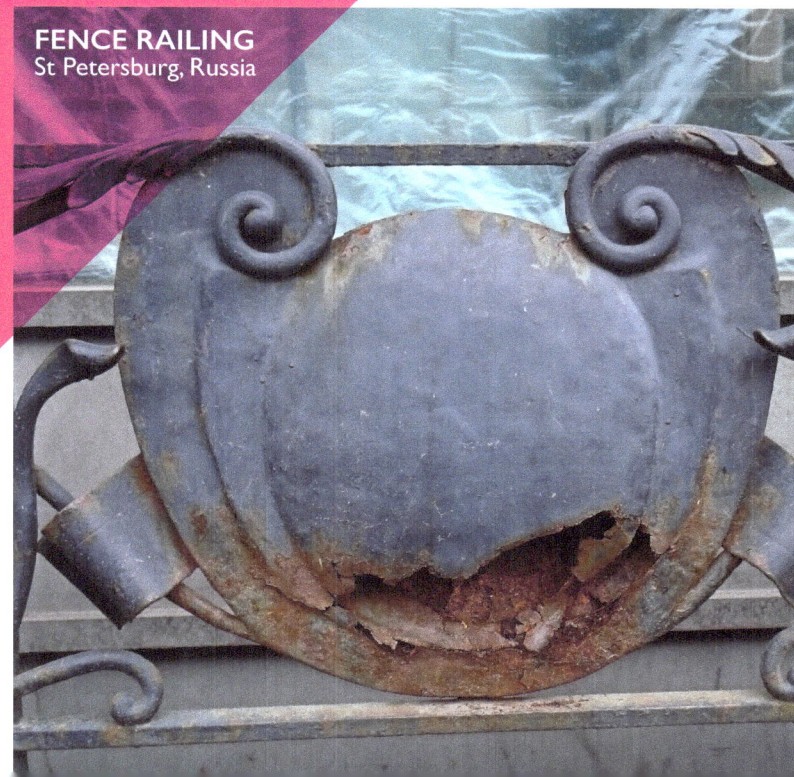

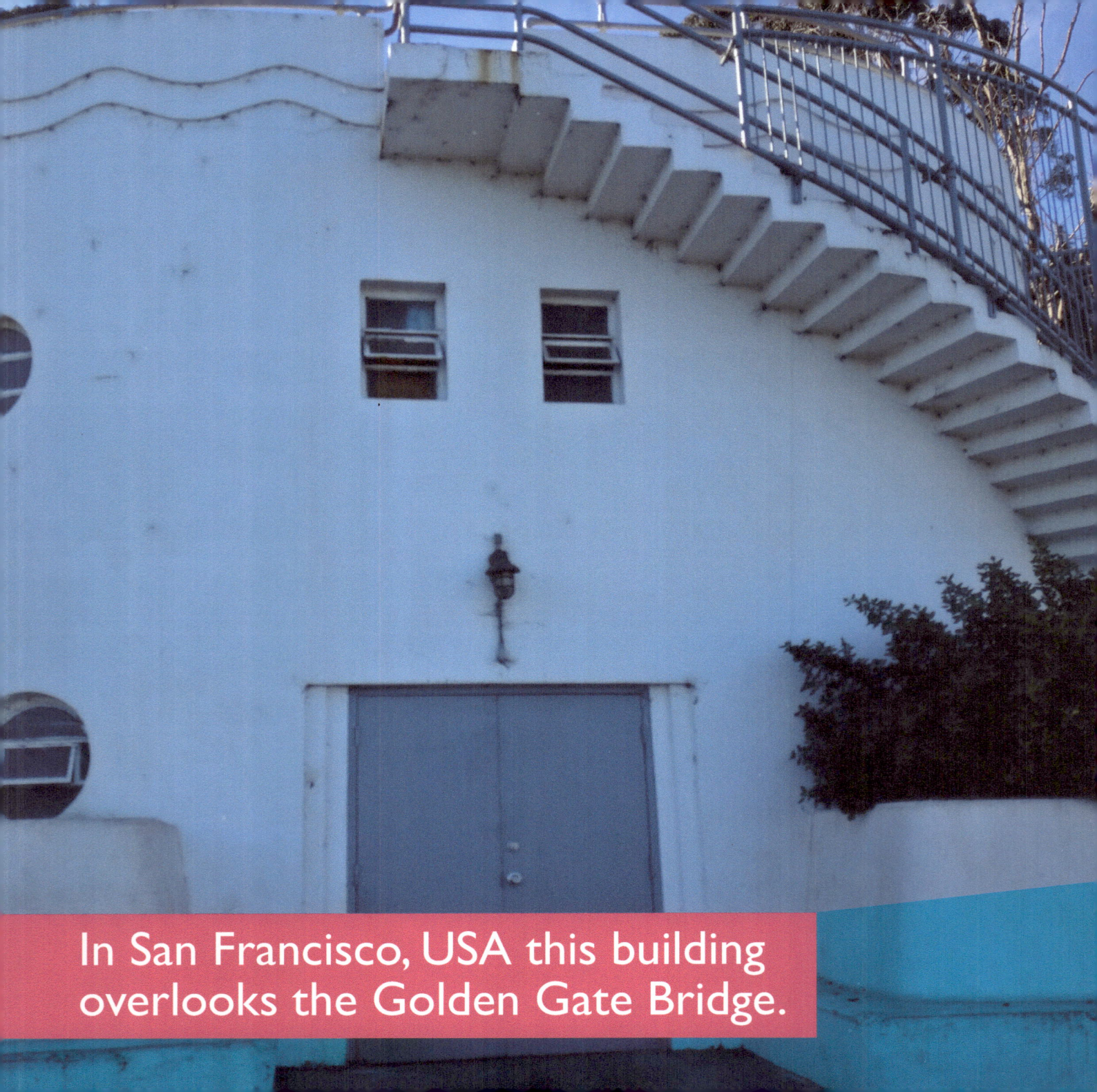

In San Francisco, USA this building overlooks the Golden Gate Bridge.

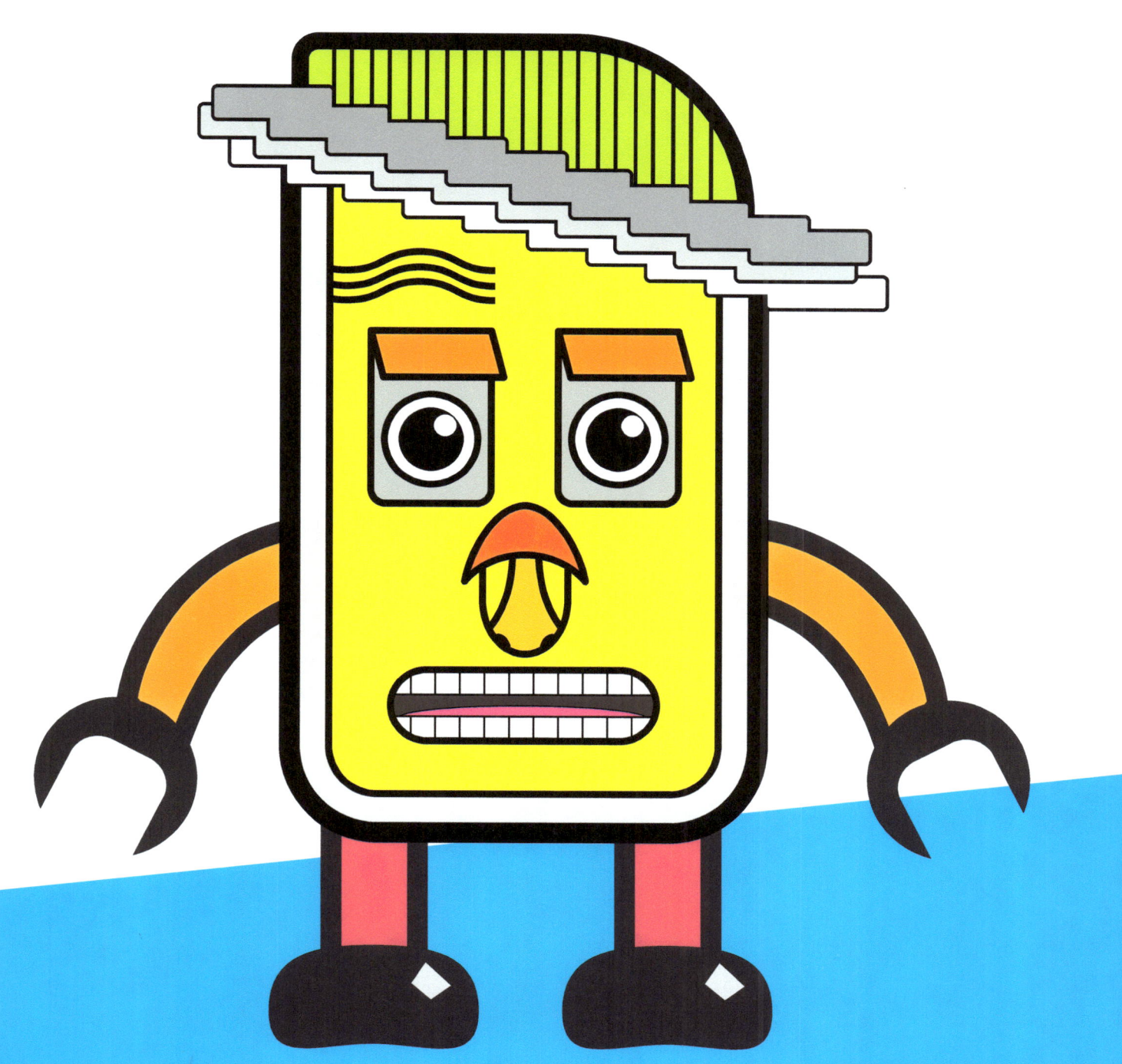

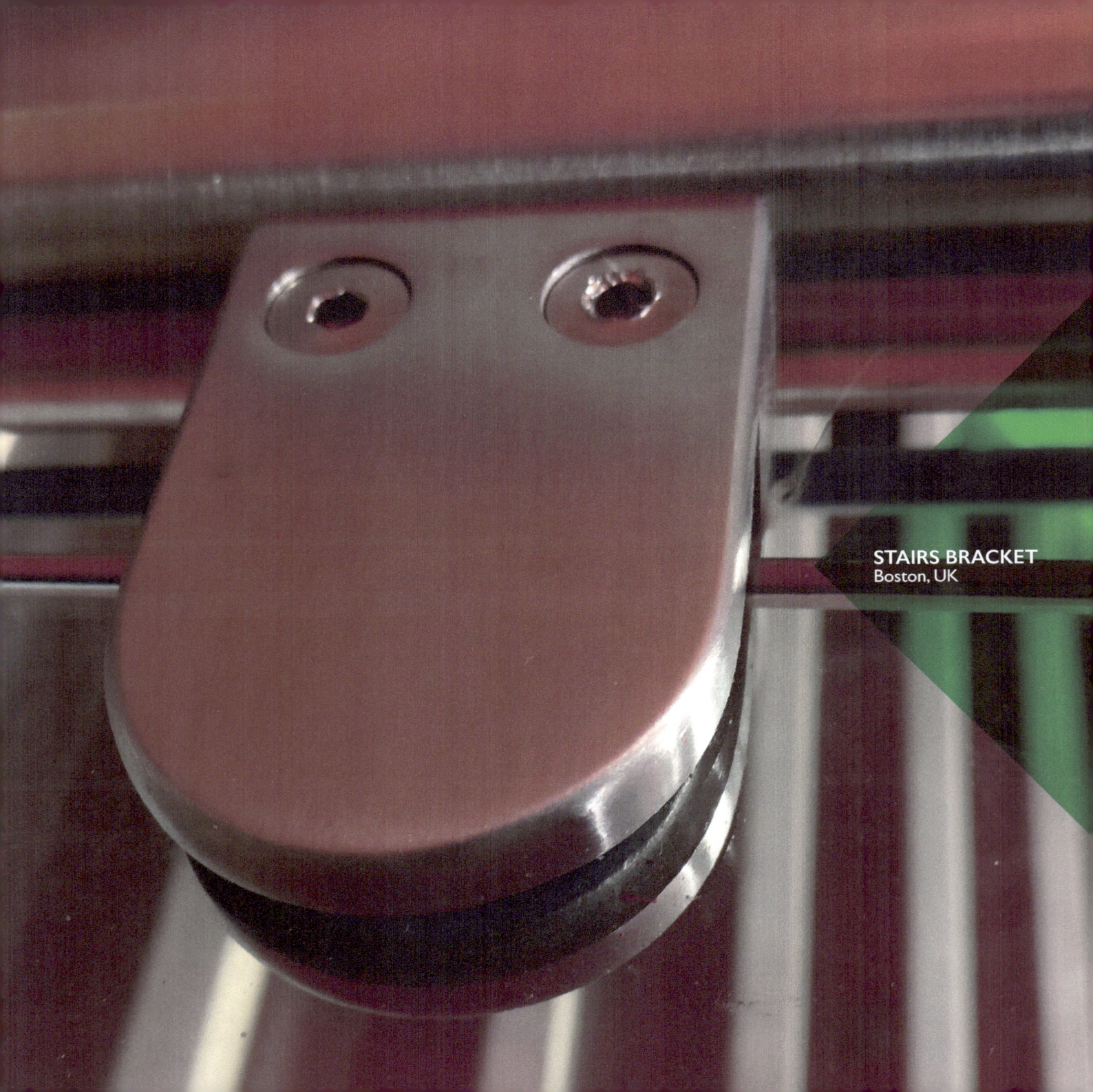

STAIRS BRACKET
Boston, UK

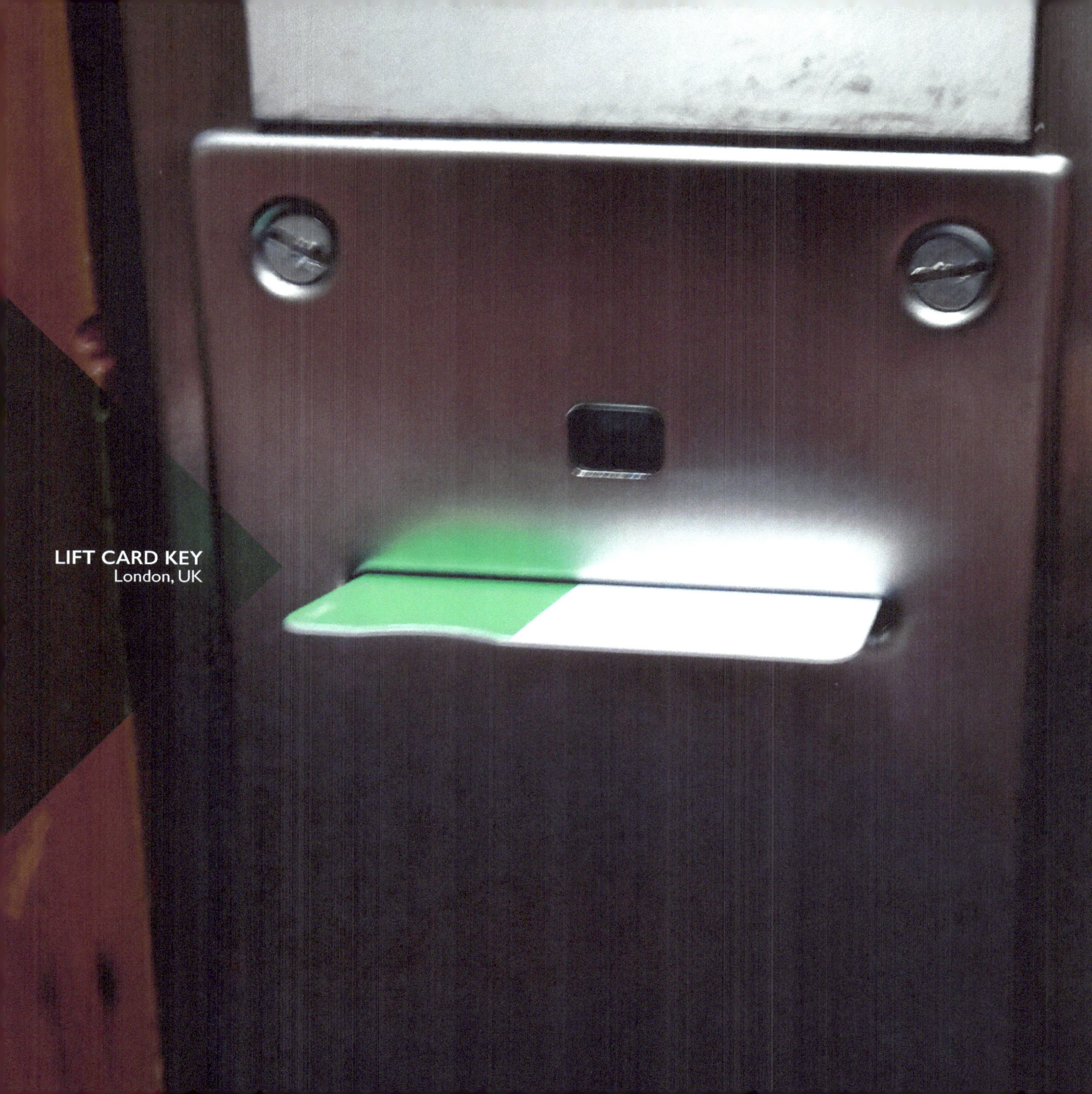

LIFT CARD KEY
London, UK

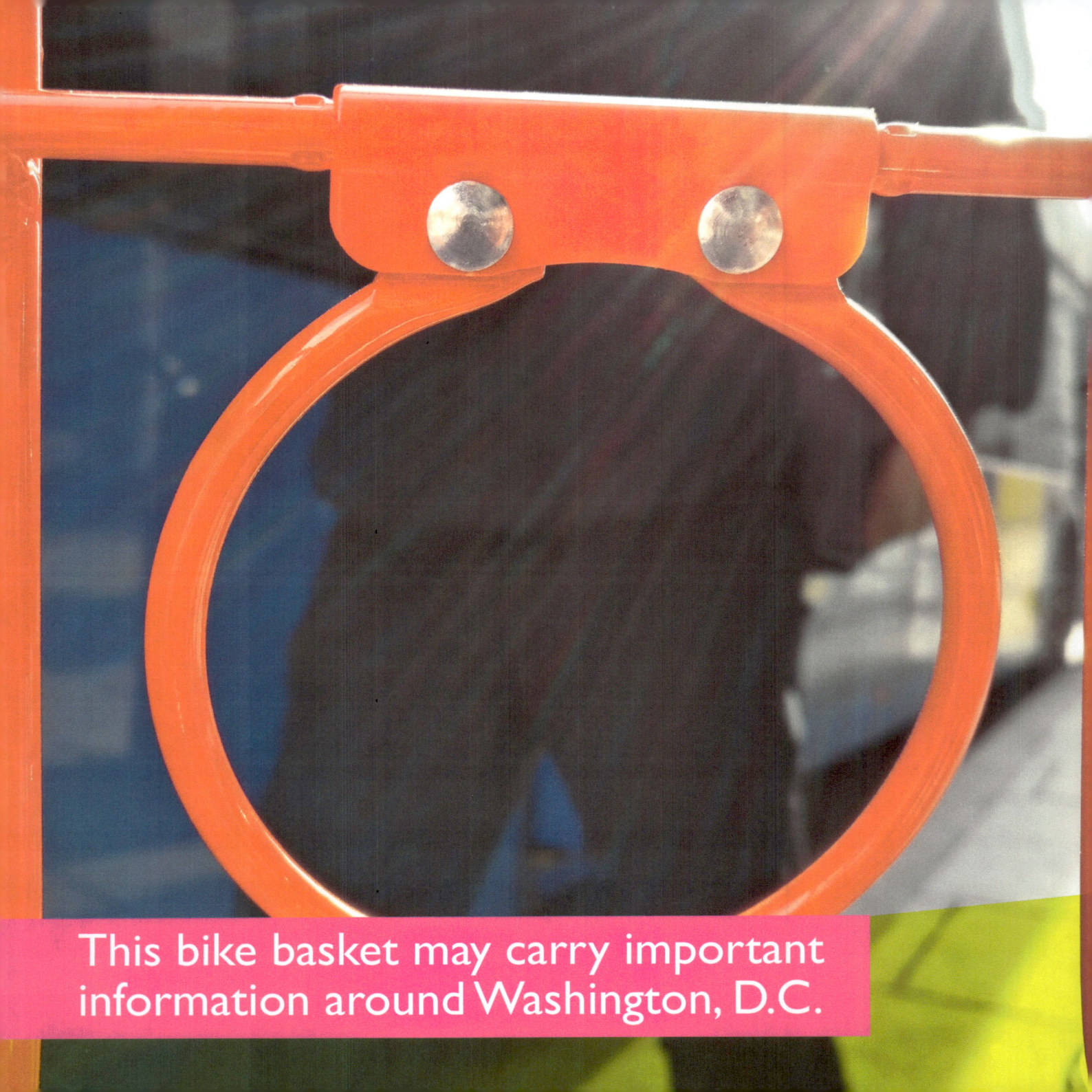

This bike basket may carry important information around Washington, D.C.

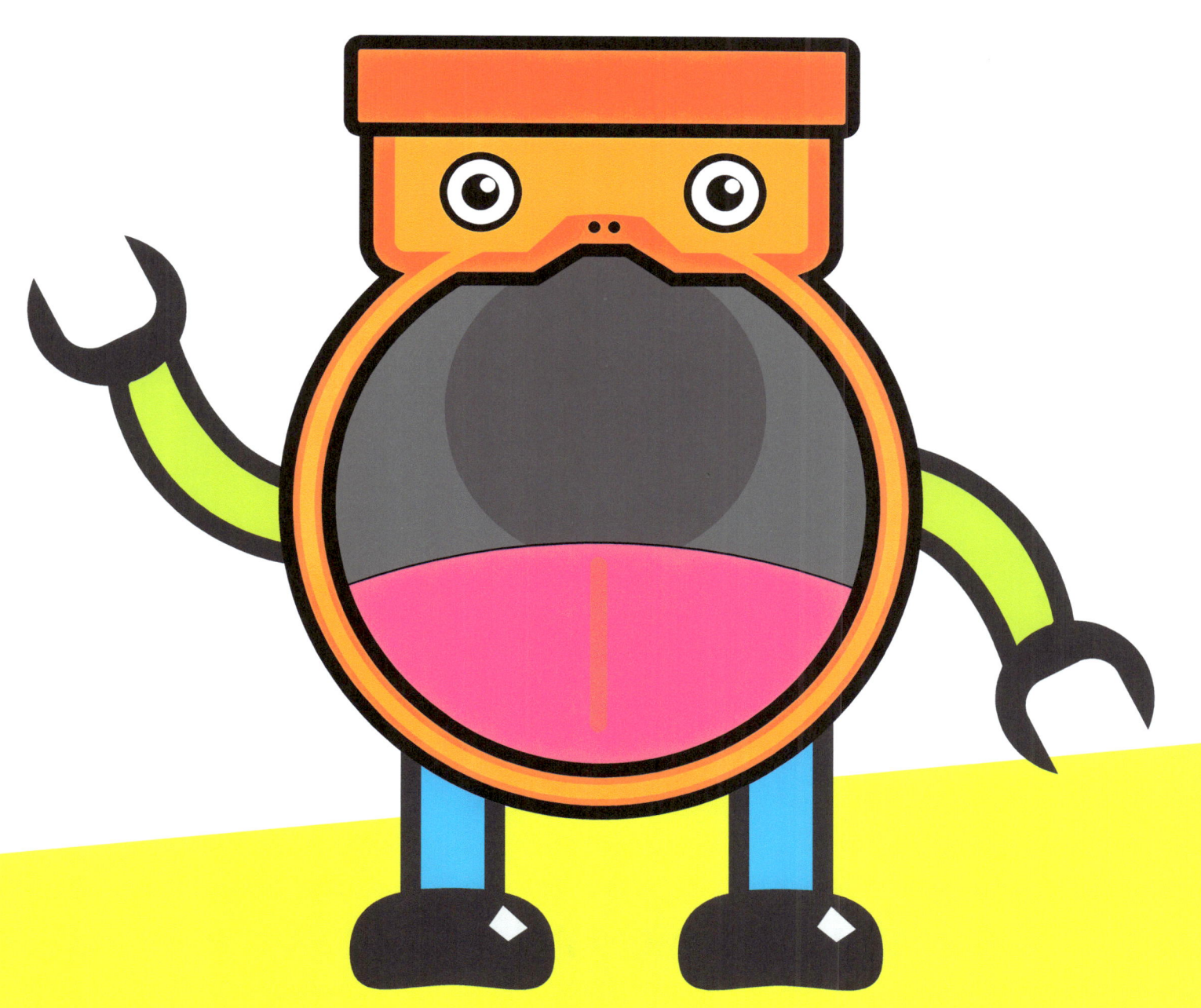

MORE BOOKS BY R&Q

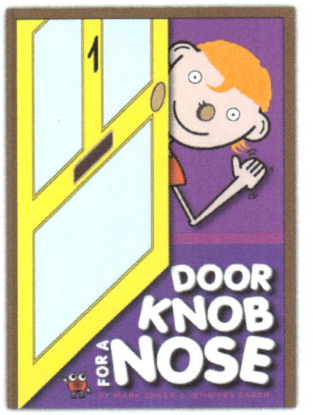

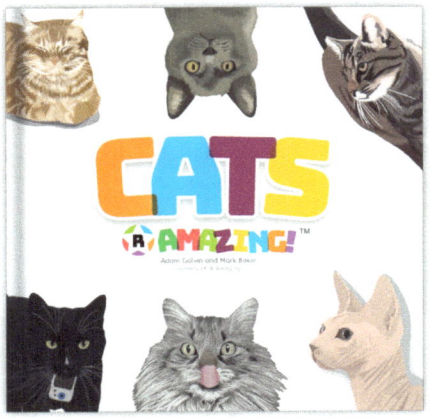

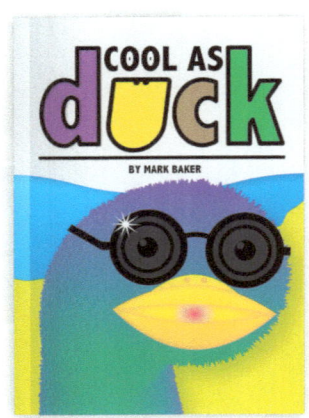

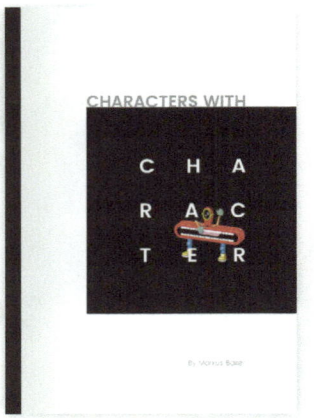

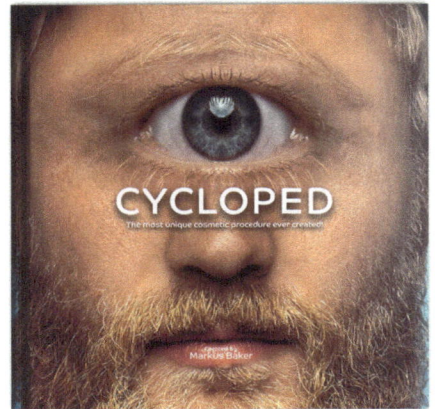

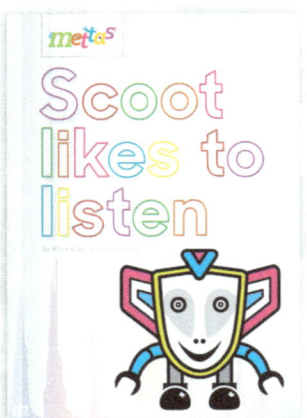

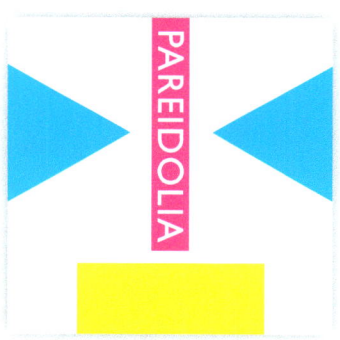